The Analysis and Design of
Computer-Based Information Systems

The Analysis and Design of
Computer-Based Information Systems

Joan C. Nordbotten
University of Bergen

HOUGHTON MIFFLIN COMPANY   BOSTON
Dallas   Geneva, Illinois   Hopewell, New Jersey   Palo Alto

Library of Congress Catalog Card Number: 84-80455

ISBN: 0-395-35707-1

ABCDEFGHIJ-H-8987654

To Svein

Contents

List of Figures

List of Tables

List of Boxes

Preface

The number of computer-based information systems (CBIS) in use has increased dramatically. This is due to the rapid growth in the number of computers available for all sizes of business and levels of government, and also to managers' increased awareness of the potentials for gaining access to increased volumes of data to provide improved support for decision making.

It remains true that if a CBIS is to be useful, it must fill some real information-processing need. Too many CBISs have been failures; they have not provided the information services that the organization needed. In many cases these systems have been technically well designed. The only real protection against system failure is to pay more attention to the analysis of information-system requirements and to the development of a system that meets these requirements.

The development of an information system consists of a series of possibly repeating tasks that generally follow the natural system life cycle. That is, the process of system analysis, design, and implementation begins at system inception with the realization that an information system is required, continues through system development, and follows through with system use, maintenance, and growth. It is not necessary for an information system to use computers for its data processing. However, for the purposes of this book, we will assume that the information system being developed will be at least partly automated.

This book is an introduction to the rather broad field of system analysis, design, and implementation for computer-based information systems. Each chapter contains a list of references to books and papers that provide further information on the chapter topic. Generally, the sequence of chapters follows the task sequence required for the development of a CBIS.

Part I provides a background for the book. Chapter 1 introduces concepts from general systems theory that are fundamental to the approach to systems analysis and design that this book takes. Chapter 2 describes a class of information systems that are especially suited to this approach to analysis and design. Chapter 3 introduces system analysis and design and discusses alternative approaches and methodologies.

Part II covers the basic tasks of information-system analysis and design and gives a methodology and tools for their execution. Chapter 4 presents problem analysis (sometimes called requirement analysis or change analysis), which is the real start of a systems development project. Chapter 5 discusses system analysis, an analysis of the current information system compared with the requirements determined in the preceding problem analysis. Chapter 6 presents the problem area of system evaluation. Evaluation techniques are needed at various stages in the system development cycle. Finally, Chapter 7 discusses information-system design, including design of the user interface and the security control system.

Information-system analysis and design is fundamentally:

- A gathering of facts and requirements
- Structuring of these facts and requirements
- An evaluation of these facts and requirements
- Finally, the design of a new or modified system

Tools that information-system analysis and design methodologies require include a graphic technique for presenting components and relationships, dictionaries for maintaining descriptions and definitions of components and relationships, and some form of analytic tool. We have chosen the graph technique presented in Lundeberg's ISAC methodology (Lundeberg et al., 1981). The proposed dictionaries closely follow ideas that are being implemented in data dictionary systems, and thus are amenable to automation. We have chosen matrices as an analytic tool, again because these can be (and have been) used as a basis for automated analysis tools.

Part III covers data-system design, including data modeling, data and file structures, and process and program specification. The emphasis in data-system design is on selecting general data processing techniques that will support the requirements of the information-system design. The data-system design should be, as far as possible, machine-independent so that it can survive changes in the available computers. Computer adaptation is viewed here as an implementation task.

Part IV discusses implementation tasks, including selection of computer support for the system, implementation planning, and system maintenance and growth. These tasks are often not included in the systems analysis and design framework; however, decisions made in this realm will often affect design parameters determined earlier in the system development cycle. Therefore we feel that these activities should be included in system analysis and design.

Part V steps back and reviews the approach to system analysis and design the book has presented. Chapter 14 discusses the users who are affected by CBISs and thus by the system analysis and design activity. These users are to be found in many different application areas, also briefly presented in Chapter 14. Chapter 15 reviews system analysis and design in general and this approach in particular.

This book has been written as a textbook for an introductory course in system analysis and design. No specific prerequisites are assumed. However, students who have an introductory-level background in computer science and knowledge of business applications will find a number of the topics easier to understand.

Each chapter includes a list of the important terms presented in the chapter, a list of references for those who are interested in further information on the topics of the chapter, and discussion questions for self-study, class discussion, or project assignments. In addition, the appendix includes an extensive bibliography, a glossary of terms, and a presentation of the model information system that is used throughout the text. It is hoped that, in addition to being useful as a classroom text, the book can be used for self-study.

ACKNOWLEDGMENTS

I am indebted to my husband Svein for much constructive criticism and for his unfailing support throughout the development of this book. I am particularly grateful to Rhoda Cahan and Pal Davidsen, of New York and Bergen, respectively, for their reviews of several sections of this text. In addition, Professors Bo Sundgren, Carol Shingles, Michael Ginzberg, and Henry M. Zbyszynski reviewed the manuscript and provided many useful suggestions. Finally, I would like to use this opportunity to thank my colleagues and students at NYU and Bergen University for their discussions and comments on early versions of this text.

J.C.N.

The Analysis and Design of
Computer-Based Information Systems

PART I
CONCEPTS, THEORIES, AND METHODOLOGIES

Chapter 1
Background

INTRODUCTION

Computer-based information systems (CBISs) are rapidly growing in number and are being applied to more and more areas within our organizations and society. Since their introduction in the early 1950s as systems for numerical analysis of scientific, statistical, and military data, they have grown into general information-processing systems capable of answering such diverse queries as the department store customer's "Where can I find sports socks?" or the sales manager's "Which product has shown the strongest sales growth in the current period?"

Governments use CBISs to maintain information on individuals, organizations, social projects, funds, and budget allocations. Businesses use them to maintain information on customers, employees, divisions, departments, products, production, and financial accounts. Private individuals use them to maintain diverse financial accounts (through banks and credit organizations), to obtain information from libraries and information services, to request services such as car or plane reservations, and for entertainment (e.g., electronic games).

Developing a CBIS is a costly and time-consuming process. Costs can often exceed $1 million, and development can require ten or more person-years of effort. The success of the resulting CBISs is commonly measured in terms of user satisfaction, that is, the perceived ability of the CBIS to provide the information services anticipated. CBISs have often been disappointing, with many reported to be total failures. Though most CBISs are useful, less than 17 percent of the 300 companies interviewed in one survey reported that they were satisfied with their systems (Kriebel, 1979).

Though there may be a number of reasons for this perceived lack of success for CBISs, many systems researchers cite the design stages of the system as the most likely source of problems, particularly the inability of the system designers to capture all the relevant user requirements for information services.

Most CBISs have been designed using methods and techniques that tend to emphasize efficiency in the automated subsystems. In terms of computer efficiency, the resulting systems are often quite good, achieving increased speed in the mechanics of data processing, and even reducing costs. However, if the CBIS is to be successful, its users must perceive it as useful and efficient. To accomplish this, the designers must emphasize determining, as completely as possible, the users' information-processing requirements and expectations.

A CBIS must serve a useful purpose, be adaptable to changing user requirements, and be developed within a given budget of time and money. We believe that a good design is necessary for a successful CBIS development project. With this background, we shall direct our attention to the analysis and design of computer-based information systems, presenting a methodology aimed at capturing user requirements and preserving them throughout the design and implementation processes for the new or modified CBIS. This approach does not ignore computer efficiency; however, in resolving conflicts, user service is given priority.

An example of an information system is presented in Chapter 2 and used throughout the text to illustrate the methods and techniques being discussed. The example system, student administration, has been chosen as presumably familiar to the readers. It also represents a type of information system common throughout business and government administration, namely, one that keeps track of an organization's product, in this case students. As such, it is expected to illustrate common and general information service problems encountered throughout our society. Finally, this system is representative of the type of administrative information system with which this text is primarily concerned.

Programming and computer technology are not topics of this text; however, readers are expected to have a basic familiarity with both topics. Since we are considering computer-based information systems, knowledge of computers and their potential and limitations will help readers appreciate some of the possibly complex presentations made here.

SYSTEMS THEORY

Systems theory as an approach to studying organizations and their behavior has its roots in physics and biology (von Bertalanffy, 1950). Its application to the study and development of computer-based systems gained particular importance and attention in the mid-1940s, with the establishment of cybernetics as a science of "control and communication in the animal and the machine" (Wiener, 1948). Credit for the initiation of a movement for a general systems theory is generally given to von Bertalanffy's 1950 paper on the theory of open systems in physics and biology (von Bertalanffy, 1950). Since then many papers have been presented describing systems and their fundamental properties, characteristics, environments, components, relationships, and regulatory capabilities.

In the following sections, we shall attempt to summarize the system theories, axioms, and concepts most relevant to understanding the role and characteristics of information systems. Readers are encouraged to explore the more general systems theory as it is applied to and influences the development of such fields as business administration, political science, sociology, psychology, anthropology, engineering, physics, and computer science.

Systems

For our study, the most basic concept is that of a system, which we can initially define as

> A group of units so combined as to form a whole and to operate in unison . . . (Webster).[1]

We note that a system is composed of a group of units. Most frequently these units can themselves be considered as systems, each of which can be composed of smaller units (or subsystems) that can be considered as systems, and so on. The system itself is also a component unit of some supersystem. In addition to the system under consideration, the supersystem is composed of one or more units (subsystems) that form the environment for the system.

When analyzing a particular system, it is necessary to fix attention on that system and then to identify

1. its supersystem, i.e., that system of which it is a component unit.
2. the environment with which the system interacts.
3. its component subsystems.

Note that the system analysis may be repeated for each of the subsystems until a depth of detail is reached that is sufficient for the analysis of the original system.

By applying this concept of a system as a component of a supersystem and composed of subsystems with sub-subsystems, etc., we can construct a hierarchical model of the system under study. Note that the system under study is placed by convention at level 1. Figure 1.1 illustrates the general system structure. In the figure, n is the number of subsystems in the system of interest, and j is the number of subsystems in subsystem 1.

We can use the hierarchical system model to create a system model for a real system, as illustrated in Figure 1.2. Here the system of interest

---

1. By permission. From the *Merriam-Webster Dictionary*, © 1974 by Merriam-Webster, Inc., publisher of the Merriam-Webster Dictionaries.

Figure 1.1 System Structure

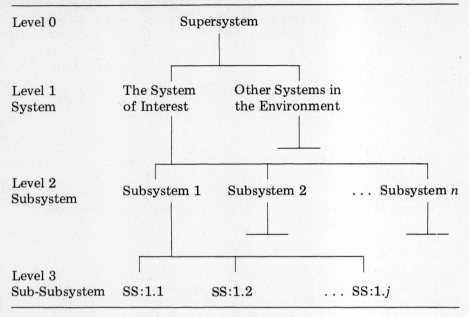

Notes : n = number of subsystems in the system of interest
j = number of sub-subsystems in subsystem 1

is the "School of Social Sciences." Its supersystem is the university, and
its primary environment consists of the other university subsystems.
The component subsystems are the departments and their major fields
of study. If we assume that the fields-of-study structure of a school is
the objective for the system analysis, this model could be considered
complete. Other models for a faculty system might consider units or
subsystems such as type of personnel or budget.

Returning to our definition, we see that subsystems are "so combined
as to form a whole." That is, there must be a system structure that relates the component subsystems into an organized whole: the system.
The system structure is defined by the relationships that exist among
the subsystems, both the hierarchical relationships and those relationships that exist between subsystems at the same level within the system.
Note that the latter (the horizontal relationships between same-level
subsystems) are not indicated in Figures 1.1 and 1.2.

The relationships among the system components define order,
sequence, interdependency, and time relationships. They enable the
system to "live," or operate. The relationships define the sequence of
actions and activities within the system. An important task of systems

Figure 1.2 University System Structured by Subjects Taught

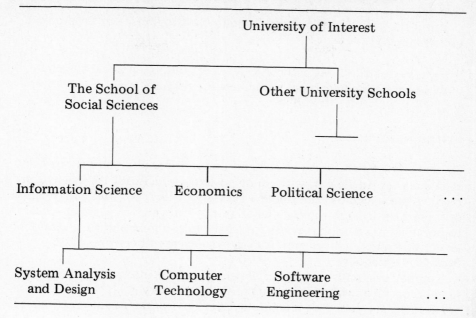

analysis is to identify and evaluate the performance of these action-defining relationships.

The system's subsystems should be able "to operate in unison" (according to our definition). That is, the subsystems must be able to interact with one another. For this to have meaning, the subsystems' activities must be goal-directed, that is, aimed at fulfilling the objectives or goals of the parent system. The primary goal for the system defines its reason for existence, that toward which the system strives. The goals for the subsystems should, in principle, be deducible from the goals of the parent system. When the system is functioning well, that is, when it is moving toward fulfillment of its goals, then its subsystems' goals will be tuned to, and supportive of, the primary system goals.

For example, a primary goal for the school of social sciences (see Figure 1.2) might be to graduate only those students who had maintained a B average. This goal can be passed on to the subsystems as a complementary goal, that is, pass only those students with a B average. Or it could generate a subsystem goal for evaluating each student.

An important axiom of system theory originates from Aristotle's statement that the whole is more than the sum of its parts. This can be interpreted as meaning that when the subsystems are goal-fulfilling at their subgoal level, the system's goals can be greater than the sum of the subgoals because of the return on coordinated cooperation. This axiom is central to our interest in determining the primary goal(s) for the system before considering the subsystem goals.

From the previous discussion, we may now rephrase our definition of a system as

System A structured, interrelated set of components (subsystems) whose combined goals act to achieve the primary goals.

System Environment

Systems are of two types: closed and open. A closed system is one that is entirely self-sufficient, with no necessary interaction with its environment. A stone can be considered a system of this type, with subsystems of molecules and sub-subsystems of atoms. Information systems exist to provide information services for their environment and thus cannot be considered closed systems. Closed systems are, therefore, of no further interest here.

An open system is one that is dependent on its interaction, that is, its relationships, with its environment. The primary goals of the system are defined in relation to this interaction. Environmental interactions or relationships fall into three classes.

1. Input, consisting of stimuli, which can take the form of resources, directives, queries, and/or information directed toward the system, and which can be used in some fashion by the system.
2. Output, consisting of the system's reaction to the input stimuli, which may take the form of results, products, and/or system state information available to the environment. Output is released to the environment, possibly initiating some feedback.
3. Feedback, consisting of messages and reactions to the output from the system. The feedback commonly generates new or modified input to the system, and as such is really a special type of input relation.

Figure 1.3a illustrates this open system concept. Applying it to the university system in Figure 1.2, we can establish that the school system, viewed as a set of areas of study, receives as input directives, students, faculty, and funds and that it outputs graduates, presumably consuming both funds and faculty (see Figure 1.3b). Graduates may generate evaluations, new requirements, and so on, outside the scope of the school system, thus possibly affecting, as feedback, the topics included within the areas of study.

In the first phase of analyzing an open system, defining the primary system goal(s), it is sufficient to consider the system as a "black box," or undefined entity, and to concentrate on the environment's interactions with the system.

Figure 1.3 System Environment

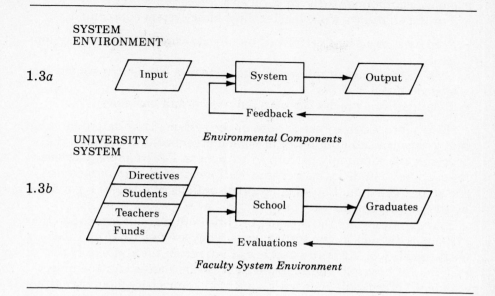

SYSTEM
ENVIRONMENT

1.3*a*

Environmental Components

UNIVERSITY
SYSTEM

1.3*b*

Faculty System Environment

System Components

We have established that the systems of interest here

1. are open systems.
2. are goal-directed.
3. obtain their goal set from interaction with their environment.
4. are composed of a structured set of interrelated subsystems.

We also know that a system may be decomposed into multiple levels of subsystems by successively considering each subsystem in turn as a system. This process ends when we have no further interest in the composition of the lowest-level subsystems. These lowest-level subsystems are considered to be the atomic elements of the system.

The atomic elements of a system are either elementary processes or system objects. Elementary processes perform some action on the system objects, typically transportation from one place to another and/or modification from one state to another. Elementary processes can be combined to form the action(s) or task of the subsystem.

What constitutes a system object will vary depending on the objectives of the system. For example, the system objects for a university administration system could be people in roles, such as students, teachers, administrative staff, and so on. In contrast, in a medical research system, humans (in general) might be the system of interest, with chemical compounds the system objects.

For our study, we will consider three basic system components:

- Processes, or actions performed on objects as required by the system goals
- Objects, or things of interest to the system (a frequent synonym for *system object* is *entity*)
- Relationships, which exist between objects and processes

System processes are the actions of the system. They determine what the system can and cannot do. In human organizational systems, the processes are commonly performed by people. For example, teachers *teach* courses, students *take* exams, staff members *maintain* records, and so on. The definition of appropriate actions (processes) is governed by the goal set for the system.

System objects are those things or entities that are of interest to the system, as defined by the system goals. They are described by those characteristics or attributes that are of interest in the context of the system. For example, the characteristic "wears glasses" for the object "student" is probably uninteresting within a university administrative system; in a medical system, however, this characteristic could be important. There are two types of characteristics, or attributes:

1. Descriptive attributes, whose values give descriptive or identifying properties of an individual object (a person's name, color of hair, account number, etc.)
2. Associative attributes, whose values identify a relationship between two separate objects (object 1 "is the son of" object 2, student A "takes" course 1, etc.)

System objects can be grouped into classes, where a class is defined as a group of individuals that have some common attribute(s) of interest to the system. For example, in a university system, the system objects "people" may be grouped into the classes "students," "faculty," and "staff."

An individual object is identified by one or more descriptive attributes whose value or values uniquely identify the individual within its object class. For example, there may be several students named Tom Jones, but only one has the Social Security number 123-45-6789.

The third basic system component is the relationship set. Relationships exist between system processes, between system objects, and between processes and objects. We are primarily interested in two kinds of relationships:

1. Structural relationships, which define the organization or structure of the system processes and objects, giving groupings and sequence

and establishing the place, within the whole system, of each of the subsystems
2. Communicative relationships, which define the interactions between the system and its environment and among the system's subsystems

Structural relationships can be clearly shown by constructing a hierarchical model, such as the one in Figures 1.1 and 1.2. These relationships are relatively permanent within the system structure and define the system's formal organization. The structural relationships commonly coincide with the movement of objects, such as material resources (money, goods, services), through the system. The structural relationships connecting the system with its environment represent the system's external relationships. Structural relationships among the subsystems are termed internal relationships.

Structural relationships also typically define the paths along which directives and control pass to and within an organizational system. Traditionally, business and governmental organizations describe their structure in terms of the reporting system of executives and departments. See Figure 3.6 for an example of such an organizational structure.

Communicative relationships exist between the system and its environment and between the system's subsystems. They may coincide with the structural relationships, but they typically include additional communication paths as well. The communicative relationships define the system's paths for exchange of information in terms of the inputs to each unit and the expected or required outputs.

It is along the communicative relationships that we can expect to find the system goals. The external relationships define the expectations and requirements of the environment with respect to the system. These requirements translate directly to the system goals. Within the system, the communicative relationships define the subsystem goals.

There are many of these relationships within a system; also, there is frequently more than one between any two system components. The internal relationships, representing the relationships between sibling subsystems, become clear when a subsystem under study is considered as a system in its own right.

The set of communicative relationships defines the information transfer of the system. This information flow can and will change over time in response to changes in the external system goals. A major task of system analysis is to identify these relationships and evaluate them with respect to the current and/or anticipated goal set.

INFORMATION SYSTEMS

In this text we are interested in the subset of systems called information systems as they occur in human organizations. With this restriction, we have defined the system environment to include humans and the organizational structures they have set up for some specified purpose. The primary goal of the information system for a specific organization can be generally stated as supporting the attainment of some aspect of the organization's goal.

From these observations, we know that the information system must be an open system and that its primary goals will be determined by the required interactions with the organization. We can formulate a working definition of an information system as

Information System A system whose goal is to provide information and information services for its environment.

This definition implies that an information system must encompass at least two subsystems, one consisting of the system's collection of information, the other providing the information services.

Information is such a common term that even persons professionally interested in information and information systems give it appreciable variations of meaning. We can start our discussion of information by analyzing the dictionary definition, which states that information is

the communication or reception of knowledge or intelligence . . . (Webster).[2]

Knowledge and *intelligence* both imply that there must be some human recipient who can interpret the message communicated and convert it into something meaningful, namely information. Thus, an information system requires human participation to interpret the messages maintained within the system.

A communication of intelligence can take any of several forms, activating one or more of our senses. For example, we may hear a drumming on the roof, feel a drop of something wet, or see a splash on a pond; any one of these could communicate the intelligence (that is, be the information message) that can be interpreted as "it is raining." Normally we think of information as implying new knowledge; repeated, identical messages quickly become uninteresting and ignored.

Humans collect information messages in their minds and memories in order to accumulate knowledge and thus reduce uncertainty in handling

2. By permission. From the *Merriam-Webster Dictionary*, © 1974 by Merriam-Webster Inc., publisher of the Merriam-Webster Dictionaries.

current, possibly new situations. People have developed a number of techniques for extending their memory capacity, principally involving the recording of information messages in accordance with some convention for future reference and use. The recording conventions must also be remembered, since recall of the messages will require knowledge of the recording conventions for proper interpretation. Consider the typical airline flight schedule; the sequence in which the departure and arrival times are stored must be known if the schedule is to be properly interpreted.

For people to be able to make use of a set of information messages, these messages must be kept in an organized way. We will call the set of information messages an *information archive*. To make this archive useful, there must be a set of functions or services by which the information messages can be both stored and retrieved. A system composed of an information archive and a set of service functions for information message storage and retrieval will be considered a basic information system.

A basic information system, containing only storage and retrieval functions for its information archive, will quickly become inadequate as an information service for a changing human environment. Knowledge upon which decisions can be made requires some processing of the basic information messages to identify trends or repetitions and to allow generalizations. Thereafter, there must be some function for communicating the information messages from storage to the intended recipient.

We can now make our working definition of an information system more content-specific by adapting Langefors's general definition:

Information System A system, including its information archive and processes, that is used to provide information (Langefors, 1973).

Information-System Structure

There are two ways of perceiving an information system. One is to view it as the set of information messages (the information archive) and to describe the information system by what it contains. The second views the information system through the set of information processes and describes the system by what it can do. It must be stressed that both components, the archive and the processes, are necessary if the system is to exist and be able to function.

For now, we will consider the information archive as a single unit for the storage of all information messages. (We will return in later chapters to the structure of the archive.) The elementary information processes can be grouped by their primary function. The following is a list of the basic information services that must be included in an information system. Note that for a system user, components 1 and 4 tend to define what the system contains and what it can do, respectively.

1. Information archive, providing a location for the set of information messages to be maintained within the system
2. Information storage, including information processes for message collection, interpretation, classification, and storage
3. Information retrieval, including processes for information request interpretation, search within the information archive, and extraction of the information messages requested
4. Information manipulation, providing processes by which a retrieved message or message group may be processed to produce new information
5. Information transfer, providing processes that, at least, transfer information messages from storage to the required output point, with possible routing to distant geographical points and necessary transformation from storage to transfer forms
6. Information dissemination, providing processes for decoding information messages from storage or transfer form to forms intelligible to humans and for possible generation of multiple copies

This basic structure of an information system is illustrated in Figure 1.4. Note that in a specific information system, a user-defined information process frequently combines several of these information services.

Figure 1.4 Information-System Structure

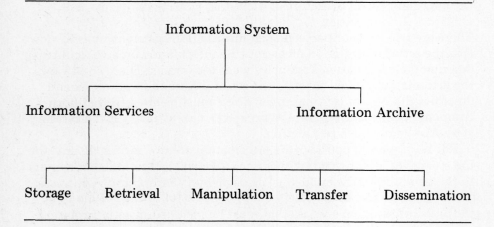

Computer-Based Information Systems

Typically, information systems are composed of both formal and informal subsystems, where the formal subsystems can be explicitly defined. Information messages within the formal subsystem may be stored in accordance with formal conventions; they are then termed data (see next section).

Since the advent of computers, storing data on computer, or machine-readable, media has become possible and increasingly economical. When this is done, the service functions for these data must be coded, programmed, or automated so that the machine-stored data can be machine-processed. Theoretically, an information system that is to serve a human organization can never be completely automated, as it will always be dependent on human interactions. If it were fully automated, it would become an automatic regulator or control process within a technical system.

The resulting partly automated information system is termed a computer-based information system, or CBIS. We can define a CBIS more formally.

Computed-Based Information System (CBIS) An information system with at least one automated subsystem and an at least partially automated information archive.

It is this subset of information systems with which we are concerned and which forms the primary subject of this book.

INFORMATION

From the preceding discussion we know that information is an intangible representation of knowledge, existing in a person's mind and subject to interpretation through that person's subjective experience. Yet we still need to capture this knowledge or set of information messages so that we may utilize collective experiences in solving current problems.

Information versus Data

The analysis and design of information systems requires that information and data and their separate processes and functions be distinguished and separated within the total information system, since the utilization of such technical aids as automation or computerization is feasible only for the formal data and data processes. (See Chapter 2 for a detailed discussion of informal versus formal information and information systems.)

In the context of automated (computer-based) information systems, the International Federation for Information Processing (IFIP) defines information and data as follows.

Information The meaning that a human expresses by or extracts from data by means of the known conventions of the representation used (IFIP, 1966).

Data A representation of facts or ideas in a formalized manner, capable of being communicated or manipulated by some process (IFIP, 1966).

Note that to be considered as data, information need not be presented in machine-readable format; it must only be recorded in accordance with some formal conventions. Thus, an accountant's books or the statistical office's publications are typically full of data to be converted to information by the prospective human reader.

From our definitions, information exists in a human mind after the perception and interpretation of information-bearing messages. Note that a necessary condition for interpretation is previous knowledge, such as the ability to read a text. Data are the result of converting information and recording it on a nonhuman medium. Data must then be reinterpreted to be converted into information. Figure 1.5 illustrates this concept of information and data. Humans use their senses to perceive *data* and previous knowledge to produce *information*. This information can then be used to increase knowledge and decrease uncertainty. The information a human acquires may be recorded, producing *data* for later interpretation by others.

In the context of this text, we are interested in the information flows and data repositories within organizations. We assume that the data are collected to describe various aspects of the organization's functioning and that the interpretation of the data is meant to support some decision-making process within the organization.

Information Value

Since establishing a formal information system, particularly a computer-based one, can be very costly, one should determine the value (to the organization) of the information to be maintained within the system. There are a number of characteristics of information that affect its value. The principal characteristics include

Figure 1.5 Information and Data

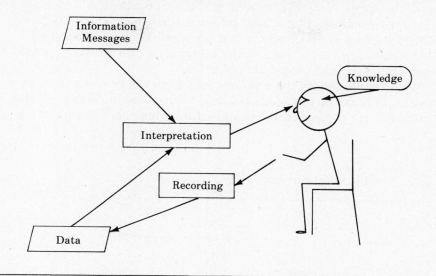

1. *Comprehensiveness.* It is generally true that an increase in the number of information messages will lead to increased knowledge or reduction of uncertainty.
2. *Detail.* The more detailed an information message is, the greater its information content. Increasing detail will, up to a point, increase the value of information.
3. *Age.* It is generally true that the older an information message is, the less useful it may be.
4. *Accuracy.* For many usages an information message must be absolutely correct; for others, such as statistical processing, it may be slightly less than perfect and still be valuable. Normally information value will decrease as accuracy decreases.
5. *Relevance.* This is critical for interpretation, but it is not always simply defined. However, we can assume that the information value will increase with relevance.

Generally it can be observed that information value does not increase steadily with an increase in any one or any combination of these characteristics. (Note that we have assumed that an increase in each characteristic, with the exception of age, will increase the information value.) The information value will reach a saturation point, beyond which it may actually fall off as the human or human organization becomes unable to absorb the increase.

Figure 1.6 illustrates the information-value curve for two common characteristics, detail and age, that frequently compete for organizational resources. Note that increasing the level of detail will increase the information value until a saturation point is reached. Thereafter, any further increase in detail will exceed the user's ability to handle the additional information. Finally, the user will be "drowned" in detail, resulting in an information value of 0.

Age, as measured by the time required from the occurrence of an event until it can be reported, will tend to decrease information value. A high volume of instantly available information is not normally feasible

Figure 1.6 Information Value

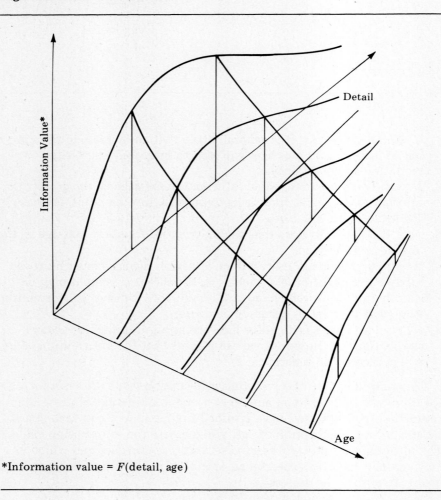

*Information value = F(detail, age)

and would not readily be digestible; rather, an acceptable level of detail and age for the information must be established.

Providing high-quality information obviously has a cost. The objective of the design of an information system should be to provide the highest-quality information at a reasonable cost. We can set up an information-quality function as follows:

$$Q = F(D, T, A, R)$$

where Q measures information quality as a function of D, the level of detail, which affects Q positively; T, the information age, which affects Q negatively; A, the degree of accuracy, which affects Q positively; and R, the relevance, which affects Q positively.

The relationship between information value and quality is illustrated graphically in Figure 1.7a. Again we note the saturation function, beyond which further information quality adds little value. Note that

Figure 1.7 Information Quality

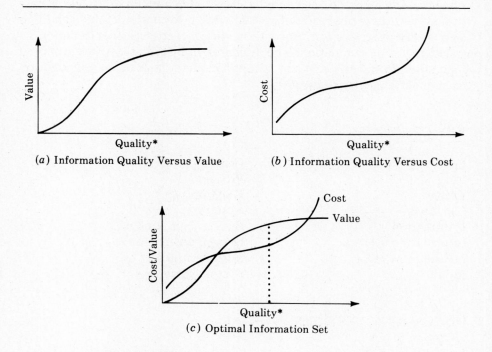

(a) Information Quality Versus Value

(b) Information Quality Versus Cost

(c) Optimal Information Set

*Information quality $= F$(detail, age, accuracy, relevance)

Figure 1.7a does not take into account the possibility that additional information quality may have a negative value after it reaches a saturation point.

The cost of providing quality information can be described by a cost function similar to that illustrated in Figure 1.7b. There will be an initial cost associated with establishing the system and making any information available. Thereafter, the cost will increase more slowly as the quality increases, until a further increase in quality is not feasible and the cost of attempting it sharply increases.

By evaluating the cost and value functions for an information system, an optimal level of cost and quality may be determined (see Figure 1.7c). This value should function as a major criterion for the design and evaluation of alternative structures for an information system.

SUMMARY

In this chapter, we have attempted to show how the concepts of systems, subsystems, input, output, feedback, and relationships from general systems theory can be applied to the description of information systems, which can be considered a subset of general systems. Information systems have six basic subsystems: the information archive and five elementary processes for information storage, retrieval, manipulation, transfer, and dissemination. The design of an information system should take into account the cost and quality characteristics of the information to be maintained by the system.

KEY CONCEPTS

CBIS	Output
Data	Process
Entity	Relationship
Feedback	System
Information	System component
Information system	System environment
Information value	System object
Input	System structure

DISCUSSION QUESTIONS

1. Define and give an example of each of the key concepts.
2. Discuss open versus closed systems. Why must information systems be considered open systems?

3. Information-system relationships can be separated into four categories: relationships with the system environment, relationships within the system, structural relationships, and communicative relationships. Discuss the degree of overlap and the distinctiveness of each of these categories. Give examples of each category of relationship.
4. How does general systems theory influence our approach to information system analysis and design?
5. Why is it important to differentiate between information and data?
6. Which information characteristics influence information value? Explain the quality and value curves given in Figure 1.7.
7. What is user satisfaction in relation to information systems? What information-system characteristics influence user satisfaction?

RECOMMENDED READINGS

J. P. Couger and R. Knapp, eds. *System Analysis Techniques.* New York: John Wiley & Sons, 1974.
> This is a collection of papers covering underlying systems theory and techniques for the analysis and evaluation of information and data systems. Of particular interest to this chapter are papers by von Bertalanffy, Ackoff, Langefors, J. Emery, and Gregory.

Emery, E. F., ed. *System Thinking.* Middlesex, England: Penguin Education, 1969.
> This is a collection of papers presenting the basic concepts and theories of general systems theory. Papers by Katz, Sommerhoff, and Simon most directly influence the concepts presented in this chapter.

Langefors, B. *Theoretical Analysis of Information Systems.* 2nd ed. Lund, Sweden: Studentlitteratur/Auerbach, 1973.
> This text forms the background for the approach used in this book.

Nordbotten, S. *Information System Analysis and Design.* Available (in Norwegian) as a compendium from the Institute for Information Sciences, University of Bergen, 5014-U Bergen, Norway, 1978.
> With the Langefors text, this text forms the background for this book.

Szyperski and Grochla, eds. *Design and Implementation of Computer-Based Information Systems.* Alphen aan den Rijn, The Netherlands: Sijthoff & Noordhoff Publishers, 1979.
> This is a collection of papers presenting the current (1979) philosophies of CBIS design and implementation evaluation. Of special interest for this chapter are papers by Kriebel, Lucas, Clausen, and Seibt.

Chapter 2
Administrative Information Systems

INTRODUCTION

Whenever two or more people or groups try to work together toward a common goal, they are likely to establish an organization in which individuals are assigned separate but supporting activities. Within the organization, an information system develops to support and document their activities. This information system, however informal, provides the communication procedures used to transfer information about the group's operations. We are interested in these information systems, particularly those in formal organizations. For this discussion we will use the following definition of an organization.

Organization A group of people cooperating to achieve a mutual goal within a legislative or statutory framework that defines their individual authority and responsibilities.

Organizations commonly establish a management section, which maintains the goal orientation of the organization, administers the communication of information between the organization and its environment, and facilitates the information flow within the subdivisions of the organization. We will call the information system used to support these activities an *administrative information system* (AIS).

An AIS typically maintains information on the employees (staff), customers (clients, members), products or services, orders (requests), shipments, funds, accounts (bills and receipts), and so on, of the organization. As a full information system, the AIS also includes the processes required to process the information. As an organization grows in size and complexity, so do its administration and its AIS. The AIS is usually perceived to be made up of a number of relatively independent information systems. For example, there can be AIS subsystems for personnel administration, production management, billing, and accounts receivable.

Since the advent of computer technology, various AIS subsystems have been automated, creating computer-based information systems (CBISs). There has been much dissatisfaction with CBISs. One complaint has been the CBIS's perceived incompleteness in providing expected or required functions or services. This problem of designing "complete" CBISs has increased interest in the study of the characteristics of administrative information systems.

A great deal has been written about information systems intended for administrative support, particularly the subset that is or can be automated. Unfortunately, the term *information system* has been given varying definitions and thus scope. The following three definitions are illustrative.

Information System (*IS*)

1. "... any system, including its processes, that is used to provide information." (Langefors, 1973)
2. "... a set of organized procedures which when executed, provide information to support decision making." (Lucas, 1978)
3. "... an assemblage or collection of people, machines, ideas, and activities that gathers and processes data in a manner that will meet the formalized information requirements of an organization." (Burch, Strater, & Grudnitski, 1979)

Definitions 2 and 3 are actually included in definition 1. In each case the definition tries to specify the kind of processes ("organized procedures"), purpose ("support decision making"), formality ("formal information"), or structure ("people, machines, . . .") of an information system. This detail, though illustrative in a given context, also limits the types of systems that are included.

For our purposes we will use the definition in Chapter 1, which extends the Langefors definition to explicitly include the information archive. This general definition lets us consider all information systems, both formal and informal. Using this definition, we can define the subset of administrative information systems as follows:

Administrative Information System (AIS) An information system, including its information archive and processes, used to provide information to support the management functions of an organization.

We can view the AIS of an organization as a single system or as a multitude of sub-information systems, each supporting the specific information needs of some subdivision of the organization.

FORMAL VERSUS INFORMAL INFORMATION SYSTEMS

We can use the traditional pyramid model of an organization, shown in Figure 2.1, to illustrate administrative structure. This figure indicates three levels of management: strategic, tactical, and technical.

Figure 2.1 Formal versus Informal Information Systems

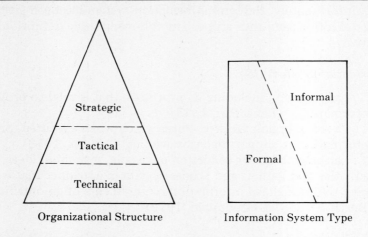

From management studies, we know that the problems faced, and thus the decisions required, by managers at these three levels differ in their level of detail, scope, and predictability. We can assume that the information systems required to support these decisions and the managers making them will also need to differ in scope and detail to satisfy the information needs of the decisions being made at each level.

An information system's degree of formality reflects our ability to define the system's structure and content, especially our ability to identify the information needed to make decisions. We know that strategic problems and decisions occur unpredictably, vary over time, and often depend on events outside the control of the organization (such as the state of the economy). Much of the information needed to support these decisions will often be based on interpretations of events outside the organization. On the other hand, we know that most of the problems and decisions faced by technical management are predictable and depend on known information generated within the organization.

For example, the decision to reorder supplies depends on the level of stock and the rate of withdrawal, both of which are generated and maintained within an inventory information system. Such a well-defined decision situation allows quite specific definition of the structure and content of the information system that supports it. The resulting system is termed a *formal system*, meaning well defined. As indicated in Figure 2.1, most formal information systems are found at the technical management level.

The term *informal information system* reflects our inability to specify precisely the decision requirements, and thus the information requirements, for a given management decision area. Typically, new decisions arise at unpredictable points in time and require a wide variety of supportive information, much of which may not be explicitly generated or gathered by the organization.

For example, selecting a building site for a warehouse depends only partly on internal space requirements. The decision must also take into account the site's proximity to transportation, cost, ground conditions, available builders, and perhaps the personal preference of the organization's owner or local political opinions. Much of this other information may not be available within the organization, or may be too costly to gather in time to make the decision. The decision will be made, and the supportive information system is termed informal to reflect its lack of definition or structure. As indicated in Figure 2.1, most informal information systems support strategic management.

Note that there is no clear, fixed line separating formal and informal information systems. As we learn more about decision making and increase our ability to capture and process information, we can expect the line to move toward the upper right in the figure, indicating that there will be a greater proportion of formalized information systems supporting high-level or strategic decisions.

Formal and informal information systems can also be characterized by the types of information messages involved. Remember that, according to our definitions of information and data, recorded, formal information is data. Table 2.1 lists the principal characteristics of the information and data required in formal and informal information systems.

Table 2.1 Characteristics of Information and Data

Property	System Type	
	Formal	Informal
Information		
Source	Internal	External
Scope	Detailed	Summary
Usage	Frequent	Irregular
Data		
Time Frame	Historical	Predictive
Accuracy	High	Variable
Organization	Structured	Ill-Defined

Formal information systems tend to contain information describing events within the organization for which frequent use is anticipated. This information is often very detailed, e.g., giving the weight, dimensions, composition, price, and quantity of each product part in the organization's inventory. The data representations for this information can be well defined, accuracy can be high, and historical data can be kept. Informal information systems have opposite tendencies.

Data Processing Systems

Data processing systems are formalized subsystems of an information system. Their goal is to provide the information system with data processing services. Data processing systems are systems in their own right. Their environment contains the informal subsystems of the parent information system, and their component subsystems consist of the formal data files and data processing routines. We can define a data processing system as:

> *Data Processing System* A system, consisting of a collection of data and a set of formal processing procedures, which provides storage, retrieval, manipulation, and communication of the data of an information system.

Data processing systems consist of five fundamental subsystems.

1. The data base, which will contain the formal records of the organization; e.g., the specific records, accounts, files, inventory data, employee and customer data, or correspondence, will depend on the information system to be served.
2. Data acquisition procedures, consisting of procedures for data receipt, verification, classification, and ordering.
3. Data storage and retrieval procedures, consisting of procedures for data storage and retrieval, maintenance of storage structures, and search strategies.
4. Data processing procedures, consisting of processes that transform the data or groups of data from one form to another. These processes record transactions, modify data values, analyze data sets, answer queries, and construct reports.
5. Dissemination procedures, consisting of procedures for reproduction and communication of the data stored or produced through any of the processing procedures.

The data processing system may be manual or fully or partially automated. A CBIS is a partially automated system with both manual and

Figure 2.2 Computer-Based Information-System Structure

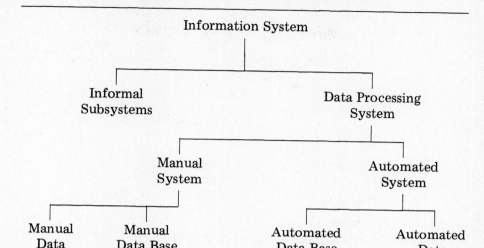

automated subsystems. Figure 2.2 illustrates the structure of a computer-based information system. Note that both manual and automated subsystems of the data processing system contain the same basic types of data processing subsystems. The manual processes work primarily with the noncomputerized data base, whereas the automated data processes work exclusively with the automated data base.

Automated Systems

As previously noted, the automated data processing system is a subsystem of the data processing subsystem of an information system. Its environment consists of the information system's informal subsystems and the manual data processing subsystems. As a data processing system, its subsystems consist of the five components listed, although in this case all are automated.

Table 2.2 Automated versus Manual Data Processing Functions

Data-System Functions	System Type	
	Manual	Automated
Data acquisition		
Capture	Most usual	Possible
Verification	Common	Increasing
Classification	Most usual	Uncommon
Ordering	Common	Common
Data administration		
Storage	Common	Common
Retrieval	Common	Common
Data processing		
Calculation	Decreasing	Increasing
Summarization	Decreasing	Frequent
Dissemination		
Reproduction	Common	Increasing
Communication	Common	Increasing

The manual and automated data processing systems are closely integrated, with the latter often automating functions previously performed manually. Table 2.2 lists the basic data processing functions by primary task and indicates the degree to which automation is currently used.

The degree of automation, or the relative size of the automated subsystem within a data processing system, will vary with each information system and with the requirements and constraints of the organization of which it is a part. The degree of automation can vary from none to almost complete. It is theoretically impossible to construct a fully automated information system for administrative support as long as people need to interact with the system to extract data in response to organization requests.

Even though the automated data processing system is only a subsystem of an information system, we will devote the rest of this book to the design of good automated systems. However, students must not assume that the automated system somehow exists by itself. All activities within the automated system must work toward satisfying one or more of the goals that the organization sets for the information system.

ADMINISTRATIVE INFORMATION SYSTEM STRUCTURE

As an information system, an administrative information system (AIS) will have the general system structure described in Chapter 1 and illustrated in Figure 1.4. However, since it is a subset of general information systems, we can expect that an AIS can be described by characteristics that are specific for it.

As previously defined, an AIS supports the administrative functions of an organization. One of the main tasks of administration is to facilitate the communication of information within and to and from the organization. A central element needed for this task is the organization's information archive. Information processes or procedures must be defined so that the information can be extracted and presented properly.

Next we will explore those system characteristics that are specific or common to AISs.

The AIS Environment

The dominant feature of any AIS environment is its people. These people typically form user groups that can be characterized by their members' similar information requirements vis-à-vis the AIS. Both user groups and individuals are referred to as system users to emphasize their relationship to the AIS. Since the AIS is basically a tool to facilitate communication between people or groups of people, it is the requirements of these people that define the ideal goals of the AIS. Importantly, an operative AIS is judged by its ability to satisfy the requirements and expectations of the various user groups.

We know that an organization's administration has managers at each decision and responsibility level: strategic, tactical, and technical. Also, the clerical staff performs the basic procedures of the AIS functions. Not always remembered in analyzing an AIS are the professional staff, who are charged with collecting and manipulating information and/or data to prepare reports on the status and development of plan details in support of managerial decision makers. Not-so-frequent, though important, AIS users are members of the production staff, who need information specific to their production-oriented tasks.

The organization's external contacts also have an important, if indirect, impact on the immediate environment of the AIS. In some instances, external user groups may also be direct users of the AIS. Users external to the organization include customers or clients, suppliers of goods or services, owners and/or shareholders, and control agencies, such as government and auditors.

Figure 2.3 illustrates the user groups that may be found in an AIS environment. Clearly not all groups are necessary for each AIS, nor does the figure illustrate the relative importance of the various groups. The exact composition of the AIS environment for each individual system must be established.

Each interest group will need specific information services from the AIS. Some of these requirements will conflict, and some will be beyond the resources and/or policy directives of the organization. The resolution of user-group requirements provides the specific goal set for a given AIS.

The AIS environment also sets design constraints for the individual system. The most important constraint is the financial resources dedicated to the establishment, operation, and maintenance of the system. Information policy, both public and organizational, also sets boundaries on the content and capabilities of the system. The available human resources, their number and skills, may also set limits on the system design. Finally, the technological facilities the system is to use will set constraints on both design and implementation.

Figure 2.3 The AIS User Environment

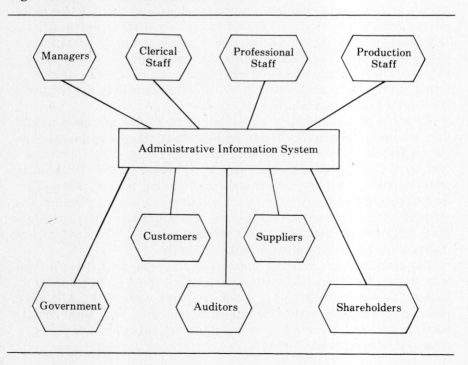

An AIS may also have other information systems and AISs in its environment. In our AIS environment system, shown in Figure 2.3, these environmental systems are embedded as a component of the owning user group. However, in dealing with a specific system, these existing systems may place serious constraints on the structure of the developing system and therefore must be identified as early as possible in the system analysis phase.

General AIS Goals

From the definition of an AIS, we know that an AIS exists and has as its primary goal "to provide information to support the administrative functions of the organization." Within the constraints set by the organization's resources, policy, obligations, and technological expertise, the specific goal set of an AIS is defined by the information requirements of the user groups directed to carry out the organization's administrative functions. Thus we can state that the primary goal of an AIS is to provide information services to the user community to satisfy their information requirements.

However true this statement is, it is too general to help us define the goals of a specific AIS. First, the general characteristics of the information services must be specified, for both the information archive and the information processes. Typically, requirements for information archives are given as desired characteristics of the information to be kept. (See Chapter 1 and Figure 1.6.) Thus a second general goal can be stated as maintaining accurate, timely, and relevant information.

Requirements for information processes must be developed from the information requirements of the separate user groups. Thus we can state a third general AIS goal as providing the information processes necessary to support the decisions and reporting obligations of the user community.

Goals 2 and 3, though true, are also too general to fully define the goal set for a specific AIS. These general goals must be supplemented by a goal set that reflects specific user requirements. To establish such a goal set, each user group's requirements must be identified and the conflicts between them resolved. Table 2.3 presents an example of a common information requirement to be expected from each of the user groups identified in the previous section (see Figure 2.3).

When working with a specific AIS, the types of requirements identified in Table 2.3 must be replaced by the specific and detailed requirements of the actual user groups the AIS is to serve. An analysis of this requirement set, reducing duplications and eliminating conflicts between requirements and conflicts with the organization's constraints, will provide the obtainable requirement set or goal set for the AIS.

Table 2.3 General User Requirements

User Group	Example of Requirement Type
Managers	Sales reports by product or section of the organization
Clerical staff	Registration of customer orders Check of order status
Professional staff	Evaluation of sales trends for products or sub-sections of the organization
Production staff	Report for each product of number on order, quantity on hand
Customers	Reports of products and services Status of own account
Suppliers	Status of own account Status of own orders or shipments
Government	Financial status of organization Employment statistics by sex, race, etc.
Auditors	Activities on all accounts
Shareholders	General status of organization

Establishing the goal set for an information system is the first task of system analysis and design. A methodology for accomplishing this task is given in Chapter 4.

Basic AIS Components

We have been considering the AIS as though it were one system supporting the whole organization. Conceptually there must be such a total system if the organization is to function as a unit. However, in reality it is more practical to consider the AIS as a system of AISs, each supporting a subsystem of the administration. This is particularly true when attempting to construct a CBIS for some subsystem of the organization.

Figure 2.4 shows a simplified model of an organization's administrative structure. Note that this model shows a traditional functional structure for an organization. It is possible to have other organizational structures without altering the assertion that there is an AIS to support the administration of each organizational subsystem. Thus we assume that the organization's AIS structure closely follows its administrative

Figure 2.4 Organizational Administrative Structure

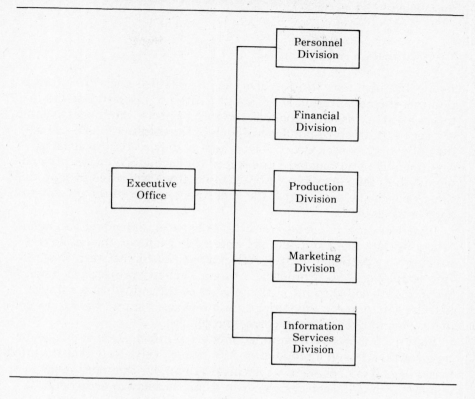

structure. Our system shows only the first-level subsystems. Each of these subsystems will usually be further divided according to the subtasks of the administrative areas. The supporting AIS may or may not be subdivided along these lines.

An AIS has the same basic components as an information system. (See Figures 1.3 and 2.2.) There are two major subsystems, the information archive and the information processes. As shown in Figure 2.2, the information processes consist of four subsystems providing the information services of acquisition, storage and retrieval, processing, and dissemination for the AIS.

In an AIS for a specific subsystem, such as the accounting system or the personnel system, the basic information services are often combined into composite data processing tasks or procedures, each of which gets its name from the primary function of the process (post receipt, record pay raise, and so on). This approach can lead to a good deal of overlap of information-processing tasks, particularly data acquisition, administration, and dissemination. Keeping these basic services separate eliminates duplication and simplifies the total AIS design. We will return to these ideas in later chapters.

The Information Archive

In an AIS, the information archive can be described as all the information that the organization keeps about entities of interest. Entities in this context are usually products, services, projects, employees, customers, accounts, or correspondence. Much of the information describing the individuals in each entity class is kept as data records in separate files (manual or automated), one record for each individual entity and one file for each entity type. For example, there will often be a product file, a project file, a personnel file, and so on, as part of the information archive for an AIS.

Interrelationships between entities or between individuals are maintained by data items and data processes. For example, the employees assigned to a particular project reflect a relationship between the entities "employees" and "projects." A data element "project assignment" is commonly added to the characteristics of the individual employee, and the data processes requiring this knowledge "know" how to associate each employee with the correct project(s).

Figure 2.5 shows two simplified models of information archives, for a personnel AIS and a production AIS, respectively. Note that the information archives of these two systems overlap. This can make maintaining the data in each system at the same currency level difficult.

Ideally, an organization should have only one information archive, from which each of the subsystem AISs retrieves information. However, this is seldom the case in practice because of the size and complexity of design of such an information archive. We will return to the analysis of information archives and the design of their data structures in Chapters 5 and 9, respectively.

Information Processes

As previously noted, an AIS must provide the basic processes of information and data acquisition, storage and retrieval, and dissemination. In addition, the set of data manipulation processes will be particular to each AIS.

The data manipulation processes of an AIS are defined by the user information requirements. That is, there is a direct correspondence between the goal set, stated as user requirements, and the information and data processes that the AIS must support.

Figure 2.5 AIS Information Archive: Examples

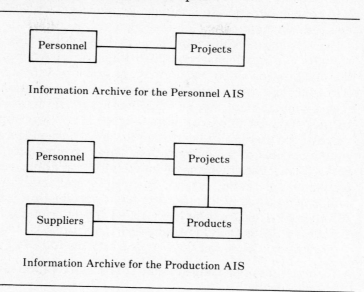

Information Archive for the Personnel AIS

Information Archive for the Production AIS

The data manipulation subsystem is the most volatile of the AIS subsystems, as it is directly affected by changes in user requirements that reflect changes in the organization's environment and the AIS environment. For this reason, as well as to separate maintenance of the data base and the processing routines, the four AIS information and data processing subsystems should be clearly identified and kept separate.

Identification and design of the data manipulation processes are central topics of Chapters 4, 5, and 10.

COMPUTER-BASED ADMINISTRATIVE INFORMATION SYSTEMS

Our concept of an organizational AIS is a collection of interrelated sub-information systems that support the administration of an organization. AIS subsystems can exist independently with varying degrees of automation, from none to nearly full. This system concept differs from the older concept of a management information system (MIS) mainly in that an MIS was envisaged as a total, relatively fully automated system.

The MIS was introduced in the early 1960s as a complete computer-based information system that would support all management decisions. Unfortunately, this ambitious goal has yet to be fulfilled, and the term

MIS has come into some disrepute. The principal problems with the MIS concept arose in determining the management level for the system and formalizing the decision-making processes.

In concept, an AIS is more general than was the MIS, as it explicitly includes not only managers, but all administrative personnel along with the organization's external contacts as primary system users. Also, the AIS concept does not necessarily imply computerization.

Attempts to implement a computer-based MIS have generally led to the development of one or more functional CBISs to support one or more of the user groups identified for an AIS (see Figure 2.3) within a functional area of the organization. These systems have been given names that reflect their major function or user group, such as accounting system, marketing system, financial system, inventory control system, personnel administration system, or production control system. (See [Brabb 1980] or [McLeod 1979] for descriptions of common functional CBISs found in business organizations.)

Functional CBISs can be classified into the following types:

- Transaction-processing systems (TPS) for technical-level information processing
- Decision support systems (DSS) for tactical- and/or strategic-level decision makers
- Office automation systems (OAS) for clerical operations
- (Libraries of) data analysis and modeling systems for use by the professional staff

Since each of these system types supports a user group within the organization's administration, they can all be said to be elements of an organizational AIS.

Transaction-Processing Systems (TPS)

Perhaps the oldest of the computerized administrative support systems, transaction processing systems have existed since the early 1960s. A major reason for this is that the TPS consists of well-defined processes that are repetitive in nature. In this context, definitions are as follows:

Transaction A formal process supporting an operational-level activity within an organization.

Transaction-Processing System (TPS) A set of transactions supporting a functional area of an organization.

A transaction usually modifies data describing individual entities of concern to the organization. For example, an order transaction will often involve one customer and one item or a small number of items, with possible initiation of one resupply order from one vendor or supplier. The transaction process will then be repeated for each order the organization receives. Status reports on individual entities, related groups of entities, or whole entity classes are included as processing modules of the TPS.

A strong motivation for developing a TPS was, and still is, a clear need to "do something" about the growing flow of paperwork, which hinders the maintenance of acceptable processing times for individual transactions. Since the work to be done is well understood and actually being performed within the manual system, an automated TPS is relatively easy to define and implement.

The principal environment of the TPS is a functional area within the organization at the operational or production level. This area maintains contact with the organization's customers (clients) and suppliers and is responsible for maintaining inventories and service levels. The organizational user groups are typically the data or information-processing personnel of the clerical staff and their technical-level managers.

The primary goal set of a TPS is to process transactions generated by the TPS environment, record appropriate data about the transactions and their effect on organizational resources, and report the status of the organization's operative-level systems upon request.

The general structure of a TPS is shown in Figure 2.6. Transactions are normally prepared by an information clerk, the person acting as the intermediary between the system users and the TPS. TPS output consists of reports initiated by the transactions. A TPS has five basic components, all of which can be automated.

1. *Data files*, which contain the data needed to process the transactions, for example, a customer file, products file, order file, suppliers file, and so on.
2. An *input processor*, which checks that the incoming transaction is valid in the context of the TPS (that the customer exists (or can be added), that the product exists, that the transaction type is valid, and so on).
3. A set of *transaction processors*, which perform the actual transaction data processing, as defined by the transaction request, including such secondary activities as adding a new customer or generating back orders.
4. A *report processor*, which presents the transaction response to the user or information clerk.
5. A *transaction library*, which contains the programs that represent the transactions and reports.

TPSs come in all sizes, from those operated by one person that activate some 10 transaction or report types for 2 or 3 files to systems with thousands of input clerks activating hundreds of transaction types for

Figure 2.6 Transaction Processing System Structure

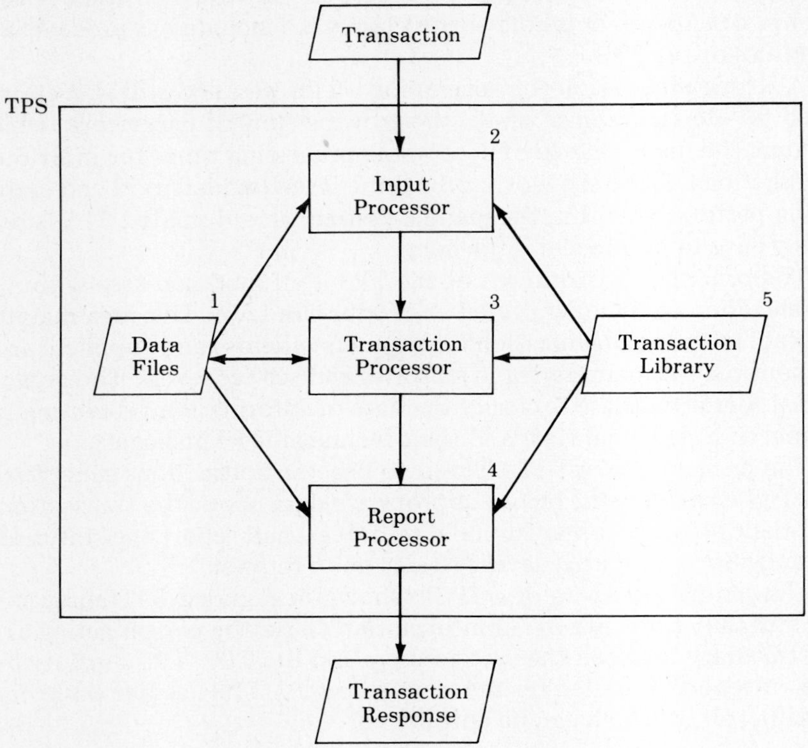

50 to 100 files, or, more commonly, a central data base. Whatever its size, the TPS structure remains as modeled in Figure 2.6; only the complexity of the components increases. Choosing a technical support system (computers and their peripherals) for a TPS is discussed in Chapter 11.

Decision Support Systems (DSS)

The MIS concept of establishing a total information system to support management-level decision making created high expectations, which could not possibly be satisfied with the rather low-level information processing embedded in the TPS, which was the major system type developed under the umbrella of MIS. At best, a TPS serves as a decision support system for technical-level management by providing information on the status of the operative system. Information that can support tactical- and strategic-level decisions is not generally available from a TPS.

To support higher-level management decisions, it was necessary to develop a system that could provide information comparing subsections and cross sections of the organization, analyze trends within and outside the organization, forecast future trends, simulate the consequences of different actions, evaluate alternative actions, and perform other similar functions. The data for these processes need not always have a high level of accuracy, currency, or detail, as aggregate trends may be sufficient. However, the data processing services must be quickly available, as the decisions that require this information cannot be delayed. Finally, this system must be easily available to non-data processing personnel—that is, to managers and their professional staff.

Technical developments that improved the scope and processing power of TPSs have made the development of reasonably high-level DSSs possible. In particular, the use of data base management technology in most of the organization's functional areas is making organization-wide data available. The development of terminals and the decline in their price have made direct access to data and results feasible. And finally, the development of user-friendly languages, such as EMPIRE, IFPS, MAPPER, and SPSS, has provided a means of communication that allows non-data processing personnel to interact with computerized systems.

DSSs have also been improved through the development of decision models for a variety of decision types and through the increased use of analytical methods for decision support. Statistical and econometric models, developed for special-case environments, are now generally available for complex analysis of data trends and forecasts. With simulation technology, impact analysis of decision alternatives takes a relatively short time.

The environment of the DSS encompasses strategic- and tactical-level management and their professional staff. The information includes both internal organization data and external data on such things as market trends.

The primary goal of the DSS is to make possible the analysis of both internally and externally generated data, quickly and easily.

A basic DSS structure is given in Figure 2.7. Note the structural similarity to the TPS. The primary differences between these two systems lie in the type of processing performed in element 3, the size and coverage of the data base, and the variety, language level, and degree of predictability of the initial input requests. The following component description is a goal statement. There are few systems available today that have all these features.

1. *Data files* or a *data base*, which can contain both internally gener-
    ated data, commonly from the organization's TPSs, and data
    collected from external sources, such as national and international
    statistical offices, market research institutes, and economic fore-
    casting institutes.
2. A *query interpreter*, which is capable of translating queries of high
    complexity, defining requests for a wide range of information proc-
    essing of diverse information, into machine processing activities.
3. A *query processor*, which can draw on a variety of analysis programs
    and an extensive data base in order to process the query.
4. A *response processor*, which can format the output data generated
    as a response to the query in a form compatible with the original
    input language used.
5. A *model library*, which contains econometric, statistical, and other
    models that can be activated during query processing.

Figure 2.7 Decision Support System Structure

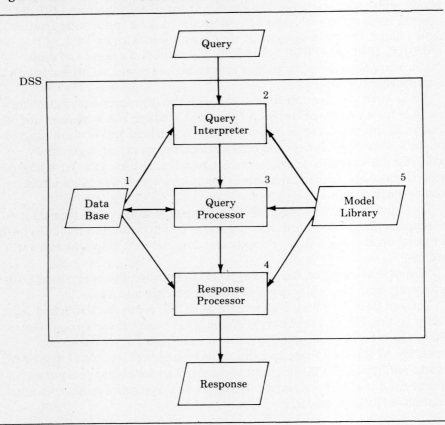

Because of the relatively large size of the data base and the complexity of the modeling programs, a full-scale DSS would require a large-scale computer environment to function efficiently. However, decision support systems are still relatively new, many in development stages. Many of their components, particularly the external data base and the modeling programs, have been developed outside the DSS owner organization. This has led to sharing of facilities through time-sharing networks, allowing smaller organizations with more limited resources to develop a DSS that can tap an information network for both data and analysis programs. There are also special-purpose DSSs for minicomputers or microcomputers. Technical configurations for these systems will be discussed in Chapter 11.

Office Automation Systems (OAS)

Transaction processing and decision support systems both provide traditional, primarily numeric data processing within the organization. They are particularly useful in the collection, manipulation, analysis, and presentation of data, including such character data as names and addresses. However, a large part of an organization's administrative effort is directed toward running the office, performing such verbal or text-oriented tasks as mail processing; preparing letters, memos, and reports; filing and retrieving textual materials (letters and reports), juggling appointments; arranging and attending meetings; and telephoning. Office automation systems try to provide support for these office activities.

Studies have indicated that office costs have doubled in recent years, increasing from 20 to 30 percent to 40 to 50 percent of an organization's expenses, without a corresponding increase in office productivity. Where automated word/text processing procedures have been introduced, productivity has increased by 40 percent and more over the manual typing pool alternative.

The environment for an OAS encompasses all office personnel: managers, assistant managers, professional staff, secretaries, and clerks. The physical environment is usually limited to one building or area; however, it can include distant geographical areas.

The goal of an OAS is to provide automated (computerized) support for office functions of the type indicated above, and particularly, to increase productivity and speed of document development, filing and retrieval of materials, and communications.

For comparison with the TPS and DSS system structures, Figure 2.8 uses a model similar to that of Figures 2.6 and 2.7 to illustrate an OAS structure. Though this is a valid model of the structure of an OAS, a

Figure 2.8 Office Automation System Structure

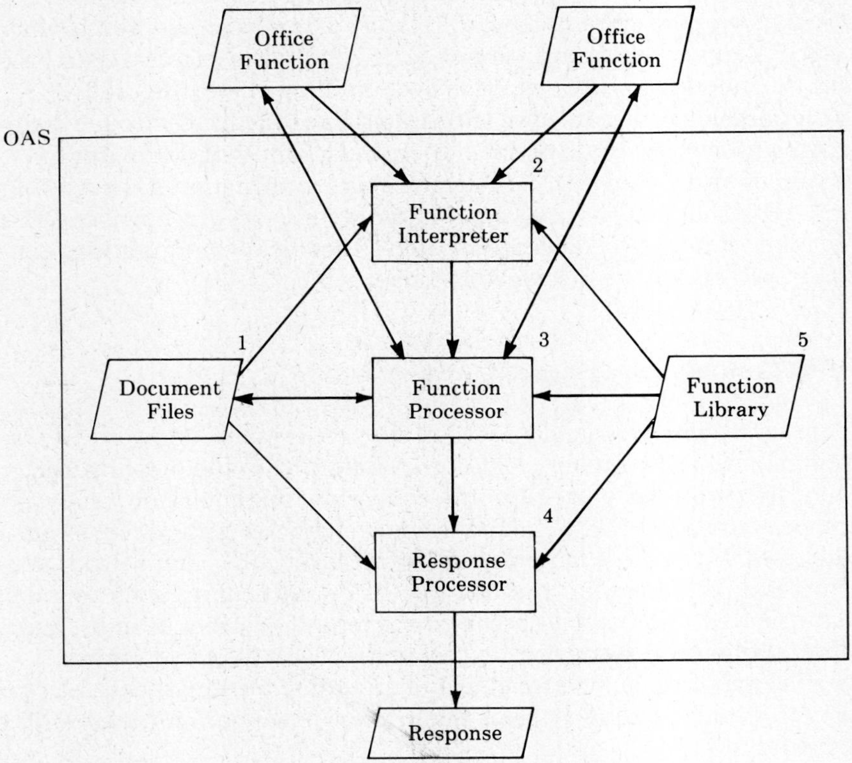

more informative model would detail the separate functions of text
processing, mail switching, calendar, and so on.

OAS components, as illustrated in Figure 2.8, include:

1. *Document files*, which contain the data necessary for supporting the
   office functions, chiefly the document collections encompassing
   correspondence, memos, and reports. These files may also be connected with or share access to the data files of the TPS and/or DSS.
2. A *function interpreter*, which in a multiple-function environment,
   selects the function to be operative and allows the user to switch
   between functions.
3. A *function processor*, which can be either a special-purpose computer or a computer program that performs the selected function
   (text processing, filing, information retrieval, mailing, appointment
   scheduling, and so on).

4. A *response processor*, often embedded in the function interpreter, which formats the responses to the user, frequently as a menu of options giving alternatives for continuing function processing.
5. A *function library*, which contains the function programs that actually automate the functions.

Note that with an OAS, the user will spend a large percentage of time interacting directly with the function processor. For example, if the function is text or document production, the user will be actively involved for the same length of time as would be needed to type a first draft manually. However, to make corrections, only the affected parts of the document will need to be retyped, and this substantially reduces correction time.

There is still relatively little automation in office procedures despite the availability of technical procedures that could be applied. Among the technical components available for OAS construction are:

- powerful word and text processing systems for document production.
- storage and retrieval systems for documents.
- message switching systems for interoffice mail.
- central calendar systems for coordinating appointments.
- inexpensive micro- and minicomputer systems capable of office applications.
- local network technology to connect multiple work stations.
- telecommunication systems for conferences.

Constructing an OAS becomes a problem of assembling these existing, available technologies and training office personnel in their use. An OAS can be implemented on any size computer. Chapter 11 contains a more detailed discussion of physical implementation alternatives for an OAS.

SAMPLE INFORMATION SYSTEM

The purpose of this text is to present students with a coherent set of tools and a methodology that will enable them to design an efficient, flexible computer-based information system for administrative support. In order to present the tools and procedures of system analysis and design, we will use examples from the analysis and design of an administrative information system for a hypothetical university.

This particular system was chosen on the assumption that all students would have at least an intuitive idea of the administrative goals and information problems of a university system. However, the examples selected are of general types that will be found in any administrative system.

Figure 2.9 shows the functional structure for the administration of the hypothetical university. Note the sample's similarity to the general administrative structure shown in Figure 2.4. Personnel administration, financial administration, and information services within a university system are very similar to the same functions in any other organization. The product of a university is its graduates, the raw material its students. We can envision production management functions controlled by the faculty administration. Our "inventory," students, can be administered through the student administration offices.

Like any other organization, a university has an AIS, which for the purposes of this book will be illustrated through the subsystem for student administration. Figure 2.10 shows the principal users of the system. Remember that it is this user set that determines the goals and thus the characteristics of the system. Establishment of the goal set will be discussed in Chapter 4, and an extension of this figure is given in Figure 4.2.

Figure 2.9 University Administration: Example Structure

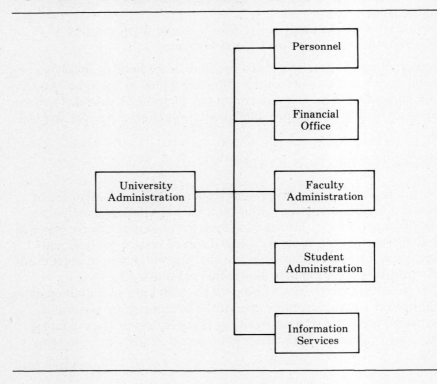

Figure 2.10 AIS for Student Administration

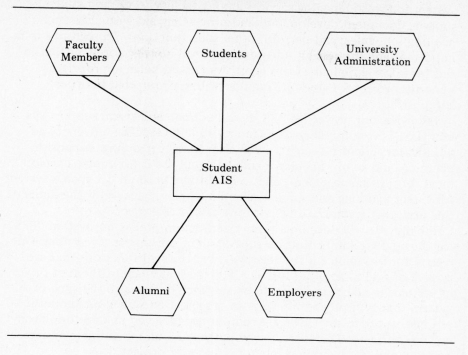

The principal entity types in the system's information archive are shown in Figure 2.11. Here each entity type is represented by a rectangle, and the inter-entity type relationships are indicated by arcs. The required information structures and the design of appropriate storage structures for the data are analyzed further in Chapters 5, 7, 8, and 9.

Figure 2.11 Information Archive for Student AIS

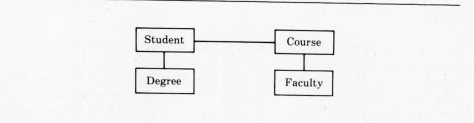

Our university AIS should include an office automation (OAS) subsystem to provide mailing services among faculty, staff, and students; support document development and processing; aid with class and meeting schedules; and perform other such functions. Though this is an important and interesting subsystem, we will not develop it further in this text. Development of this subsystem could be an appropriate semester project for students familiar with or interested in office administration.

Likewise, our university AIS should contain a decision support system (DSS) for administrative planning at all levels. The university administrators could use such a system for budget planning, expansion planning, and so on. Faculty members could use it for course development, project management, and so on. Students could use such a system for career planning and subject selection. Again, because of the limits of this text, this system will be left for a semester project.

Finally, we will develop a (mini) transaction-processing system (TPS) for the student administration subsystem of our university system. One reason for this choice is the relatively well-defined functions that are typical of a TPS. Another is that a TPS is usually one of the first types of systems in an organization to be automated. It is also the type of system that typically administers an organization's own data about itself and its processes. Clearly, a sample system given in a textbook cannot be complete. Therefore, development of a more complete system, possibly one for real use, is left for a semester project.

The purpose of this system, a CBIS for student administration, is to provide a background example that will demonstrate how system analysis and design tools can be used to develop a specific system. Text examples will necessarily be fragmented and oriented toward illustrating the tool or phase under discussion. For a more coherent and complete example, see Appendix C.

The conventions used to construct the graphic models in this chapter will be described in detail in the chapters in which they are introduced as a system analysis and design tool, principally in Chapters 4, 5, 8, and 10.

SUMMARY

In this chapter, we have identified a set of information systems, administrative information systems (AIS), that are commonly found in organizations in the form of CBISs. An AIS is used at all levels of an organization to provide information-processing services for the management of the organization and its business. We have further identified three types of subsystems commonly found in an AIS: transaction-processing systems (TPS), decision support systems (DSS), and office automation systems (OAS). These subsystems are often candidates for automation and are thus of special interest in this book. Finally, we have introduced a sample information system, a TPS for student administration, that will be used as a background example throughout this text.

KEY CONCEPTS

Administrative information
  system (AIS)
AIS goals
Data processing system (DPS)
Decision support system (DSS)
Formal IS
Functional IS
Informal IS
Information archive

Information clerk
Information processes
Information system (IS)
Management information system
  (MIS)
Office automation system (OAS)
System user
Transaction
Transaction-processing system (TPS)

DISCUSSION QUESTIONS

1. Define and give an illustrative example of each of the key concepts.
2. Discuss the similarities and differences between formal and informal information systems. Is there a clear boundary between these system types, and will it remain constant? Defend your answer.
3. Data processing systems may have manual and/or automated subsystems. Discuss each subsystem and the possibility of automating it.
4. Developing an all-encompassing CBIS has been a tempting goal for over 20 years. What is envisaged by this idea? With this background, discuss the similarities and differences between an MIS and an AIS.
5. Current CBIS technology has led to the development of three types of system discussed in this chapter: the TPS, DSS, and OAS. How are these system types similar and dissimilar? Use examples for each, and discuss the user groups served.

PROJECTS

1. Adapt the text sample system to your university. Identify and give priority to the system users. Discuss the type(s) of CBISs that would be applicable to this system. Based on this discussion, select a set of subsystems as a basis for a term project.
2. Repeat the same steps as in Project 1, but replace the university system with another administrative information system from some other organization, real or imagined.

RECOMMENDED READINGS

Brabb, G. J. *Computers and Information Systems in Business*. Boston : Houghton Mifflin Co., 1980.
    This text describes the use of computers in business. Chapter 3 discusses management information systems, and Chapter 4 details the structure of the most common computer-based functional information subsystems.

Martin, J. *Telematic Society—A Challenge for Tomorrow*. Englewood Cliffs, N.J. : Prentice-Hall, 1981.
    This book discusses the impact of telecommunications and cheap computers on our ways of doing business.

McLeod, R., Jr. *Management Information Systems*. Chicago : SRA, 1979.
    This text covers topics important to understanding the concepts and techniques employed in computer-based management information systems (MIS). Part 4, Chapters 10 to 13, presents functional information systems in considerable detail.

Chapter 3
Information-System Analysis and Design

INTRODUCTION

Information-system analysis and design (ISAD) refers here to the processes involved in preparing the specifications for an information system. In our context of developing information systems, the term *system analysis and design* is used most frequently to refer to the development of computer-based information systems (CBISs). However, the basic approaches are quite applicable to the development of general, nonautomated information systems. In fact, one positive outcome of the ISAD process would be a decision not to construct a CBIS.

INFORMATION-SYSTEM LIFE CYCLE

The development of information systems follows the life-cycle pattern of systems in general. That is, first a need for an information system is identified, then goals and objectives for the system are determined, the structure and functions are developed, the system is used, and finally it is replaced when it becomes obsolete. System analysis and design activity works within this life cycle, observing, designing, modifying, developing, and controlling information-system development.

The Development Cycle

Figure 3.1 illustrates the development cycle of information systems.

Information-system conception, stage 1, occurs when it is realized that there should be an information system to support some communication activity. Typically this occurs when some problem arises in human correspondence, for example, when desired information is not readily available. System conception also refers to the point at which modification, usually major, of an existing information system is desired.

Goal specification, stage 2, must follow system conception in order to identify what information the system is to contain, how this information is to be used, and who is to use the information. In other words, goal specification involves identifying the system environment, specifi-

Figure 3.1 Information-System Life Cycle

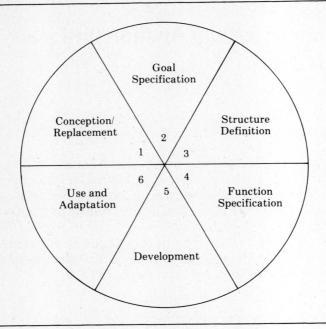

cally the users, their organizations, and their requirements for support from the IS.

Structure definition, stage 3, involves the determination of the subsystems and their interrelationships. Remember that system relationships define both the hierarchical structure and the information flow throughout the system. An IS that is to support some human activity may have one of many different structures. The "best" structure depends on the system environment, its expectations, and its resources.

Function specification, stage 4, provides the details of how each subsystem is to perform its activities and responsibilities. In this stage technical aids for task achievement are selected and any automated subsystems will be defined.

System development, stage 5, includes those activities required for

- establishment of operational procedures
- development of reports and forms
- implementation of job specifications
- implementation, programming, and testing of all computerized subsystems
- training the users in the operation of the system

System usage, stage 6, begins when the new or modified IS starts operation. All of the earlier activity was aimed at providing the best possible system. From experience, it may take two to three years for a CBIS to reach this stage, in which it will remain for some five to ten years. The system will continue to be adapted to altered requirements during this stage.

System replacement, stage 1, occurs when the system can no longer be adapted to satisfy new requirements or goals. At that time a major modification of the current system or an entirely new system will be needed. Note that system replacement is actually a return to system conception and that the cycle will be repeated.

Information systems are continually at some stage of their life cycle. More specifically, there are really no new information systems, only revisions, modifications, or improvements to the previous system. However, the effort of converting a manual information system to a computer-based information system is usually so great that the CBIS will be perceived as a new system. Also, substantial modifications will lead to the perception that a new system has been established.

Development Costs

Depending on the scope or size of the information system, the system definition and specification stages, 1 to 4 in Figure 3.1, will usually take from one to six months of analysis and design effort. The length of the development stage, including testing, will also depend on the size and complexity of the project, but a medium-sized, new CBIS can often take three calendar years and up to 100 person-years of effort. The operative life span of a CBIS is typically five to eight years, depending on the stability of the organizational environment. Because of the large investment needed to develop a CBIS, increasing attention is being given to the system analysis and design stages.

Experience has shown that design errors are very costly to correct. Figure 3.2 provides a schematic illustration of these escalating costs. If a design error remains undiscovered, it will influence later design and implementation decisions, necessitating more extensive action to eliminate the error. Later-stage errors will have a more limited influence and will thus be somewhat easier (less costly) to correct.

Figure 3.2 Cost of Errors Originating in Different Development Stages

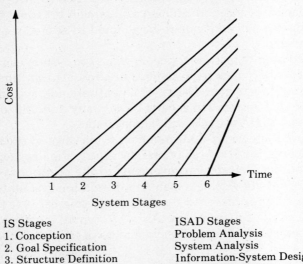

IS Stages
1. Conception
2. Goal Specification
3. Structure Definition
4. Function Specification
5. Development
6. Use

ISAD Stages
Problem Analysis
System Analysis
Information-System Design
Data-System Design
System Implementation
System Operation Evaluation

REQUIREMENTS FOR INFORMATION-SYSTEM ANALYSIS AND DESIGN

The stages of information-system analysis and design, identified in Figure 3.3, follow the life cycle of information-system development. Figure 3.3 differs from Figure 3.1 only in its orientation. Figure 3.1 identifies the separate life-cycle stages of an information system, whereas Figure 3.3 identifies the primary stages of ISAD as it addresses each life-cycle stage.

Similar IS development models, differing only in the names given to the ISAD stages and, in some cases, in the determination of stage boundaries, can be found in the literature. We shall use this model, as it emphasizes the problem analysis and information-system design components, which are crucial to designing a successful system.

The ISAD activities required for IS development are the following:

1. Problem analysis involves identifying the information requirements for the information system and analyzing them in detail. The result of the problem analysis is a detailed list of goals for the information system.

Figure 3.3 Information-System Development Cycle

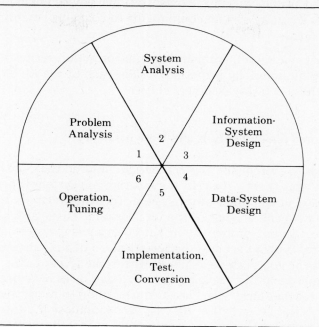

2. System analysis involves a detailed examination of the existing information system to determine the extent to which the goals identified
   during problem analysis are being attained. The purpose is to identify the subsystems that need to be improved or replaced to enable
   the information system to achieve its goals.
3. Information-system design develops the specifications for a new or
   modified information system that is expected to raise the goal
   achievement level.
4. Data-system design develops the design specifications for the data
   processing subsystems of the new or modified information system.
   In this text, we assume that a major portion of the data-system
   design effort is concerned with developing specifications for the
   automated or computerized subsystems of the information system.
5. Implementation, test, and conversion involve the implementation
   (programming), operative test, and introduction of the subsystems
   of the new or modified information system. The last part of this
   stage involves training the users in the operation of the system.
   Usually the most time-consuming task will be the implementation
   of the automated subsystems.

6. Operation and tuning cover the use and adaptation of the new or modified system within the organizational environment. Tuning involves adapting system components to changing environmental requirements.

The most general requirement for an information-system analysis and design methodology is that it consider each of the IS development stages, with their tasks, as indicated here.

Information-System Analysis and Design Theory

Approaches to system analysis and design build on the concepts of general systems theory. That is, the information system is perceived to be composed of a number of subsystems that interrelate in some way to achieve the general goals of the total system. The analysis problem then reduces to one of identifying the goals and subsystems and their interactions. Design becomes the specification of the subsystems in such a way that the goals can be achieved with some level of efficiency.

Many approaches to the analysis and design tasks have been proposed. These approaches have been classified according to their "system construction view," i.e., whether they try to decompose the total system into its components before designing each, or whether they start with system components and try to build a total system. These approaches cannot follow one direction exclusively, but each approach philosophy follows the direction indicated by its name.

1. Top-down approaches emphasize goal and structure analysis first, before the detailed specification of any subsystem is prepared. System analysis and design follows the hierarchical structure from the total system down through each successive system level (see Figure 1.1).
2. Bottom-up approaches emphasize identification, specification, and construction of the lowest-level subsystems, considering them the building blocks upon which the total system can be constructed. As low-level subsystems are designed and implemented, they are used as elements in the construction of higher-level subsystems until the full system has been developed.
3. Inside-out or outside-in approaches emphasize an iterative approach to analysis and design in which, as a subsystem takes form, a reanalysis of its place in the total system becomes necessary. The rationale here is that a subsystem's characteristics are determined as implementation alternatives are selected. These new characteristics may have an impact on the characteristics of this system's neighbors: its sibling subsystems or parent or grandparent systems. Thus, an impact analysis is required to maintain total system design coordination.

We will present a modified top-down approach. The modification involves an emphasis on the need for iteration as the analysis and design project proceeds in a top-down sequence. The rationale is the same as the arguments presented for the iterative aspects of the inside-out approach. The principal argument for the top-down direction of the ISAD approach is that without careful analysis of the system's goals and its environment, it will be difficult or impossible to construct an information system that truly serves and supports its human users.

Information-System Analysis and Design Methodologies

Generally, the components of an ISAD methodology can be considered as stages or tasks that must progress from identification of an information problem through implementation of a system that addresses the problem. Presenting these ISAD stages or tasks in a series of chapters or lectures further strengthens the perception that there can be a serial progression through each stage. However, in execution, the stages are not mutually independent or strictly serial in nature, although each uses the results of earlier stages.

The analyst must be prepared to repeat any of the earlier stages to obtain further clarification or detail for a specific problem. For example, in the implementation stage, a decision must be made between an on-line, interactive system and a more traditional, and less costly, batch-processing system. (Chapter 10 discusses these system types in detail.) The decision depends on the response time requirements, which are, or should have been, determined during problem analysis. If this information is not available, the analyst must return briefly to the problem analysis stage.

Also, details required for later stages, particularly the data-system design stage, tend to turn up early in the analysis stages. For example, the analyst usually knows from the beginning how much of the data looks—how many characters are used for names and addresses, or how many decimal places are required for prices and salaries. This information should be collected as soon as it becomes available, then passed on to the ISAD stage that requires it, here the data-system design stage. These activities support a desirable level of parallelism between the ISAD stages (Muller-Merbach, 1978).

Figure 3.4 illustrates the iterative nature of the ISAD stages. Note that from each stage there are three possible directions: (1) continuing to the following stage, (2) returning to an earlier stage, or (3) exiting and terminating the ISAD effort.

The outputs of the ISAD stages, given in the right-hand column of Figure 3.4, provide the documentation of each stage and its conclusions or proposals. At the end of each stage, the project status must be reviewed to ensure that the designers and management agree on the scope of the project. Aborting further design of a computer-based information system is a valid and not uncommon decision, particularly if the costs are felt to exceed the possible benefits, or if it is determined that the problem is actually not an information-flow problem.

In addition to the directional approach, top-down or bottom-up, there are two general orientations for existing ISAD methodological approaches, one toward identifying what the system can do (the process-oriented approach), the other toward identifying what information the system contains (the information-oriented approach). The orientational approaches coexist with the directional approaches—one can have a top-down information-oriented approach, a bottom-up information-oriented approach, and so on.

Figure 3.4 Stages in Information-System Analysis and Design

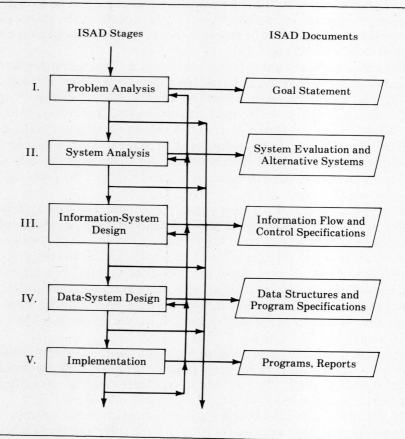

Process-Oriented Methodologies

Process-oriented ISAD approaches study an information system in terms of "What do we want to do?" This tends to lead to identification of the information processes first, then secondarily to the information needed to perform each function. The resulting system tends to have a strongly integrated set of processes with a loosely related set of data files. Figure 3.5 illustrates a typical model of a process-oriented system, applied to the student administration example.

The process-oriented approach tends to be or become a bottom-up approach in which the basic processing functions are combined into higher-level procedures. The approach leads relatively quickly to the implementation of subsystems, which are later combined into higher-level subsystems until the full system is established.

The principal problem is in inter-subsystem communication and the sharing of common information or data, as the structure of information messages and stored data tends to become fixed in a form that was efficient for the first process implemented. Another problem is that the resulting system tends to be fairly rigid and difficult to change as environmental requirements change.

Process-oriented approaches are often chosen when quick results are required for subsystems, or in situations where the scope of the system is unclear and the possibility for disturbing organizational change is present. Proceeding subsystem by subsystem makes it possible to abort construction of the system at an earlier stage, should this be necessary.

Figure 3.5 Process-Oriented Information System

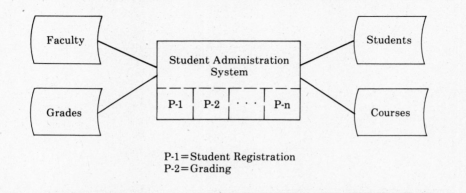

P-1=Student Registration
P-2=Grading

Information-Oriented Methodologies

The information-oriented approaches study an information system in terms of "What information do we have or want?" This leads to a fairly extensive search through the communication messages, queries, and reports being used in the current system in order to find the entities about which the organization keeps information. How this information is processed is determined in the course of this search.

The result of this search for information messages and the entities about which information is kept is the early establishment of an information directory, detailing the organization's information collection. Processes are then defined in a way that enables them to retrieve information from a central information store. This approach leads directly to the data-base approach advocated for large-scale CBISs and tends to lead to the establishment of a relatively complete collection of information that is accessible to the total system.

Figure 3.6 gives a typical model of an information-centered system. Note that it includes the same processes as the process-oriented system (Figure 3.5). The difference between these models and the resulting systems will be in their primary orientation and their structure, not in their functions.

Figure 3.6 Information-Oriented Information System

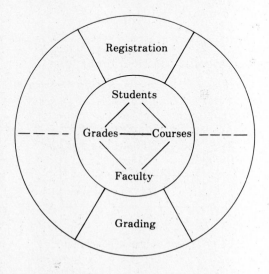

Information-oriented approaches tend to be top-down, at least during the problem and system analysis stages. The resulting system will have a relatively highly integrated data base with a fairly loosely integrated set of processes. Typically, the process set resembles a TPS (transaction-processing system) in which new processes can be added relatively easily.

The primary problem is the additional time required for system analysis and the resulting delay before any subsystems are in operation, i.e., the approach is perceived as slow. Also, individual information processes may operate less efficiently as a result of more complex procedures for data retrieval, since the data base is oriented toward serving the total system.

The information-oriented approaches are preferred when many relatively small subsystems must be integrated. This approach is often used when the total system is well formalized. Separate subsystems can be implemented within the context of the whole system, while design and implementation effort is also directed toward the development of a data base that is common to all subsystems.

Selecting a Methodology

Since an information system, by definition, must contain both an information archive and a set of information-processing subsystems, both approaches must necessarily lead to the development of both. The main difference between these approaches is in their primary emphasis, one on the processing subsystems, the other on the information archive. Each approach tends to result in a suboptimal design for the secondary subsystem, the information archive or the information-processing subsystems, respectively.

We believe that the information archive is the most stable subsystem within an information system and that the majority of required changes will involve new or modified processes for using existing information. We also expect the growth of the information archive to involve new information types rather than changes or deletion of elements. Therefore, we believe that the information-oriented, top-down approach to information-system analysis and design will produce the most stable and most adaptable CBISs. It is this ISAD approach that is developed in this text.

THE SYSTEM ANALYST

Generally speaking, a system analyst is a person who designs systems; in our context, a system analyst is a person who designs information systems, often computer-based information systems. The high cost of correcting design errors, particularly in CBISs, and the high incidence of dissatisfaction with the information-system services provided by CBISs (see Chapter 1) are forcing system analysts to pay increasing attention to the design of the total information system of which the automated data system is to be a part.

Commonly, the scope of the information system under study is such that one person is unable to satisfactorily cover all its details or be knowledgeable about all its subsystems. In this situation, a system analysis team made up of a group of people is needed. Since the ISAD tasks for both large and small systems are basically identical, differing only in the amount of work and coordination required, we shall use the term system analyst to refer to both an individual and a group assigned to perform the ISAD tasks.

System Analyst A person or group of persons whose job is to (1) establish the objectives for an information system, (2) evaluate the performance of the information system, and (3) prepare design alternatives for improving the existing system's ability to achieve its goals.

An information system exists to provide information services to some group of people, the system's current or prospective users. It is these users who know the information-system requirements. If the system analyst is not the primary user of the proposed system, then the analyst must establish close contact with the prospective users. In order to function well as a system analyst, the person or group needs to have the following:

1. A good understanding of the organizational goals for the environment of the information system
2. A working knowledge of the functional area to be supported by the information system
3. Knowledge of information-system structures and operation
4. The ability to identify and evaluate information-system requirements
5. The ability to evaluate in detail the current information system and its environment
6. Knowledge of computer technology

In organizations with an established electronic data processing (EDP) department, the system analyst is usually a member of the EDP staff, particularly a member of the system development group (refer to Figure 3.7). However, the analyst may well be employed in the functional area of the organization that is concerned with the information system under study. For example, the analyst may belong to the accounting, personnel, operations, or some other department. Not infre-

Table 3.1 The System Analyst

Origin of System Analyst	Principal Strength	Probable Weakness
EDP staff	EDP insight	Lack of application-area expertise
Functional area within organization	Knowledge of area requirements and functions	Lack of EDP expertise
Outside consultant	Knowledge of general CBIS design principles	Lack of knowledge of specific organization requirements

quently, the system analyst is an outside consultant brought into the organization to help resolve the perceived information problem.

Depending on the origin of the system analyst, he or she will bring certain strengths and weaknesses to the analysis and design task, as outlined in Table 3.1.

The System Analysis Team

The skills needed by a system analyst are such that it is difficult, if not impossible, to find them all in one individual. In order to provide all the necessary skills, the system analyst should work within a group that can supplement the analyst's knowledge about the system environment and organizational constraints. The system analysis team should include representatives of the various groups who interact with or are responsible for the information system. The system analyst should primarily function as the group's secretary, making sure that all important factors in the design and evaluation of the information system are taken into account.

A typical analysis team should be composed of representatives from the following groups:

1. Top management—a person responsible for the functioning of the information system who can ensure support for and commitment to the analysis and design project, as well as providing information concerning constraints on the resources that the organization can allocate to the information system.
2. User group(s)—members of the clerical and operative staff, supervisory personnel, EDP staff, and external control organizations who

Table 3.2 User Involvement in System Analysis and Design

ISAD Stage	System Development Task	User Participation
1	Problem specification Goal statement Feasibility analysis	Management, staff Management, staff Management
2	System evaluation Alternative systems Cost/benefit analysis	Management, staff System analyst, EDP Management
3	Information-system design	Management, staff, system analyst
4	Data-system design	EDP, system analyst
5	Implementation Testing Acceptance Conversion	EDP EDP, staff Management, staff Staff, management

can supply the input/output requirements for the information flow to and from the system.

3. The system analyst—who is responsible for recording the information requirements and the system constraints, and proposing an information-system design that will maximize goal achievement given the constraints.

If the group is to function well, its size should be limited to three to seven people. For larger projects, where many user groups are affected, these groups should be kept current through meetings, and proposals should be given to them for comment before the interim and final reports are submitted for approval.

Analysis team membership may change during the project life cycle. Table 3.2 illustrates the particular areas in which the various user groups may participate in the analysis and design of an information system. The stage numbers correspond to the system stages outlined in Figure 3.3. The tasks are the principal tasks within each stage. In the early stages of the project, representation should be weighted toward the system users, while during data-system design and implementation planning, more weight should be placed on EDP representation.

Organizational Placement of the System Analyst

Information and data are important resources in an organization. Many business-system researchers feel that these resources are as important as the personnel and financial resources of the firm. In order to be most useful, the information must be well managed.

One organizational structure involves the establishment of an information systems department, possibly including the data processing department, reporting at the vice president level within the organization. Many researchers advocate such a centralized approach to information management (McLeod, 1979; Burch et al., 1979). This department functions as a service unit for both information-system design and data processing services for the entire organization. It is felt that this organization will facilitate control and integration of use of the organization's information.

Figure 3.7 presents a possible organization for an information systems department. The special area of system analysis and design reports to the manager for systems development. The ISAD area will serve as

Figure 3.7 Information Systems Department Organization

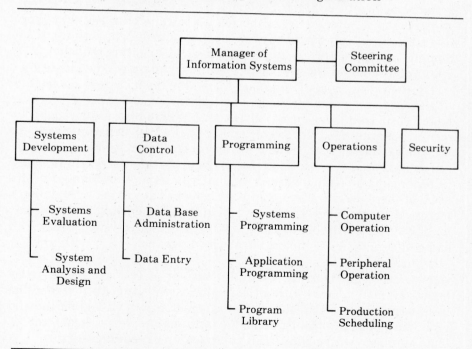

the communication link between this department and the other sections of the organization. Within the department, the ISAD group must establish special relationships with the other groups, especially

1. management, for presentation of system evaluations and new system proposals.
2. the data center, for such data processing services as data-base administration facilities, application and subroutine library facilities, and data entry and report generation support.
3. programming, for implementation of design specifications for the system software.
4. operations, for data processing facilities.
5. security, for establishing security and control procedures for each system.

This organizational structure has the advantage of central control over CBIS design and implementation and ensures that the organization's data processing facilities are used appropriately and are in accordance with the total organization requirements. It also provides an opportunity to maximize the use of information while maintaining control over its use and growth.

A particular problem of system analysts being centrally located during system design is the emphasis it places on the EDP expertise of the system analysts, as noted in Table 3.1. This problem can be offset by good communication between the analyst and the prospective system users. The team approach to system analysis and design, with users dominating the analyst team, is recommended to ensure that the appropriate goal set for the new or modified system will be identified.

The decreasing cost of computer hardware, the increased availability of standard application packages, the aggressive promotion of "complete" CBIS solutions, the rapidly increasing data processing requirements (appetite), and the lagging ability of the EDP department to provide expanding services have all encouraged users to press for decentralization of the information and data processing services. In many larger organizations there are already many computer installations. The users of these decentralized computer centers want to get or maintain increased control over them. The development of decentralized information systems will require the development of intersystem control and communication if the organization wishes the total system to be coordinated.

In a decentralized environment, the system analyst is more apt to be organizationally placed within the functional department. It will still be necessary to supplement the analyst's expertise with EDP expertise and with knowledge of organization-wide information policy. Again, the team approach will facilitate this combination of requirements.

The idea of a central information systems department is still valid. However, in a decentralized environment its function will be one more of planning and coordination than of computer center operation.

ANALYSIS AND DESIGN TOOLS

Although the ISAD methodologies actually in use vary among individual practitioners, some of whom consider ISAD an art rather than a clearly defined methodology, there are a number of generally accepted tools that can aid in the ISAD tasks. All ISAD methodologies consist of a number of tasks, the results of which are presented to the "owners" of the information system for approval or corrective comment.

ISAD tools aid in collecting, analyzing, and presenting the task information and results. These tools can be classified according to their basic form and their primary use.

- Questionnaires typically consist of a series of questions intended to elicit from the users of a system information about their information requirements or about their evaluation of the system being studied. This tool is particularly important in collecting information about the system environment.
- Scoring models are a formal tool for organizing and evaluating system characteristics. They are particularly useful in evaluating nonquantifiable characteristics of a system. (See Chapter 6.)
- Flowcharts are used to develop a model of the system, particularly of the sequence of its processes and their use of information. They can be used to model the dynamic characteristics of a system.
- Matrices can be used to show the relationships between users and general system requirements, data and processes, and so on. They provide a very concise model of the static characteristics of the system.
- Dictionaries are used to define the terms, information and data elements, and processes included within the system.
- Data models are used to show the relationships among data elements within the system.
- Text is necessary to make the system analysis and design reports readable by everyone interested in the system and its design, operation, and service characteristics.

Table 3.3 lists these seven categories of tools, and indicates which tools are especially useful in each of the system analysis and design stages. (Stages 1 to 5 are the same as those in Figures 3.3 and 3.4.) Note that stage 6, evaluation, is actually a component of each of the other stages.

Table 3.3 System Analysis and Design Tools

Tools	ISAD Stages*					
	1	2	3	4	5	6
Questionnaires	X	X				X
Scoring models	X	X				X
Flowcharts		X	X	X	X	
Matrices	X	X	X	X	X	X
Dictionaries		X	X	X	X	
Data models			X	X	X	X
Text	X	X	X	X	X	X

*1. Goal analysis   4. Data-system design
 2. System analysis   5. Implementation
 3. Information-system design   6. Evaluation

Several of these tools may be applicable to the tasks of any one stage, and one tool may be useful in several stages. For example, questionnaires, scoring models, and matrices are useful in charting and analyzing user requirements for the information system. Matrices can provide a compact, detailed description of system relationships. They are useful in all stages of the analysis and design process.

Each of these tools provides a concentrated picture of some aspect of the analysis or design task in which it is used. However, the tools must be accompanied by text documentation giving the background and assumptions used in determining the particular design alternatives chosen for the system. Text documentation is vital for identifying the decision points encountered during system evaluation and design. Without knowledge of the background considerations used for the evaluation and design, it will be quite impossible to evaluate the quality of the design document.

All ISAD tools exist in a manual form. The main problem with using manual tools for any reasonable-sized system is analyzing the quantities of information collected. A secondary problem is the time required to prepare presentable graphs and tables for discussion, evaluation, and acceptance by the users.

A number of research projects have been directed toward automating sections of the ISAD tasks; examples are ISDOS (Teichrow, 1974), CASCADE (Solvberg, 1973), and SYSTEMATOR (Aschim, 1982). In general, these systems provide a set of automated tools for recording collected information, allowing it to be analyzed, and generating readable reports from it. At present the analyst must still make the actual design decisions in accordance with the specific parameters and constraints of the system under development.

Manual Tools

All complete ISAD methodologies separate the ISAD process into stages, each containing a set of tasks, which aim at:

- defining the system requirements.
- evaluating (analyzing) the current system.
- preparing the design specifications for a new or modified system.

The methodology then outlines the procedures to be followed in collecting information, analyzing it, and preparing the design specifications. Often the methodology will emphasize a particular tool set as "ideal" for supporting the ISAD tasks. These tools are chosen from the categories in Table 3.3.

Questionnaires are particularly useful in collecting information about the system environment. Important questionnaire components must elicit information

1. identifying the current and desired system users.
2. identifying the information elements each user requires.
3. identifying the information-processing services required, including
   a. input forms desired.
   b. transformations or processes to be enacted on the information.
   c. controls.
   d. output forms.
4. specifying the anticipated activity of each user, giving number of requests per time period and allowable time before response.
5. specifying the relative priority of each user within the user community.
6. identifying user control requirements.
7. determining user evaluations of the current system.

Responses to the questionnaire must be compiled to provide a description of the system environment, a list of the "ideal" system goals in terms of information content and information services, and an evaluation of the current system.

Scoring models are particularly useful in presenting qualitative data from a questionnaire for evaluation and selection of alternatives. The model lists components with their relative priorities and, sometimes, an evaluation of their relative importance or the anticipated cost or benefit to the system. The model is then completed by providing data about at least three alternative system designs. By convention, alternative 0 is the current system, against which alternatives 1, 2, . . . *n* can be compared. Chapter 6 discusses the use of scoring models.

Flowcharts first became a common ISAD tool in the late 1950s, when they were used to give a graphic presentation of the steps that make up a computer program. Since then they have been used to represent whole processing systems involving many programs, to represent the data flow to and from the processes, and to document the control flow from one subsystem to the next within the system. These charts are also used (in a modified form) to illustrate the organizational structure. Because of their many uses, the term "flowchart" is commonly preceded by a term indicating its current application, such as "data flowchart" or "program flowchart." There is a standard (ANSI, 1970) definition of the graphic figures to be used in constructing a program flowchart. Unfortunately, there is no comparable standard for other graphs constructed on these principles. The conventions used in this book follow the proposals of the Scandinavian school of informatics (see Chapter 7) for presentation of the information-system model, and the most common data-base methodology forms for presentation of data models (see Chapter 9). The standard program flowchart symbols are used in Chapter 10.

Matrices and dictionaries are used in combination throughout this text to define the system relationships. The matrix illustrates a binary relationship between the vertical-axis components, here those identifying and describing the requirements of users and processes, and the horizontal-axis components, here the information or data elements. The matrix body will provide a relationship descriptor code that depends on the relationships being described. For example, the matrix of Table 3.3 uses a descriptor code "X" to indicate that there is a relationship between the matrix axis "tools" and the matrix axis "ISAD stages." An empty matrix cell indicates the absence of a relationship.

A dictionary or directory provides detailed definitions of the elements of the system. There should be a dictionary for users, for information and data elements, and for the information and data processes. The relationships among the information in the separate dictionaries are defined in the system matrices.

Data models are used to illustrate the information and data structures found within the information and data systems, respectively. In an information-centered ISAD approach, these models are one of the most important system design tools. Again, unfortunately, there are no standards for constructing a data model, as different research groups want to use their own models to highlight particular data characteristics. The model conventions used here are presented in Chapter 9; they generally follow the conventions proposed by the CODASYL 1971 report.

Automated Support Systems

Since the early 1970s there has been much concern about the increasing amount of time needed to develop operational computer-based information systems. A number of research projects were undertaken to explore the possibility of developing tools and methodologies for computer-aided design of information systems. Many partially or entirely computer-based ISAD methodologies have been described at recent IFIP working conferences (Olle et al., 1982; Schneider, 1982). These methodologies provide either automated tools or automated support for basically manual tools.

Most of the automated ISAD support projects have been aimed at generating operative codes, often in the form of a COBOL program or a program in some other high-level language. The most successful projects have resulted in "application generators," programs for automatically creating programs from specifications. These projects have focused ISAD attention on data-system design, our stage 4, and particularly on program design.

Unfortunately there is still no comprehensive set of automated tools that will support all the system analysis and design tasks, from problem analysis to system tuning. However, there are important aids available. In addition to application generators, which aid in the implementation tasks of programming and file design, there are data dictionary systems for collection, analysis, and generation of reports on the data elements to be included in the system. The more advanced of these systems include a subsystem for automatic generation of a data base (see Chapter 9).

Choosing Tools

The methodology used in this text emphasizes matrix presentation to document the system relationships. For example, matrix presentation can document the relationships between users and goals, users and information elements, users and information service, information processes and information, or data processes and data. A matrix records relationships in a very detailed manner. However, it is also very cryptic and must be supplemented by definitions of the matrix-axis elements. We will use data, user, and process dictionaries to store the element definitions.

Most ISAD methodologies rely heavily on graphic presentations, and in the literature there are many types of graphic forms proposed for designing flowcharts and data models. Although we will use one set here, analysts are free to select a different standard. However, the graphic forms used should be consistent within the framework of a specific project. As graphic tools are meant to facilitate communication with the system users about the system design, it may be best for the analyst to choose graphic forms with which the users are familiar, if these forms can capture the important aspects of the design.

The tools recommended in this text will be presented in the chapters in which they are first used. The ISAD methodology presented here is, or, more precisely, can be used manually. When automated tools such as data dictionary systems or flowchart generating systems are available, these can and should be included among the analyst's tools. Currently, work is being done at the Institute for Information and Computer Science, University of Bergen, Bergen, Norway, on developing a comprehensive automated support system for this methodology.

SUMMARY

In this chapter, we have discussed the general characteristics of information-system analysis and design, its background theories, methodological approaches, and tools. The aim has been to give readers a feeling for the breadth of approaches and thinking on this general topic. We have been deliberately general in this chapter, but we have tried to make a case for choosing an iterative, top-down, information-oriented approach to system analysis and design. In Parts II and III of this text. we will develop such a methodology.

KEY CONCEPTS

Bottom-up ISAD	IS goals
Data-system design	IS life cycle
Development cycle	ISAD stages
Goal specification	ISAD tools
Implementation	Problem-oriented ISAD
Information-oriented ISAD	Problem analysis
Information-system analysis	System analysis
and design (ISAD)	System analyst
IS design	System analysis team
IS development costs	Top-down ISAD

DISCUSSION QUESTIONS

1. Define and give an example of each of the key concepts.
2. Using a hypothetical system, for example, the student administra-

tion system of your school, discuss the stages of an information-system life cycle. At what stage is your information system? Explain.

3. Discuss system development costs as they are illustrated in Figure 3.2. Why do the figure lines not intersect? Is this reasonable? Explain.

4. Discuss each of the stages of information-system development. Why are problem analysis and system analysis considered two separate stages? What are the major objectives of these two stages? Should these stages be combined? Explain.

5. Compare the top-down and bottom-up approaches to system analysis and design. Can either of these approaches be followed exclusively? Explain.

6. Compare process-oriented and information-oriented system analysis and design methodologies. Can two ISAD methodologies, one using each approach, give the same system design? Defend your evaluation.

7. Discuss and defend the list of skills needed by a system analyst as presented in this chapter. Where would one expect to find a good system analyst? Why would one choose a source other than the ideal for a system analyst? How could your second choice be complemented?

8. Discuss the size and composition of a system analysis team. Would it be possible to compose such a team for an analysis of your school's student administration system? Explain.

9. Using Table 3.3, discuss the usefulness of each of the ISAD tool categories listed. What are the system analyst's primary considerations in choosing ISAD tools? What tools do you think would be available to your system analysis team (Question 8)?

ISAD PROJECT

Divide the class into an appropriate number of system analysis teams. Assign team positions to each team member. Discuss the member responsibilities of each member.

ASSIGNMENT

Using your school's student administration system, have each team member prepare a position paper describing his or her relation (as a member of the system analysis team) to this information system. Include the member's view of the system's goals and problems.

Call a team meeting to prepare a collective review of the information system's goals and problems for class presentation and critique.

Alternative 1: Use individual projects instead of a team approach.

Alternative 2: Replace the student administration system with some other system of general interest.

Alternative 3: Have each group or individual select an interesting system for study.

RECOMMENDED READINGS

Couger, J. P., and R. Knapp, eds. *System Analysis Techniques*. New York : John Wiley & Sons, 1974.

(See Chapter 1.) Papers by Couger, Murdick, Chapin, CODASYL (#13), Teichrow, and Rhodes are particularly relevant to the topics of this chapter.

Lucas, H. C., Jr., F. F. Land, T. J. Lincoln, and K. Supper, eds. *The Information Systems Environment*, 1980 IFIP Conference Proceedings. Amsterdam : North-Holland Publishers, 1980.

This is a collection of the papers and discussions of a working conference of IFIP's Technical Committee 8. Of particular interest are papers by Szyperski, Winkelhage, Hoyer, Blokdijk, and Land.

Olle, T. W., H. G. Sol, and A. A. Verrijn-Stuart, eds. *Information System Design Methodologies: A Comparative Review*. Amsterdam : North-Holland Publishers, 1982.

This is a collection of twenty-five papers, each presenting a solution to a given problem, organizing a conference, according to a different ISAD method.

Schneider, H. J., and A. I. Wasserman, eds. *Automated Tools for Information Systems Design*. Amsterdam : North-Holland Publishers, 1982.

This is a collection of the papers presented at the IFIP WG 8.1 Working Conference held in New Orleans, January 26–28, 1982. The 1982 state of the art in concepts and operative systems for computer-aided system analysis and design is described in these papers.

Szyperski, N., and E. Grochla, eds. *Design and Implementation of Computer-Based Information Systems*. Alphen aan den Rijn, The Netherlands : Sijthoff & Noordhoff, 1979.

Of special interest to this chapter are the papers by Mumford and Clausen.

PART II
INFORMATION-SYSTEM
ANALYSIS AND DESIGN

Chapter 4
Problem Analysis

INTRODUCTION

The development of any information system must start with an analysis of the organizational problems (the system environment) that have led to the conclusion that a new or improved information system is needed. It is not unusual for some of the problems thought to be information-system problems to be alleviated by changes in other systems in the organization (reorganization of the sequence of activities, redefinition of some tasks, changes in personnel location, changes in technical support systems, and so on).

The purpose of a problem analysis is to explicitly define (1) who has information problems, (2) what these problems are, and (3) which problems are in fact attributable to the service levels of the information system. When performing a problem analysis, the system analyst must:

- identify the system users.
- identify the information problems.
- group information problems so that system boundaries can be identified.
- specify the information requirements.
- resolve requirement conflicts.
- perform a feasibility analysis for satisfying the requirements.

An information system exists to support some user environment. It is the users' requirements and problems that define the goals and objectives of the system. As discussed in Part I, the primary system users are people or groups within the organization who need information to solve organizational, work-related problems. The information-system environment will also frequently include user groups outside the organization who need information about the goods, services, and/or status of the organization. Both current and prospective users must be identified and their information requirements analyzed.

In the following discussion, we shall assume that the problems identified are truly information problems. These information problems need to be grouped, by user group and by function, to determine whether one or a number of information systems are required. The decision to separate an AIS into several information systems is often a design decision and will differ from one organization to another. We shall assume that there is to be one information system. The system boundaries then define (1) the system environment, its users, and interacting systems, and (2) the system components.

The information requirements of all users provide the basis for establishing what information and which information processes the information system must supply. The total set of information and information-processing requirements will contain conflicts that must be resolved. Priorities must be set for users, user groups, information, and information processes. This will assist in the construction of a single information requirement list, which is the goal statement for the information system.

Finally, the goal statement must be evaluated in terms of the organization's financial, personnel, technological, and legal constraints, in order to establish the feasibility of providing an information system that will support the given goal statement.

Information problems form the basis for identifying the system users and for establishing the goal statement for the information system. It is the goal statement, representing the users' information requirements, on which the system analysis and evaluation must be based and in accordance with which system modifications or a new information system will be designed.

GOAL ANALYSIS

The objectives of goal analysis are to identify the information requirements of the separate users and user groups, assign priorities to these requirements, resolve conflicts, and adjust the requirement set to conform to organizational constraints. The resulting list of requirements will be the goal set for the information system.

The primary goal of an information system is to provide information and information services to its users. An information system is expected to contain "complete, accurate, timely, and relevant information" within the context of the organization (goal 2, Chapter 2), and to provide services that present this information in a useful format, quickly and easily (goal 3). Information problems arise when the information system fails to perform to expectations in either or both of these fundamental areas.

Normally, an information system is studied when problems within the organization are attributed to a faulty or insufficient information system. Information problems are commonly expressed by such statements as:

- "I cannot get information on . . ."
- "It takes too long to get an answer about . . ."
- "It takes too long to process this . . ."

- "It is difficult (or time-consuming or impossible) to make changes in . . ."
- "This report does not contain the information I need."
- "What will be the impact of closing shop A?"

The purpose of goal analysis is to explicitly define who has information problems, what these problems are, and what information services are required to resolve the problems. Performing a goal analysis requires:

1. identification of all the system's users.
2. determination of their information problems.
3. identification of the information services, information and processes, required to resolve these problems.

System Users

Chapter 2 discussed user groups commonly found within the environments of most administrative information systems. These groups were shown in Figure 2.3. As noted there, users are typically found in groups who perform some common task and/or require the same type of information from the information system. User groups may be either inside (internal users) or outside (external users) the organization.

The user community consists of both suppliers of information (to the system) and recipients of information (from the system). Users interact with an information system as either information suppliers or information recipients at any given time. Some user groups are both information suppliers, typically of information about themselves and their relationship to the organization, and information recipients, typically of records of services and/or goods received from the organization.

Figure 4.1 illustrates the primary association of an administrative information system's user groups, indicating whether they are primarily information suppliers or information recipients.

Note that there are several user groups that are both information suppliers and information recipients. In particular, the clerical staff operates on both sides of the information system because of their role as communicators between the system and other users. Also, customers or clients and suppliers of services and/or products to the organization tend to be both suppliers and recipients of information although not of the same information.

In defining the specific user community for a given information system, it is easiest to start by identifying the information recipients—those who require information or *outputs* from the system. Output requirements are the basis for identifying the information processes required to produce them. They also indicate the information that the system must have available, i.e., information that at some prior time

Figure 4.1 Information Suppliers and Recipients

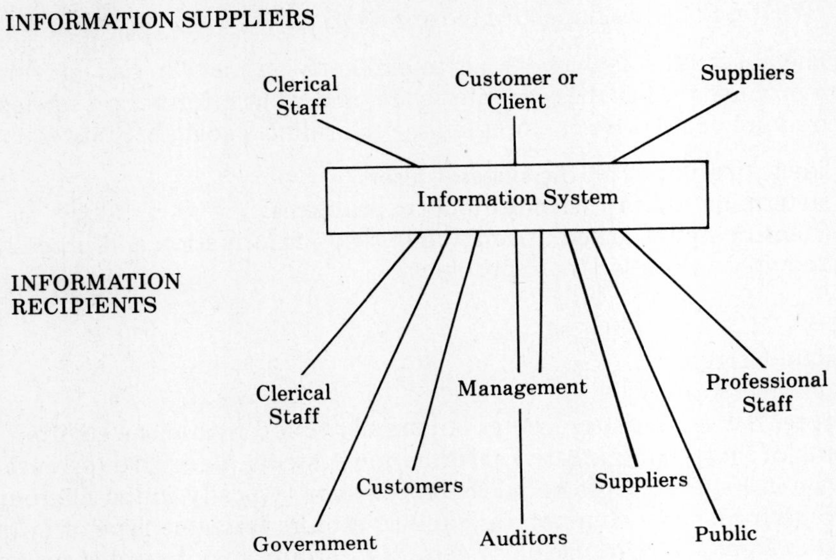

INFORMATION SUPPLIERS

Clerical Staff   Customer or Client   Suppliers

Information System

INFORMATION
RECIPIENTS

Clerical Staff   Management   Professional Staff

Customers   Suppliers

Government   Auditors   Public

must have been presented to the system as a system *input*. Those users responsible for providing this information, the information suppliers, are then identifiable.

For example, let us consider the student administration subsystem of the university system presented in Chapter 2 (Figure 2.9). The tasks of student administration could be supported by a student administrative information system, *student AIS*, for which potential information recipients could include:

- University administrators, receiving information on

  1. an individual student's academic status, financial status, housing, medical records, parents' address, extracurricular activities.
  2. ratio of students to faculty.
  3. projected rate of growth of student body.

- Faculty, receiving information on

  1. an individual student's academic status, academic background, academic goals, faculty association, current performance, or nonacademic activities.
  2. registrations for a given class.
  3. prognosis for a new topic.

- Students, receiving information on

    1. their own academic status, financial status, or class status.
    2. class schedule.
    3. course or degree prerequisites.

Other information recipients could include alumni organizations, student organizations, government offices, such as the Department of Education, national scholarship foundations, accreditation agencies, other universities, employers, and so on.

Defining the user community, and thus the environment, determines the scope of the information system. Clearly a student AIS could be defined that would serve only internal university user groups, some subset of the user groups listed, or more user groups than those listed.

Given that we want to define a student AIS that will support the information recipients indicated in Figure 4.2, we must locate information suppliers who can supply information on students, curriculum, academic status and progression, scholarships, employment requirements, government requirements, and so on. Suppliers of this informa-

Figure 4.2 Users of a Student AIS

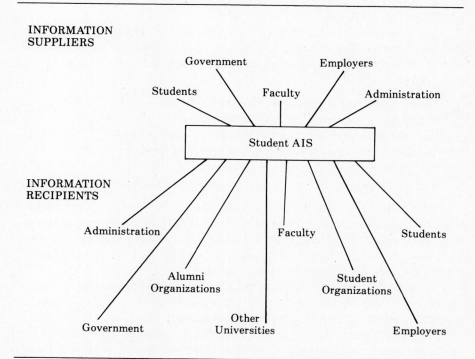

tion could include (see Figure 4.2)

- students, giving identification and location information, career and educational goals, and so on.
- faculty, providing individual student academic achievement, general curriculum, specific curriculum, and so on.
- administration, providing financial and academic status information, housing, career and funding information, and so on.

Secondary sources of information would include government agencies and employers. This secondary-source information is usually entered into an information system by information clerks within the administration (as assumed in our example).

Problem Statement

Once the user groups are established, each individual user and user group must be interviewed to determine their information problems, requirements, and priorities. Practically speaking, a user group's requirements and problems can be solicited from a representative of the group. However, when this is done, the resulting list of problems and requirements should be given to all the group members for discussion and possible extension.

Whenever the user community includes more users and/or user groups than the system analyst knows well, the interview technique will need to be used. For all systems, the following information must be gathered:

1. The identity and composition of the user community
2. The types of information the users require
3. The problems the users have in obtaining information
4. The users' priorities for various information services
5. The quantities of information required
6. The frequency of information service requirements

Box 4.1 lists the basic questions that must be answered to provide a relatively complete description of the user community, the problems it perceives regarding the information system, and its priorities in resolving these problems. Details of questions 2 and 5, on what information is required, are discussed in the next section.

The system analyst must be aware that the information problems identified in this fashion are those that are current, with only a slight orientation toward future information requirements. Thus this initial interview can never provide a complete, future-oriented picture, and the user community's information problems and requirements should be reviewed on a regularly scheduled basis. Most important, a review should

Box 4.1

INITIAL USER INTERVIEW QUESTIONNAIRE

1. User Identification
   - User name and position
   - Organization address

2. Information Required
   - Objects (entities) of interest
   - Characteristics (attributes) of each entity
   - Relationships among entities
   - Information processes required
   - Reports required

3. Information Problems
   - Detailed list of problems encountered:
     - Delays on information receipt?
     - Difficulties in transaction initiation?
     - Unavailability of information?
     - Confusing or redundant processing?

4. Priorities of Information Services
   - How important is each of the problems listed?

5. Quantities of Information Required
   - How long, in number of lines or number of objects reported on, are the required reports?

6. Frequency of Use of the Information System
   - How often is each process and report used?

be performed after the new or modified system has been functioning for a month or two. Then further reviews should be made, for example at the half-year point, then at yearly intervals.

After the initial interview, its results must be analyzed to clarify priorities and problems, and resolve potential conflicts. Conflicts are commonly found in the evaluation of the importance of particular problems, i.e., in setting priorities. Also, a common problem with interview results involves the use of nonstandard names for information elements and/or processes. The analyst must identify the conflicting identifiers and establish a standard system-wide naming convention.

The interview results can be presented in a problem analysis table (PAT). The PAT identifies each user's problem(s), describes each

Table 4.1 Problem Analysis Table (PAT): An Example

User ID*	Problem ID †	Problem Description	Priority
U-1	Pr-1	Receipt too late	High
U-2	Pr-1	Unavailable	Medium
	Pr-2	Receipt too late	High
U-3	Pr-3	Receipt too slow, too many alterations	High
.	.		
.	.		
.	.		

*U-1 Student   †Pr-1 Transcript preparation and distribution
 U-2 Faculty   Pr-2 Class roster preparation and distribution
 U-3 Administration Pr-3 Grade reporting and recording

problem, and indicates the importance of this problem to this user. Note that several users may share a problem, but give it different priorities. Also, a given user may well have several problems. Table 4.1 illustrates a PAT for the student AIS.

Two versions of the problem analysis table (PAT) should be prepared. The first details the information problems encountered in each user group, ordered by user priority. This version should be returned to the users to confirm that the interviewer has in fact interpreted the user's problems correctly. Not uncommonly, the interview will focus the user's attention on the information system and problems with it. New requirements can be added at this review stage. The second and final PAT version includes the results of an analysis of the total user community and orders their problems in accordance with a system priority. This final version must again be agreed to by the user community, for it provides the basis for setting priorities throughout the following system analysis and design.

Information Requirements

Formulation of the information requirements for an information system involves the preparation of a detailed and specific statement of what information is required to resolve current and anticipated information problems. The two primary sources for establishing the information requirements are the problem statement and the current information system.

As discussed in Chapter 1, information consists of the facts that people know about things. These things are real objects, events, and relationships within the organization's frame of reference (or interest). What we know about things are certain characteristics of interest. For example, if we are interested in the grades that students get on their exams, then the things of interest are students and courses, and the characteristics of interest are student name, perhaps student identification number, a course identification, and the grade achieved.

In information-system design, the following terms are commonly used:

Entity A thing of interest, for example, one student.

Entity type A group of entities sharing a common characteristic. For example, (all) students could be referred to as the entity type *student*.

Attribute A characteristic, for example, a student name.

Attribute value The value of a characteristic (attribute) for a given entity. For example, Tom Jones could be the attribute value of the attribute "student name" for a given student. An attribute value may also be called a data item.

In a goal analysis, we are interested in identifying the entity types and the attributes for these entity types that are of interest to the information system being studied. For example, the student AIS would include such principal entity types as students, faculty, courses, curriculum, degrees, transcripts, and bills. It is not uncommon for an AIS to have 25 or more principal entity types, i.e., entities directly describing real objects of interest to the organization.

Entities are described by some set of their characteristics or attributes. The particular set of attributes of interest will vary depending on the scope of the information system being considered. For example, relevant attributes describing the entity type *student* within a student AIS environment could include student name, address, telephone number, degree program, current courses, grades, completed courses, and so on. It is not uncommon for each of the primary entity types in an AIS to have more than 100 attributes, and thus for there to be more than 2500 attributes within the system.

Figure 4.3 presents a graphic tool that can help with the entity description process. The graph presents a model of an entity type or a group of related entity types, giving the set of attributes of interest to the system. If possible, a single graph should include all entity types of interest so that shared attributes can be easily identified. However, for

Figure 4.3 Entity Model: An Example

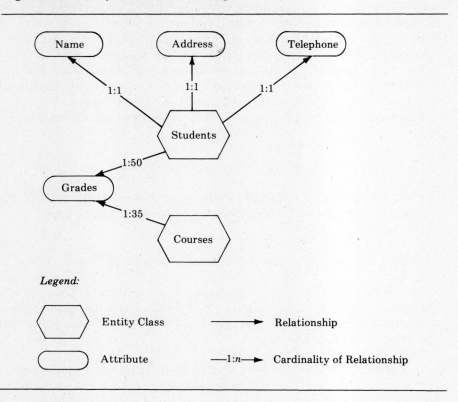

Legend:

| | Entity Class | ——————▶ | Relationship |
| | Attribute | ——1:n——▶ | Cardinality of Relationship |

information systems with a large number of entities and attributes, a series of graphs, modeling individual entity types or closely related groups of entity types, is often needed.

Using the *students* entity type as defined in Figure 4.3, one entity, one student, can be described by attribute values for the attributes name, address, and telephone number. For example,

(Jane Doe; 123 Main Street, Home Town, USA; 123–4567)

Some attributes actually define characteristics of relationships between entity types. In Figure 4.3, the grade attribute is shared by the entity types students and courses. This attribute is actually a characteristic of the relationship between these entity types: students take courses, or courses taken by students. Any one student will have one grade for one course. The directed arcs between entity types and their attributes indicate the cardinality, or the number of occurrences of the attribute for the entity type. In our example, each student will have one name and between 1 and 50 grades.

Whether to consider a shared attribute as an attribute for a number of entities or as a separate entity type representing the relationship is an information-system design decision. We will return to this problem in Chapter 9, where its resolution is important for data-system design.

As part of the information requirements, volume characteristics for the identified entity types and attributes must be specified. In particular, entity types are populated by numerous individuals. For the data-system design, it is important to know the anticipated maximum number of entities of an entity type. It is also important to know the maximum and average number of instances of each shared attribute, for example, the maximum number of students or the maximum number of grades that an individual student can have.

Attributes are characterized by their attribute values or *domain sets*. Where applicable, the domain range (the set of valid values for the attribute) should be specified. The domain set characteristics include:

- range, low and high numeric values for ages, salaries, grades, and so on.
- code definition, for status indicators, postal codes, and so on.
- unit of measure, for example, dollars, years, pounds, kilograms, and so on.
- check-sum definition, for identification numbers.
- a valid alphabet, for text attributes, and so on.

An individual user or information process will rarely, if ever, need the complete attribute set for an entity. Therefore, when defining information requirements, it is necessary to identify each user's attribute requirements, then incorporate them into the user community's definition of the entity types.

Processing Requirements

Processing requirements state the information processes that are needed to extract, modify, and/or transform the information stored in the system's information archive to the information needed to support resolution of the work problems or decisions named in the problem statement.

There will be at least one processing requirement for each identified problem. Often a problem will specify a slow organizational procedure, such as the processing of an order from receipt to shipment, that contains a number of information-processing tasks. In this case, the system analyst should define each task as a separate processing requirement. It is not uncommon for an AIS to have more than 200 information processes representing the basic procedures of a functional unit within the organization. These 200 processes form the basis of the information-processing requirements.

Each processing requirement specification must define the information to be acted upon, the information manipulations to be performed, and the form in which the results are to be presented. More simply, a process can be specified by its

$$\text{input} \longrightarrow \text{process algorithm} \longrightarrow \text{output}$$

Information process characteristics include the expected frequency of use per time period and the required response time, i.e., the desired time interval from process initiation to presentation of results. These characteristics also include a description of the process users, giving the identity of the primary user of the process, which other system users have access to this process, and the geographic distribution of the process users.

THE GOAL STATEMENT

The goal statement is a presentation of the results of the goal analysis that defines the user specifications for a desired (not necessarily existing) information system. The goal statement documents contain definitions of the desired system environment and user community, the information problems to be resolved, the information that the system needs to support resolution of the information problems, and the information processes required to serve the user community.

The goal statement is the first major document in the system analysis and design procedure. It serves as the basis for determining whether or not to go ahead with an analysis of the current information system with the goal of proposing system improvements. The goal statement must be reviewed and approved by both the proposed system users and the members of the organization's management who are (or will be) responsible for the proposed information system. Once the goal statement has been approved, further system analysis and design work can be performed.

The goal statement is the document against which the current system will be evaluated, any modifications will be proposed, and the new or modified system will be designed. It consists of four central documents containing the data and specifications derived from the problem analysis:

1. The user directory
2. The information dictionary

3. The process dictionary
4. The requirement matrices

These documents define and relate the users, information content, and processing requirements for the desired information system. They must be developed concurrently, as new users and requirements are determined during the problem analysis process. Their content may be modified during the feasibility analysis as the system specifications are adjusted to reflect organizational constraints.

The goal statement documents must be presented in a problem versus goal analysis report that defines the assumptions made in assembling the documents. These assumptions give the organization management responsible for the development of the information system the information they need to evaluate the validity of the report content.

The User Directory

As users of the information system are identified, a *user directory* must be established. The directory contains a full description of each user with his or her information and information service requirements, behavior patterns as a system user, and priority within the user community. The most important components of the user description are listed in Box 4.2.

Note that a system user, although normally a person or group of persons, may also be another information system or an external (to the environment of the AIS) organization. From the point of view of the information system, and therefore also of the user directory, any supplier of information to or recipient of information from the system is a system user and must be defined in the directory. If the system environment contains many different categories of users, the user identification section of the directory should be expanded to include a specification of the user category.

The layout of the user directory should include a graphic presentation of the user community, like that shown in Figure 4.1. The user definitions should be placed in the directory in an order that will make locating an individual user convenient. Cross-indexing will also be necessary, so that a user can be located by name, membership in an organizational unit, or some usage characteristics for either information or information services.

Most commonly, if the current system has a user directory at all, it will be contained in the previous system analyst's notes. It must be made formal and generally available, as the directory defines the system environment, from which the judgment of system success or failure will be made. The users are also the source of all system goals.

Box 4.2

USER DESCRIPTION COMPONENTS

1. The user identification, giving:
   - full user name
   - organization address
   - code name for use within the information system
   - priority level within the user community
   - access authority to system subsystems
   - account number(s) for system use billing

2. The information requirements for each user, giving:
   - entities and attribute sets to be used
   - interentity relationships used
   - information supplied by the user
   - output forms required

3. The information-processing requirement, giving:
   - the information processes to be used
   - the frequency of use of each process
   - the response time requirements for each process

The directory is a good candidate for automation, and some existing "data dictionary systems" do provide for user definition, if not to the extent indicated here. Data dictionary systems are actually tools developed for use during the data-system phase of system development. These systems will be discussed in Part III.

The Information Dictionary

As the information requirements are identified, an *information dictionary* must be established. The information dictionary contains a complete definition of each information element—entity, attribute, or relationship—to be included in the information system. Box 4.3 lists the definition components needed to describe each information element.

The information dictionary is the basic document for file and database design; it will be the basis for constructing the data dictionary during the data-system design phase. However, in compiling the information dictionary, the storage method to be used for the information element should not be considered, as this is a data-system design consideration; this will be discussed in Chapter 9.

Box 4.3

INFORMATION DEFINITION COMPONENTS

1. The information-element identification, giving:
   - full name as element is known by users
   - synonym name(s) as required by users
   - code name for use within information system
   - reference number or name(s) as used on system-design graphs and/or matrices

2. The element definition, giving:
   - a full verbal definition
   - the type of element: entity, attribute, or relationship

3. The element characteristics, giving for each:
   entity class:
   - the complete attribute set
   - the identifying attribute(s)
   - the relationships associated with this entity
   - the cardinality of the entity set
   attribute type:
   - the entities and/or relationships this attribute describes
   - the attribute value domain set type: alphabetic, numeric, coded, date, other
   - the quality requirement for the value set (age, accuracy, relevance, source, scope)
   - the valid value range for attribute values
   - for coded attributes, the code definitions
   - desired presentation format(s)
   relationship:
   - the entity classes related
   - the attribute set describing the relationship
   - the cardinality of the relationship

4. The element usage characteristics, giving:
   - names of the information processes that refer to the element
   - names of the processes that modify element values

5. The security requirements for the element, giving:
   - the user responsible for the element
   - users allowed to change element values
   - users allowed to use but not modify element values
   - security code(s) or level assignment

The information dictionary can be kept as a manual reference list of element names in alphabetical order, or by entity class with associated attributes. However, storage as an automated file would make searches and analysis of the usage characteristics of the various elements easier. One of the more general data dictionary systems can be used to establish and generate reports for the information dictionary. (We will return to these systems in Part III: Data-System Design.)

The Process Dictionary

As the user directory and problem statement are developed, information-processing requirements are identified and defined. These definitions make up the content of the *process dictionary*. Box 4.4 lists the components needed to define information-processing requirements.

The process dictionary will be used during information-system design to establish the information procedures that must be included in the information system, and again during data-system design to specify both manual and automated data processing tasks.

The process dictionary should be kept as a separate document, as it is the basis for specification of the programs and procedures that will make up the automated portion of the data system. Like the information dictionary, it may be compiled as a reference manual. Analysis and cross-referencing between the user directory, information dictionary, and processing dictionary are easier if all are kept as automated files.

Automated design aid systems for program specification can be used to develop the process dictionary. (See Teichroew, 1974, for a description of the PSL/PSA specification language.) However, the system analyst must also capture process requirements that are not candidates for automation, and must then use the automated tools in a context wider than many of them have been designed for. We will return to developing the specifications for automated procedures in Part III, Chapter 10.

Requirement Matrices

Matrices can present large quantities of information for analysis in compact form. During goal analysis, a number of matrices are useful for cross-referencing and analysis of the information and data collected in the dictionaries and directories. Particularly useful matrices include:

1. A user/problem matrix to supplement the PAT table and specify the relationships between user and problem(s)
2. A problem/process matrix, useful when a single problem relates to more than one process

Box 4.4

PROCESS DEFINITION COMPONENTS

1. The information process identification, giving:
   - process name as known to the users
   - synonym name(s) as required
   - code name used within the information system
   - reference name or number(s) as used on system design graphs and/or matrices

2. A process definition, giving:
   - objective(s) of the process
   - specific algorithm(s) utilized
   - modifications to stored data elements

3. The information requirements, giving:
   - input information elements required
   - stored information/data elements required
   - volume of stored data required by process
   - type of data access required (selection of one item, a subset of items, or the entire entity class)
   - result presentation format(s)

4. The usage characteristics, giving:
   - frequency of use per time period
   - minimum response-time requirement
   - number of individual users
   - highest priority within the user group

5. The security requirements, giving:
   - user responsible for process functioning
   - users allowed to use this process
   - security level for the process

3. A user/information matrix, giving the information elements needed by each user and the users of each information element
4. A process/information matrix, giving the processes for each information element and the information elements for each process

Figure 4.4 illustrates the basic layout for a requirement matrix. The convention followed puts the principal component being described (user, problem, user, and process, respectively, in the preceding list) on the horizontal axis. The usage requirements are then located on the

Figure 4.4 Requirement Matrix Structure

Principal Axis	Usage Detail Axis	
	Information Elements Used	Frequency · Priority
User ID	Element Section	Usage Characteristics Section

vertical axis in such a way that each matrix row describes the system usage characteristics for one user, problem, user, or process, respectively.

Note that a requirement matrix has two vertical sections, with the leftmost describing items used by the individual and the rightmost defining the usage requirements for the item set. In the "elements used" section, an X in the cell where a user and an information element cross indicates that this user "uses" this information element. A blank indicates that the user has no interest in the element. The frequency column indicates how often, within a given time period, the user makes use of the elements indicated. The priority indicates the relative priority of this user or process among all users or processes.

This basic matrix form is used extensively in this text as a tool for analyzing ISAD information. As the ISAD project develops, the matrix contents become more specific. These details will be discussed as they are used (see particularly Chapter 5).

Figure 4.5 illustrates the process/information requirement matrix, using a few processes from the student AIS. According to the matrix, P-1, registration, uses information elements i1, student name; i2, address; and i3, course identification. This process is executed five times as many times as there are students, once for each course each student registers for. The priority is high.

In its final form, the matrix should give the high-priority rows first, and the most used element columns should be on the left. To reduce the system scope, in terms of number of processes or number of information elements included, one could then delete "bottom" rows and "rightmost" columns, or develop them as later-phase projects. Note that Figure 4.5 shows only a trivial example; a real system may well have more than 100 process rows and several thousand element columns.

If the goal analysis dictionaries and directories have been compiled and stored using an automated design aid, this tool will normally contain a facility for producing and ordering requirement matrices. If a manual collection process has been used, the matrices must also be produced and analyzed by hand.

Figure 4.5 Process/Information Matrix: An Example

Process[a]	Information Elements Used[b]					Frequency (Executions per semester)	Priority
	i1	i2	i3	i4[c]	...		
P-1	X	X	X			5 × Number of students	High
P-2	X		X	X		5 × Number of students	High
P-3	X	X	X	X		Number of students	High
P-4	X		X			Number of courses	Medium
.							
.							
.							

a. P-1 Registration
   P-2 Grade recording
   P-3 Transcript
   P-4 Class roster

b. X used by process

c. i1 Student name
   i2 Address
   i3 Course identification
   i4 Course grade

FEASIBILITY ANALYSIS

The initial goal statement for a new or improved information system contains many user information and information service requirements that the current system is not fulfilling satisfactorily. Providing these services will require changes in the existing system, and this will require organizational resources, and probably revision of current task procedures, while the changes are being implemented. The objective of performing a feasibility analysis for the goal statement is to ensure that (1) the changes indicated are really desired and (2) they can be accomplished given the resources of the organization.

The system analyst should provide several alternatives for system improvement and rank these alternatives by expected level of goal achievement. Generally, techniques ranging from improving manual procedures to full (or nearly full) automation can improve (speed up) information flow. Other improvement techniques might be changes in the person-machine interface, upgrading of computer hardware (without changing the user interface), making personnel changes, and so on.

It is up to the organization management to decide what level of goal achievement is required and which improvement techniques should be applied to the information system. Although it is generally the system analyst who will present the feasibility analysis to management, the analyst will not have a great deal of the benefit information readily available. Therefore, several iterations of the feasibility analysis between the analyst and management will probably be needed.

A number of constraints will influence the implementation of system changes. Usually the chief concern is the investment cost in dollars of the new or modified system and the expected monetary benefit. The analyst must be prepared, wherever possible, to present system alternatives in terms of their expected monetary costs and benefits. However, other constraints and considerations must also be taken into account. System changes may also involve operational, technical, social, and possibly legal costs and benefits. These costs and benefits must also be evaluated in the feasibility analysis.

Options for System Improvement

Options for changing an information system to improve its capabilities vary with the level of technology currently in use. The current information system may be a fairly loosely perceived manual system with no automation, or it may be a highly automated CBIS. Generally, improvement techniques include some combination of the following:

1. Rearrangement of the physical environment and components of the system to follow the information flow through the organization more closely
2. Reassignment of the information-processing staff to better match staff assignments with the labor requirements of the individual information-processing tasks
3. Addition or modification of information and/or information processes
4. Expansion of the size of the information-processing staff
5. Increasing the technical level used

Improvement tactics 1 and 2 require little capital outlay and are relatively easy to implement from an organizational point of view. Tactics 3, 4, and 5 require both a monetary outlay and an increase in the educational or skill level of the information-processing staff.

Basically, these improvement tactics can be applied to different types of information problems: inefficient information flow patterns, congestion points within the system, unavailable information or information services, overload of information-processing transactions, accuracy and scope of information required, respectively. Each of these tactics can affect, positively, the rate of information flow through the system.

Table 4.2 relates the improvement tactics to the type of information problem. Note, however, that this relationship is not absolute. The usefulness of each tactic depends on the current system's efficiency and implementation tactics. The evaluations in Table 4.2 assume that the current system is a loosely defined manual information system. The

Table 4.2 System Improvement Tactics

Information Problem Type*	Physical Environment	Staff Assignment	New Tasks	Staff Size	Technology Level
IP-1	Good	Possible			
IP-2	Possible	Good		Good	Possible
IP-3			Good		
IP-4		Possible		Good	Good
IP-5		Possible			Good
IP-6	Possible	Possible		Good	Good

*IP-1 Inefficient information flow
IP-2 Congestion in information flow
IP-3 Unavailability of information or information service
IP-4 Overload of work for information system
IP-5 Insufficient accuracy and scope of information
IP-6 Slow response time

effect of an improvement tactic on higher-level technical systems will not normally be as great.

When preparing a system improvement proposal for the goal set, the system analyst should assign alternative strategies for attaining each goal. At least two, and preferably three, alternatives should be developed. Typically, the analyst starts with alternative 0, keeping the current system unchanged. Alternative 1 changes the most central processes, commonly introducing or improving automation. Alternative 2 changes more processes than alternative 1, and so on. The feasibility analysis then assesses each proposal against organization constraints. The "best" proposal must be appropriately modified until an acceptable proposal is developed.

Constraints on System Change

The constraints on construction and/or modification of information systems come from sources both inside and outside the organization. Generally the constraints fall into the following categories:

1. Financial
2. Operational
3. Technological
4. Social
5. Legal

Financially, an organization will always have limited monetary resources to allocate to improvement of the information system. Since the goal statement reflects changes and additions, one must expect the new or modified system to require a clear cost outlay. Therefore, the new system must be justified by the benefits it is expected to provide. An acceptable improvement proposal would be one for which the anticipated monetary benefits outweigh the costs. In the feasibility analysis, both direct monetary benefits and costs must be estimated, since real development costs and operational benefits will not be known until later system design and development stages are completed.

Operational constraints concern the time available for implementing the system improvement proposal. In addition to the time needed to program and test the system, operational constraints consist of time to train personnel in the use of the new system, personnel to operate the system, and operational funding. Again, the system improvement proposal must estimate the operational resources required and evaluate the organization's ability to provide these resources.

Technical constraints are closely related to both financial and operational constraints. New technology requires a financial outlay, sometimes of substantial size. It also requires an operational staff, which, even if it is available within the organization, will require training. The costs of technical components can usually be established fairly well at goal analysis time. Again, equipment from several alternative vendors should be presented for evaluation.

Social constraints involve the system's human environment. People may have been hired for specific tasks and be unwilling or unable to be retrained. The system proposal may involve layoffs that would be unacceptable to the workers, unions, and/or management. Customers and/or suppliers may respond negatively to aspects of the proposal. And finally, some aspects of the system may change the organization's public image. As far as possible, the social implications of the system changes must be estimated and their acceptability to the people involved evaluated.

Legal constraints are set by government laws and regulations, organizational directives, union contracts, and normal organizational ethics. The system proposal must be checked for information collection and/or processing aspects that could conflict with these constraints.

The Analysis

A feasibility analysis is an evaluation of the system improvement proposals against the constraints in each of the categories discussed as set by the organization and its environment. The best, i.e., the most feasible, proposal provides the objectives or goal statement against which the current system can be evaluated and a new or modified system designed.

Each of the goals in the goal statement must be evaluated against each of the constraint criteria. Each element of the improvement proposal must be evaluated positively if the proposal is to be acceptable.

The feasibility analysis tests two conditions: conformity with the system constraints and a positive cost/benefit ratio, i.e., the system is expected to improve the organization's information processing capabilities. The first entails an evaluation of each of the proposal's provisions as acceptable or unacceptable. The second is more complex.

A cost/benefit analysis of the goal statement is at best an estimate of expected (hoped-for) benefits and anticipated costs. A full financial analysis is not possible, since the system has not yet been designed, and thus the specific costs are unavailable. However, price ranges can be used as a guideline. Also, benefits are very difficult to estimate, since the specific implementation design has not been developed. Again, the goals set an optimum achievement that can be compared with the estimated costs.

A further problem with performing a cost/benefit analysis for the goal set is the weight to be placed on nonmonetary considerations, particularly the operational, social, and legal aspects of the system. Chapter 6 returns to this problem in the context of preparing a specific set of system design proposals for evaluation.

SUMMARY

Problem analysis must be the first phase of any ISAD project. In this phase, current information problems are identified. From this problem set, it is possible to identify the users of the information system, the system's boundaries, and content. Once the users are known, their information requirements can be determined, and a combined goal statement for the new or modified information system can be established. Finally, before continuing with a detailed system analysis and/or a new system design, the goal set must be tested for feasibility given the framework of the organization's constraints.

KEY CONCEPTS

Attribute	Entity type
Cost/benefit analysis	Feasibility analysis
Domain	Goal analysis
Entity	Goal statement

Information dictionary
Input supplier
Output recipient
Problem analysis

Process dictionary
Requirement matrix
User directory
User group

DISCUSSION QUESTIONS

1. Define and provide an example of each of the key concepts.
2. What is the objective of a problem analysis? Why is it so important? Why should it be the first thing the system analyst does when asked to perform a system analysis and design?
3. What is a goal analysis, and how does it relate to the problem analysis? Who has problems of interest to the system analyst, and how can these problems be determined?
4. Discuss the differences between internal and external users. Why are external users important to a system analyst concerned with an internal information system?
5. What are the components of information? Are these components unique categories, or could an information element be classified as differing components? Who decides the classification of an information element? Use an example to illustrate your discussion.
6. What is a processing requirement, and how is it defined? Must a processing requirement be subject to automation? Why?
7. What are the components of a goal statement? Who prepares it and who approves it? When? Why?
8. Why are requirement matrices valuable? Can one goal statement contain more than one requirement matrix? Why? Discuss the use of this matrix.
9. How can information systems be improved? Is automation a good first choice? Why?
10. What constraints apply to changes in information systems? Discuss what is meant by social constraints. Should these constraints be of concern to a system analyst? Why?

PROJECT

Using an organization of your choice,

1. Prepare a complete goal statement for an information system to serve four to six user groups. Include at least one external user group.
2. Prepare a feasibility analysis for the system proposal, using real costs wherever possible.

RECOMMENDED READINGS

Burch, J. G., Jr., F. R. Strater, and G. Grudnitski. *Information Systems: Theory and Practice.* 2nd ed. New York : John Wiley & Sons, 1979.

Chapters 3 and 11 discuss important aspects of information requirements specification and feasibility analysis, respectively.

Lundeberg, M., G. Goldkuhl, and A. Nilsson. *Information Systems Development.* Englewood Cliffs, N. J. : Prentice-Hall, 1981.

Chapter 3 discusses "change analysis," which has objectives similar to those of goal analysis in this chapter.

Rockart, John F. "Chief Executives Define Their Own Data Needs." *Harvard Business Review*, March–April 1979.

This paper details the problems of extracting management information for decision support from operations-level transaction-processing systems. It also presents a method of specifying information-system goals using "critical success factors."

Chapter 5
System Analysis

INTRODUCTION

The objective of system analysis is to determine *where* the current information system needs to be changed to provide more satisfactory information services for the user community. More specifically, a system analysis studies the current information system to locate the points that need to be changed in order to relieve the information problems identified in the goal analysis, and proposes alternative system structures and techniques that can be used to implement these changes. Designing the modified information system and its supporting data system are part of later system development stages that build on the system change proposal that results from the system analysis.

Prior to a system analysis, a goal analysis has established:

1. The scope of the information system under consideration
2. The user community for the information system
3. The information problems perceived by the user community
4. The feasibility of resolving the problems, given the organizational and social constraints
5. A feasible goal statement for the information system

System analysis actually consists of two tasks:

1. A description and analysis of the current information system to determine the content and structure of the system and to identify the modifications and additions that are necessary to satisfy the goal statement. This is the topic of this chapter.
2. An evaluation of alternative system structures for implementing the proposed system modifications. This is the topic of Chapter 6.

The result of a completed system analysis is a proposal for information-system modifications that

1. satisfy the goal statement.
2. are cost-effective.
3. are within the constraints of the organization.

System evaluation will be discussed in Chapter 6. In this chapter we will develop a technique for the first stage of system analysis, system description.

The first objective of system analysis is to determine the extent to which the current information system actually contains the information and information services necessary to satisfy the goal statement; the next is to identify the information and information services that must be added or modified in order to satisfy the goal statement.

The analysis of an information system starts with documentation of its interactions with its environment. The environment of an information system is termed its *object system*. The analysis proceeds in two steps:

1. *Activity Analysis* This describes the activities in the object system and their points of interaction with the information system.

2. *Information-System Analysis* This isolates and describes the information system and identifies those points that must be modified to improve goal achievement.

The results of the system analysis for the current information system are:

1. Complete documentation of the current information system
2. A list of the information and information services that must be added or modified to provide a system that can satisfy the goal statement
3. Suggested system structures and implementation strategies for incorporating the proposed changes

As discussed in Chapter 3, methods of system analysis fall into one of two categories: information-centered or process-centered approaches. This text uses an information-centered method, chosen on the belief that the information archive is the most constant component of an information system and that problems that arise from a lack of information are more costly to resolve than those that require new or modified information processes. The methods and techniques presented here have been developed from the work done originally at the University of Stockholm on information-system theories, methods, and development techniques (Langefors, 1973; Lundeberg, 1974).

System analysis concentrates on describing a system so that it can be understood and evaluated against the goals set for it. The primary tools used for object- and information-system description are:

Graphs to document material, information, and data flows.

Matrices to document cross-references of identified activities or processes with the information messages they act upon.

Dictionaries to document the characteristics of the activities and information elements.

The system analyst uses these tools to develop a model of the system and to document the details of the system (matrices and dictionaries). The major input to the analysis phase is information solicited from the users, through formal and informal conversation (questionnaires and meetings). The second major input will be whatever documentation of the current system may exist.

OBJECT-SYSTEM DESCRIPTION

We know from Chapters 1 and 2 that an information system is "a system, including its information store and processes, that is used to provide information" for its (human) user community. The user community is found in the organizational system that contains the IS and in that organization's external environment. The main interests and objectives of the organizational system concern such business activities as manufacturing, selling, providing services, and so on. The information system exists to support one or more of these business activities.

There will be many business activities within an organization, each with one or more supporting information systems. We will call that portion of the organization that provides an information-system environment the *object system*. The object system encompasses one or more of the business activities of the organization, its employees, products, customers, suppliers, and so on, and its information system(s).

An information system maintains both information about the object system and the information processes that support the object system's activities. For example, an organization's personnel office, the object system, will have an information system containing (1) information on employees, such as names, addresses, and salaries, and (2) information processes, such as registering a new employee, production of the monthly payroll, and so on.

Figure 5.1 illustrates this layered model of an object system and its information system. Again, we use the university system, which here contains subsystems for administration, buildings, faculty members, library, student body, and supplies. The information system for student administration contains data and processes for student registration and grading. Note that an object system may have components, such as buildings and supplies in the model, that are not represented in the information system being studied.

The first step in describing an information system is to perform an activity analysis, that is, to identify the object system and its points of interaction with the information system. We can concentrate our attention on those sections of the total object system that we expect will have interactions with the information system being studied—in the model in Figure 5.1, the administration, faculty, and student body. We must be sure to include all possible users of the system.

Figure 5.1 The Object System

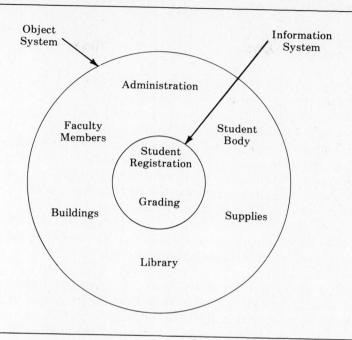

Material versus Information Flow

The movement of information through an information system usually follows the flow of people, goods, and/or money through the object system. For example, a manufacturing company will have an information system tracking orders from their receipt through manufacturing, packing, shipping, possible resupply, possible delayed partial shipment, and payment for the received order.

The flow of goods, services, and/or materials typically follows the production structure of the organization. Storing and processing information about the material flow, for example, order servicing, is a principal function of the information system. The information flow so strongly reflects the material flow that the structure of the information system is often implemented as a direct model of the pattern of material flow through the object system.

Analyzing an object system to determine its interactions with its information system focuses on describing the material flow and the information use and requirements as they occur throughout the object system. Documenting the material flow within the object system is usually easier than documenting the information flow, since the material flow involves concrete things or entities about which people, the information system users, are concerned.

Activity Analysis

An *activity analysis* is used to develop the description of object-system activities that need information-system support. Activities of concern include those that provide input, receive output, and require specific data processing services from the information system. This is the first step in a system analysis, the objective of which is to document the object system and its interactions with its information system. Once the object system has been defined, the information system may be extracted and the appropriate information analysis performed.

Restated, we can define an activity analysis as:

An analysis and description of those activities of an object system that affect information-system functions.

A number of methods and techniques for preparing an activity analysis have been proposed. The method presented here is based on ideas and techniques developed in the ISAC approach (Lundeberg et al., 1981). The principal premise of an information-centered system analysis approach is that the information an information system maintains must be related to real object-system requirements. Thus, before designing the system, the system analyst must perform a detailed analysis of the users and their information requirements, i.e., what information the users need.

An activity analysis is performed as a top-down analysis of the object system, with special attention paid to the information flow that supports the material flow through the object system. The analysis is top-down in the sense that the object system is viewed as a whole that receives certain inputs (e.g., orders, queries, and so on) and produces specified outputs (e.g. products, reports, and so on). For the outputs to be produced from the inputs, certain activities must take place within the system. Each activity is in turn considered a system with specified inputs, outputs, and activities. System decomposition continues until the lowest-level activities are established, i.e., until further decomposition gives no further information about the system's functions. (Note that the number of system levels analyzed will differ for different major subsystems.)

An activity analysis documents the content and structure of the object system by developing a set of activity graphs, one for each system and subsystem. These graphs illustrate the flow of information and material through the object system. Along with the graphs, a set of matrices are used to cross-reference the users (activities) and the information elements identified. Information and process dictionaries, with the same format as those developed for the goal analysis, should be developed to document the existing system. These will form a basis for comparing the current system with the goal statement.

The activity analysis may uncover activities and users that were overlooked during goal analysis. If these new activities or users cannot be served under the goal statement, it will be necessary to return to the goal analysis stage and study the impact of the new information requirements. If the expected impact of the new activity or information element is limited, this return to the goal analysis can be put off until the full system analysis is completed.

Activity Graphs

Graphs are often used to display models of systems. A graph is a useful tool for focusing attention on and initiating discussion about the system of concern, since rather large systems can be modeled in a single graph. Graph nodes represent the objects of interest, in our case the activities, materials, and information of the system. Graph arcs represent the relationships, structure, or sequence (flow) between the system objects.

Activity Graph A graph with two types of nodes, one identifying activities, the other identifying materials and/or information. The arcs represent (1) the sequence of occurrence of the activity nodes and (2) the information and/or materials passed between activities. An activity graph documents both the material and information flows and the activities (processes) involved in an object system.

In this text we will use the graph notation proposed by Lundeberg (Lundeberg, 1974). The symbols used are shown in Figure 5.2. Note that there are two basically different symbols for information or materials and for activities, the rhomboid and dot, respectively.

In an activity graph each node is identified by a number. Activities, indicated by dots (small 'o' in the figures in this chapter), are identified by a multidigit number *nnn...* that gives the subsystem level of the activity. For example, in Figure 5.3, there are three level 1 subsystems: 4, curriculum development; 5, registration; and 6, class administration. Figure 5.5 is a level 1 model of subsystem 6, class administration. Here the activities are identified as 61, 62, and 63, indicating that they are subsystems 1, 2, and 3 of subsystem 6.

Information elements and materials, indicated by rhomboids, are identified by a number:letter combination. The number identifies the activity that generated or introduced the information or material entity. Each initial information element is assumed to come from some activity

Figure 5.2 Activity Graph Notation[1]

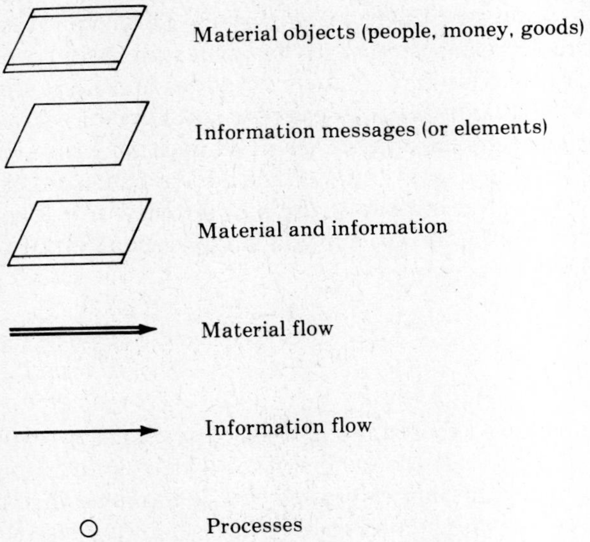

Material objects (people, money, goods)

Information messages (or elements)

Material and information

Material flow

Information flow

Processes

1. Lundeberg, Goldkuhl, and Nilsson, *Information Systems Development: A Systematic Approach*, p. 98. © 1981. Reprinted by permission of Prentice-Hall, Inc., Englewood Cliffs, N.J.

outside the system under study. Thus the first internal activity will always have an identifier > 1. See Figure 5.3.

Figure 5.3 illustrates a level 0 activity graph for the student AIS. The three inputs 1A, 2A, and 3A are assumed to come from three separate external activities. Activity 4, curriculum development, is the first internal activity defined. It produces information element 4A, course offerings, which in turn is an input for activity 5, registration. In this example, only activity 6, class administration, produces external output, i.e., output from the system, here 6B, experienced faculty; 6C, evaluations of students; and 6D, graduates.

An activity graph actually has two sections, the graph itself and a text page that elaborates and further defines the elements of the graph. See Figure 5.3.

During an activity analysis, a hierarchical set of activity graphs is developed. Each graph models the activities of some subsystem, identifying its primary inputs and outputs, of both material and information, and its major subsystems. The initial graph, level 0, presents the system as a whole and identifies the major subsystems. Level 1 graphs, one for each of the major subsystems, model the subsystems and identify their

Figure 5.3 Activity Graph, Level 0: Student AIS Example

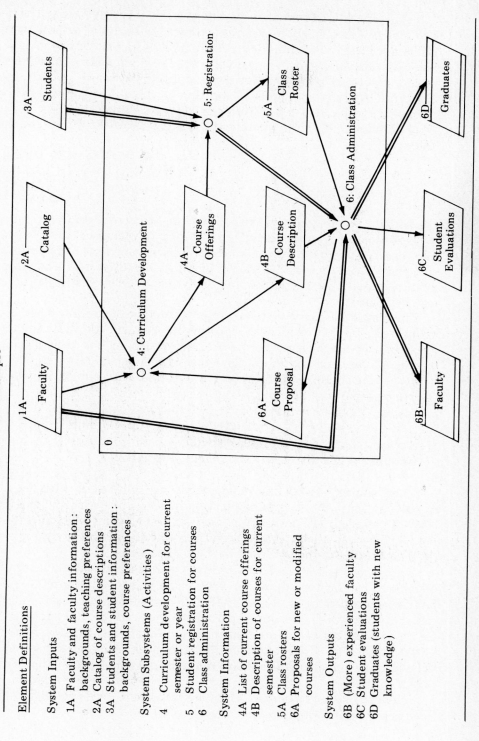

Element Definitions

System Inputs

1A Faculty and faculty information :
    backgrounds, teaching preferences
2A Catalog of course descriptions
3A Students and student information :
    backgrounds, course preferences

System Subsystems (Activities)

4 Curriculum development for current
   semester or year
5 Student registration for courses
6 Class administration

System Information

4A List of current course offerings
4B Description of courses for current
    semester
5A Class rosters
6A Proposals for new or modified
    courses

System Outputs

6B (More) experienced faculty
6C Student evaluations
6D Graduates (students with new
    knowledge)

sub-subsystems, and so on. In the example, level 1 activity graphs would be identified as 4, 5, and 6 and would describe the activities and material and information flows for curriculum development, registration, and class administration, respectively. See the example in Figure 5.5.

The set of activity graphs developed during the activity analysis defines the structure, components, and flow of the object system. The number of graphs developed during an activity analysis depends on the level of detail required to document the activities of the object system fully.

Activity Matrix

An activity graph identifies the activities and the information or materials of the object system and describes their flow through the system. An *activity matrix* documents the cross-references between activities and the entities these activities use. Since we are interested in the information system, we will include only information elements in the activity matrix.

The matrix has three vertical sections: the first contains the activity identifiers, the second gives the information-element use, and the third describes the usage characteristics of the activity, such as how often it occurs, its priority, and so on. Each row of the matrix describes one activity. The columns of the matrix show which activities have overlapping element use or similar usage characteristics.

We can define an activity matrix as follows:

> *Activity Matrix* A matrix that documents the cross-references between system activities and information elements.

There should be only one activity matrix for the set of activity graphs, so that the activity/information relationships of the whole system can be seen. The activity and information-element references should be those used as graph identifiers so that a matrix row can be quickly related to the appropriate graph elements.

Figure 5.4 illustrates an activity matrix for the activity graph set established so far for the student AIS, namely, level 0 (Figure 5.3). We've assumed that the student AIS under consideration covers 5000 students, each taking 5 courses per semester out of the 1000 course sections being offered. Note that the activities are identified as A-4, A-5, and A-6 to correspond with the references in the activity graph. The information elements are also referred to by their graph identifiers, 1A, 2A, etc.

Activity characteristics (AC) that are important for an activity analysis of an information system are:

Figure 5.4 Activity Matrix: Student AIS Example

Entity / Activity[a]	Entities[b,c]										Activity Characteristics[d]		
	1A	2A	3A	4A	4B	5A	6A	6B	6C	6D	AC-1	AC-2	AC-3
A-4	X	X		X	X		X				2	1	2000
A-5			X	X		X					1	1	5000
A-6	X		X		X	X	X	X	X	X	1	1000	35

a. A-4, curriculum development.
   A-5, registration.
   A-6, class administration.
b. See element definitions in Figure 5.2.
c. X: The entity is used or referenced by the activity.
d. AC-1, priority: 1, high; 2, medium; 3, low.
   AC-2, frequency: executions per semester.
   AC-3, volume: inputs per execution.

Priority (AC-1) In an activity analysis all activities are important, but some will be more actively used, have more critical time constraints, or be more vital to the functioning of the total system than others. The priority indicates the relative importance of the activity within the total system. The manager of the system must set priorities to ensure that the total system functions satisfactorily. Individual priorities can be stated as high, medium, or low.

Frequency (AC-2) The frequency characteristic of an activity indicates how often, within a given time interval, the activity is used. A common time interval for all activities should be used to allow comparisons of activity frequencies. In Figure 5.4, the number of occurrences per semester was chosen. Other options would be to compare occurrences per day, week, or month. This is a particularly important characteristic during data-system design; it can supersede the priority characteristic in certain instances.

Volume (AC-3) Volume is an indicator of the quantity of inputs used during any one execution of the activity. For example, if the registration system requires all students to register for courses before it can terminate and produce any output, then the volume characteristic would be a number equal to the number of students times the number of courses for which they can register.

The Activity Analysis Report

The activity graphs and activity matrix provide graphic models of the system. Although these models provide an excellent overview of the system and its details and facilitate communication between the system analyst and the user environment, they cannot provide full detail because of their compact form. They must be supplemented with textual information that can be readily located using the activity or information-element name (reference identification). The element descriptions should be kept in the information and process dictionaries being developed for the system.

Object-system activities are processes that should be documented in a process dictionary with the same format as that used during goal analysis. Most of the activities documented during system analysis should already have been identified during goal analysis; if they were, the definitions need only be copied in the process dictionary documenting the current system. Some activities may not have been recorded, either because the users were so satisfied with their functioning that they were forgotten or because they are actually irrelevant and therefore are not used. Some processes from the goal analysis are not in the current system, but are part of the goal set for extension of the system.

Information elements are the attributes and entities of the object system that are of interest. The information dictionary for the current system should have the same format as that used during goal analysis. This dictionary is used to document the status of the information already kept in the current system. Again, new entities may be identified during the activity analysis, and there may also be missing entities that appear as information requirements.

The activity analysis report is a readable document that describes the object system, its components, and system flow. This report is illustrated by the activity graphs and matrix and will have as an appendix the information and process dictionaries.

The activity report gives the current status of the object system's use of its information system. This report provides the basis for defining boundaries and the required inputs and outputs for the information system.

If problem areas that were not identified during goal analysis are identified during the activity analysis, it will be necessary to return to the goal analysis to determine the impact of these problem areas on the goal set for the system. These problem areas are of particular concern in the information analysis and system design that will follow.

Activity Analysis Example

An activity analysis of a real system can produce more than 50 graphs covering four or five system levels. Normally, defining the object system to three or four subsystem levels is adequate. If further detail is needed, it can be provided at later stages. With the graphs will be a combined activity matrix, with more than 100 rows and possibly more than 1000 information-element columns. Obviously, it will be necessary to partition this data or, better, to use some automated documentation tool, such as ISDOS, SYSDOC, or a commercial data dictionary system.

For our model, we will present only one level 1 graph: that for subsystem 6, class administration, from Figure 5.3. Figures 5.5 and 5.6 give level 1 graphs and an activity matrix for this subsystem.

In a complete activity analysis, there would be second-level graphs for subactivities 61, 62, and 63 from Figure 5.5 and activity graphs for the subsystems of activities 4, curriculum development, and 5, registration, from the primary system (Figure 5.3). The number of graph levels required depends on the complexity of the primary system and the separate subsystems. Having different numbers of graph levels for the different primary subsystems within the graph sets is quite feasible.

Each graph should be supplemented by a text page containing the long version descriptors for the graph components (see Figure 5.5). These descriptors should be so explicit that the reader can understand the graph without having to go to the information or process dictionaries.

Normally there would be one activity matrix for the primary system and one for each of the major subsystems. The matrix can link several graphs and thus provide an overview of the system.

Boxes 5.1 and 5.2 illustrate an entry for an entity, student, and an activity, evaluation, in the information and process dictionaries, respectively. Note that these entries are incomplete. More detail will be added as the specifics of the system are developed in the analysis and design stages. Refer to Chapter 4 for the outlines for complete dictionary entries.

INFORMATION SYSTEM DESCRIPTION

An information system is a subsystem of the organizational system (the object system) that it serves. The people, activities, and material flows of the object system, which interact with the information system, are the entities of the system environment about which the information system collects and processes data.

Figure 5.5 Activity Graph, Level 1: Student AIS Example, Class Administration

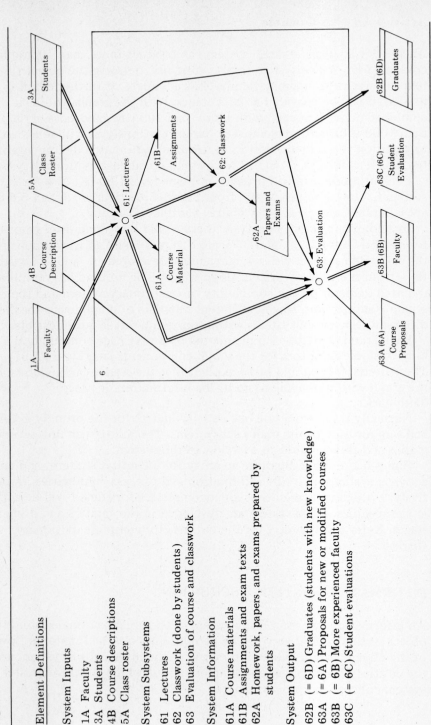

Element Definitions

System Inputs

1A Faculty
3A Students
4B Course descriptions
5A Class roster

System Subsystems

61 Lectures
62 Classwork (done by students)
63 Evaluation of course and classwork

System Information

61A Course materials
61B Assignments and exam texts
62A Homework, papers, and exams prepared by
     students

System Output

62B (= 6D) Graduates (students with new knowledge)
63A (= 6A) Proposals for new or modified courses
63B (= 6B) More experienced faculty
63C (= 6C) Student evaluations

Figure 5.6 Activity Matrix, Student AIS Example: Activity 6, Class Administration

Entity Activity[a]	Entities[b]											Activity Characteristics[c]		
	1A	3A	4B	5A	6A	6B	6C	6D	61A	61B	62A	AC-1	AC-2	AC-3
A-6	X	X	X	X	X	X	X	X				1	1000	35
A-61	X	X	X	X					X	X		1	15	35
A-62			X					X	X	X	X	1	15	35
A-63	X		X	X	X	X	X		X	X	X	1	16	525

a. A-6, class administration.
   A-61, lectures.
   A-62, classwork.
   A-63, evaluation.
b. See element definitions in Figure 5.5.
c. AC-1, priority: 1, high; 2, medium; 3, low.
   AC-2, frequency: executions per semester.
   AC-3, volume: inputs per execution.

Box 5.1

INFORMATION DICTIONARY—STUDENT AIS EXAMPLE

3A   STUDENTS

    Also: STUDENT

    Definition: Persons who are currently taking courses at this university

    Type: Entity Attributes: s-id, name, address, . . .

                               list of courses taken with dates and grades,
                                   list of current courses

Identifier:	student identification number, s-id
Relationships:	to COURSES - 1:40
Cardinality:	5000

    Associated
    Activities: 5: REGISTRATION
                 6: CLASS ADMINISTRATION
             61: LECTURES
             62: CLASSWORK

Box 5.2

PROCESS DICTIONARY—STUDENT AIS EXAMPLE

A-63:   EVALUATION

Also:	COURSE EVALUATION
Objective:	Prepare evaluation of course and students
Inputs:	Course description and materials, class roster, and student papers and exams
Outputs:	Course modification proposals Student evaluations (grades)
Frequency:	Course proposals: once at end of semester Student evaluation: as work is graded
Users:	Faculty and administration, students
Priority:	High
Security:	High

An information system contains only information and information processes. It is activated by receipt of an input message from the object system requesting some information service. The system produces an output or information message relevant to the input message. In the information system, the input message may be recorded, transformed, processed, and reformatted before the desired output message is formed. The procedures that handle the input message while it is in the system are the information processes.

Information can be considered the most important component of an information system, since without adequate and accurate information the information processes will not be able to perform to desired standards. The information-element types (not values) are also the most stable component, since the entity types an organization is interested in tend to remain constant, with the principal change being the addition of attributes for existing entity types.

Information processes, on the other hand, tend to be continually changing as quality and efficiency are improved and new functions are added.

Based on these observations, we will define an information system by documenting first the information types required, then the information processes required to produce this information. This is not strictly possible; however, we will emphasize identifying the information elements first. In practice, an information process is identified immediately after the identification of the information elements it produces. System description is actually an iterative process of identifying entity types with primary attributes, identifying information processes for these entities, identifying secondary attributes required for the processes, identifying new processes, and so on.

Information-System Analysis

Information-System Analysis The activity that defines the components of an information system and evaluates the extent to which the system achieves its goals.

Identification of the information component of a system begins with documentation of the information flow to and from the object system. The information processes can then be considered as the actions necessary to produce the required output message(s). And input messages are those messages that (1) trigger an output message or (2) provide initial information to the system.

The information element description must present a detailed documentation of the system's

- input, expressed as input messages or input statements.

- output, expressed as output messages or report formats.
- stored data, expressed as the entity and attribute types stored within the system.
- relationships between entity types and connecting entities and attributes.

Information-process description provides a detailed documentation of the processes within the system, giving

- information elements used and produced.
- frequency of use of each process.
- information volumes required.
- priority within the system.
- response time requirements.
- special algorithms used.

Useful analysis tools for developing and evaluating the information-system description are graphs, dictionaries, and the information matrix. These are basically the same as the tools used for the activity analysis and are discussed in detail in the following sections.

Information-System Graphs

An information graph presents a model of the information component of the information system. It should include a statement of what information is input to, output from, and resident in the system. Also, the graph should outline the information flow through the system, i.e., in which processes the information is used. The information model does not define the information processes; however, it states their place in the information flow.

We can define an information graph as follows:

Information Graph A graphic model of the information component of an information system, showing input, output, and resident information with information flow.

The information-system graph will actually be a set of graphs, one for each subsystem analyzed. In structure, the graph set will follow the activity graph set closely. In practice, the information-system graph set tends to be more detailed than the accompanying activity graph set, as the information elements are reduced to their elemental parts.

Several graphic models for presenting the information component have been suggested. The one used here is the complement of the activity graph used in the preceding section as proposed by Lundeberg (Lundeberg et al., 1981). The graph notation uses only the information and process symbols, i.e., the single-edged figures and the small circle from Figure 5.2.

Constructing an information graph for a system for which an activity graph set is available involves simply lifting the information-system component from the activity graphs. Thus we can construct (extract) the information system for the student AIS from Figure 5.3, as shown in Figure 5.7. Note that, like the activity graph, the information graph also has an accompanying page for the element definitions.

Note that the information graph differs from the activity graph in that only information and information processes are included. The activity graph will also include a model of material and personnel flows.

By convention, system inputs are presented at the top of the graph and outputs at the bottom, and resident information is shown within the system boundaries. Details of the components of these information structures will be presented in the successively lower-level graphs. Also, the information processes will be presented in detail as the graph set is developed. Remember that the information processes are considered the subsystems during the system decomposition and documentation.

The information graph set provides a model of the information-system structure. By its nature, however, the graph cannot contain all the details required for system documentation. Therefore the graph set must be accompanied by documents that can contain the needed detail.

The information dictionary, begun during the activity analysis, should be extended to include the information gathered during information analysis, whenever new elements or new details become known. Similarly, the process dictionary should be expanded to include new or modified information as it is identified.

Information Matrix

The information matrix details the cross-references between the information elements and the information processes as they are established through the system analysis. It is similar in form to the activity matrix, but its content is changed to document the information usage of the processes. Also, since the information-system analysis is more detailed than the earlier analyses, there will be more elements along both the information and process axes.

Figure 5.8 illustrates the information matrix, using the information-system graph components from Figure 5.7. We have assumed that the student AIS is a completely manual system.

There are two principal changes from the activity matrix in Figure 5.4: the element use description is more detailed, and the processing characteristics description has been extended.

Figure 5.7 Information Graph, Level 0: Student AIS Example

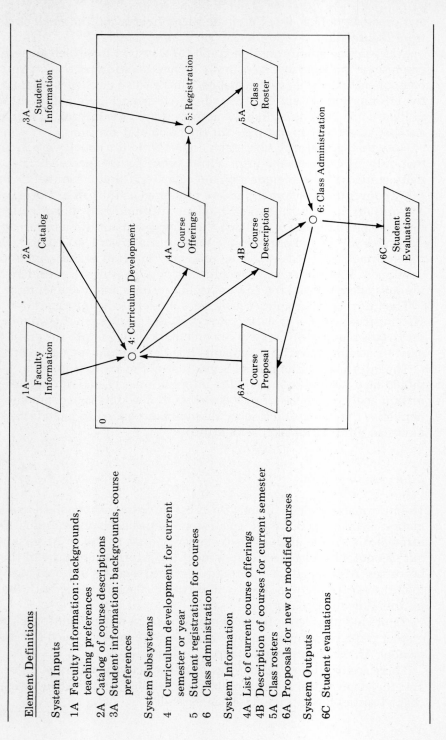

Element Definitions

System Inputs

1A Faculty information: backgrounds, teaching preferences
2A Catalog of course descriptions
3A Student information: backgrounds, course preferences

System Subsystems

4 Curriculum development for current semester or year
5 Student registration for courses
6 Class administration

System Information

4A List of current course offerings
4B Description of courses for current semester
5A Class rosters
6A Proposals for new or modified courses

System Outputs

6C Student evaluations

Figure 5.8 Information Matrix, Student AIS Example

Information Process[a]	Information Elements[b,c]									Activity Characteristics[d]				
	1A	2A	3A	4A	4B	5A	6A	6B	6C	AC-1	AC-2	AC-3	AC-4	AC-5
IP-4	I	I		O	O		I			2	1	2000	S	M
IP-5			I	I		O		O		1	1	5000	G	M
IP-6			I		I	I			O	1	1000	35	S	M

a. IP-4, (supports A-4) curriculum development.
   IP-5, (supports A-5) registration.
   IP-6, (supports A-6) class administration.
b. See element definitions in Figure 5.7.
c. I: The information element is an input to the process.
   O: The information element is an output of the process.
d. AC-1, priority; 1, high; 2, medium; 3, low.
   AC-2, frequency: executions per semester.
   AC-3, volume: inputs per execution.
   AC-4, data access: D, direct; G, group; or S, serial.
   AC-5, processing type: M, manual, or A, automated.

The element use description specifies, for each information process, whether the information element is an input I to the process or an output O of the process. Information elements resident in the system may be both inputs to and outputs from a process. This happens when the objective of the process is to change the element value, e.g., to modify an account balance. This can be documented by using the symbol I:O.

The processing characteristics are expanded to include more detail than has been captured until now. Clearly, these characteristics could have been described earlier, and alternatively, specification of their values can be delayed if a completely new system is being developed. Since we have assumed that we are documenting an existing system, the new characteristics document:

- AC–4: type of information element access used:
  - D: direct, to one element or record occurrence
  - G: group, to a subset of the data
  - S: serial, through all the available data
  - (See Chapters 8 and 9 for more detail.)

- AC–5: processing type:
  - M: manual
  - A: automated

The Information-System Analysis Report

The information-system analysis report is a refinement of the activity analysis report. It takes the form of a text with the information graphs and matrix as illustrations. The completed information and process dictionaries are appendices to the report.

The IS analysis report documents the current information system. It explains the processing characteristics of each component and provides the basis for evaluating the system against the goal statement. This report also provides the basis for proposals for alternative system structures. Such proposals typically involve a structural or implementation technical change to some portion of the information system in order to improve system performance as measured by goal achievement.

The initial IS analysis report documents the current system, and new reports should be developed for each alternative system developed. The analysis of each IS proposal must then be evaluated against the goal set and the current system to establish the degree of performance improvement that can be expected.

Information-System Analysis Example

The following discussion continues the development of the student AIS. So far it has been developed through the activity analysis, as shown in Figures 5.3 through 5.6. Figures 5.7 and 5.8 illustrated the level 0 information graph and matrix for the system. Figures 5.9 and 5.10 give the information graphs for subsystems 6, class administration, and 63, evaluation, respectively.

Note that as the system is broken down into smaller subsystems, the definitions of the processes and information elements become more specific. Definitions of additional processes and information elements must be added to the process and information dictionaries, respectively. Also, the descriptions of the major processes and entities must be revised to include their component elements, i.e., subprocesses and attributes.

If our example were complete, there would be information graphs for each of the activity graphs developed during the activity analysis. We would also expect there to be one more level beyond the low-level activity graphs to document the information systems for these activities. This level would normally include enough detail to document the information system supporting the object system.

The information matrix can be expected to be very large, as it is not uncommon for principal entities to be described by more than 100 attributes. Also, the main processes commonly consist of many subprocesses. One method of constructing the information matrix is to break it into several matrices, one for each entity type. The major disadvantage of this is the loss of the description of interentity relationships as they are used by the processes.

The information matrix will be the principal document for the subsequent evaluation, since it is a composite of the existing information elements and processes. These components are then evaluated against the goal set and used as a basis for formulating proposed modifications to improve the system.

SYSTEM VERSUS GOAL ANALYSIS

Goal analysis, which should precede system analysis, is performed to establish the information-system objectives as required by the user community. The goal analysis report contains the user requirements and is referred to as the system's goal statement. The goal statement is a list of activities and information requirements, ordered by priority; this is the basis for all further analysis and design work.

Figure 5.9 Information Graph, Level 1: Student AIS Example, Class Administration

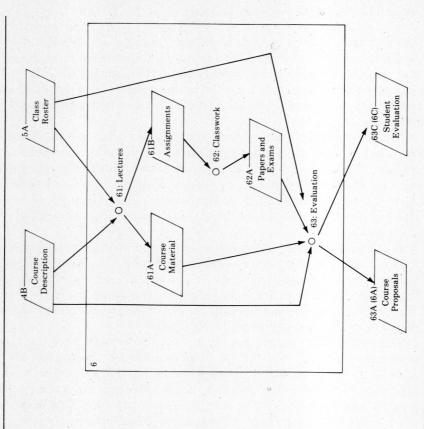

Element Definitions

__System Inputs__

4B Course descriptions
5A Class roster

__System Subsystems__

61 Lectures
62 Classwork done by students
63 Evaluation of course and classwork

__System Information__

61A Course materials
61B Assignments and exam texts
62A Homework, papers, and exams prepared by
     students

__System Output__

63A (= 6A) Proposals for new or modified courses
63C (= 6C) Student evaluations

Figure 5.10 Information Graph, Level 2: Student AIS Example, Evaluation

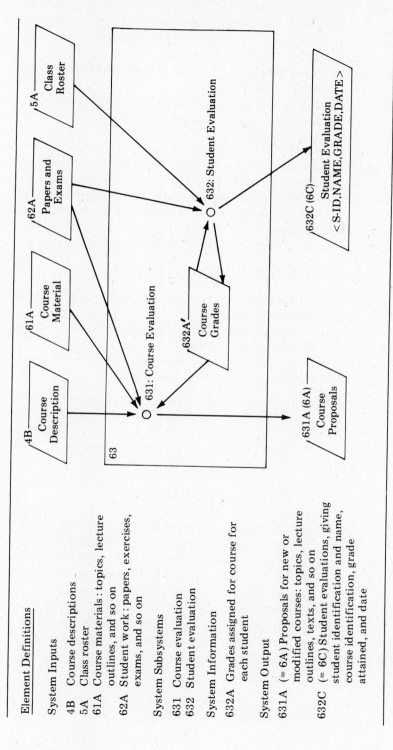

Element Definitions

System Inputs

4B   Course descriptions
5A   Class roster
61A Course materials : topics, lecture
     outlines, and so on
62A Student work : papers, exercises,
     exams, and so on

System Subsystems

631 Course evaluation
632 Student evaluation

System Information

632A Grades assigned for course for
      each student

System Output

631A (= 6A) Proposals for new or
      modified courses: topics, lecture
      outlines, texts, and so on
632C (= 6C) Student evaluations, giving
      student identification and name,
      course identification, grade
      attained, and date

System analysis is performed to document and evaluate the components and functioning characteristics of the current system. The analysis has two parts: a system description and a system evaluation. The system description requires an object-system analysis, an activity analysis, and an information-system analysis.

Both goal analysis and system analysis produce descriptions of system processes and information elements kept in the process, and information dictionaries of the goal analysis and system analysis reports, respectively. The process dictionaries can be analyzed to determine how much overlap there is between the information-processing requirements and the current system facilities. The information dictionaries will also indicate the overlap between the information requirements and the current information store. Identification of these overlaps is an important result of this stage of the analysis, as they indicate the extent to which the current system contains the elements required by the goal statement.

The initial system analysis report contains:

1. the structure of the current system, modeled by the activity and information graphs and matrices.
2. the overlap of system activities (processing facilities) required by the goal statement and those found in the current system.
3. the overlap in information requirements defined in the goal statement and those found in the current system.

A comparison of the goal statement (GS) and the system documentation (SD) also identifies those sections of the information system that can, should, or must be enhanced in order to improve system performance. We can formulate a model for the derivation of system improvement alternatives (SI) as:

$$SI = F(GS - SD)$$

In order to best derive system improvement alternatives (SI), the system description documents, the GS and SD, should be presented in the same format to facilitate comparison and evaluation. We have presented a report format that will allow comparison of the goal statement, current system documentation, and alternative system structure proposals in the information graphs, matrices, and dictionaries.

System evaluation determines the feasibility and economics of the goal statement, current system design, and alternative system proposals. This evaluation will be discussed in detail in the next chapter.

SUMMARY

This chapter has presented one method of describing an existing information system. This method starts with an analysis of the system environment, the object system, to determine where information is required. Then an information-system analysis is performed to determine how the system is structured, what information is maintained, and what processes are involved. The analysis reports are documented by activity and process graphs and matrices. Information and process dictionaries are developed to maintain element definitions and characteristic descriptions.

The information and process dictionaries of the system analysis reports have the same structure as those of the goal statement to facilitate comparison and evaluation of the current system against the goal statement.

KEY CONCEPTS

Activity analysis
Activity graph (A graph)
Activity matrix (A matrix)
Information dictionary
Information flow
Information graph (I graph)

Information matrix (I matrix)
Information-system analysis
Material flow
Object system
Process dictionary
System analysis

DISCUSSION QUESTIONS

1. Define and give an illustration of each of the key concepts.
2. Why should a goal analysis be done before a system analysis? If there were no goal analysis, what would be the possible results of a system analysis?
3. What are the tasks of a system analysis? What is the advantage of documenting both the object system and the information system?
4. What tools are useful for system documentation? Why? Give an illustration.

PROJECT

1. Develop an activity and information-system analysis report for process 5, registration. Use activity and information graphs and

matrices to model the system. Develop the appropriate dictionary entries. Be sure that your report states the assumptions you have made.

2. Same task as project 1, but for a self-selected system.

RECOMMENDED READINGS

Langefors, B. *Theoretical Analysis of Information Systems.* Philadelphia : Auerbach, 1973.

   This text gives a theoretical foundation for analyzing an information system by decomposing the components into their elemental information messages and processes.

Lundeberg, M., G. Goldkuhl, and A. Nilsson. *Information Systems Development—A Systematic Approach.* Englewood Cliffs, N.J. : Prentice-Hall Inc., 1981.

   Chapters 4 and 5 present the ISAC method of activity study and information analysis, from which the graphics used in this text are derived.

Chapter 6
System Evaluation

INTRODUCTION

System evaluation, for an information system, is that process that seeks to determine the extent to which the facilities and services provided by an information system meet the requirements of the goal statement as set by the user community. An evaluation may be performed at any time during the life cycle of an information system (see Figure 3.1). The stage at which the evaluation is performed will determine the precision of the evaluation results.

As a system analysis and design project progresses, the analysis and design proposals must be evaluated to ensure that they are consistent with the intentions and constraints of the user community. Thus an evaluation report is an integral part of the system development report that concludes each stage of the analysis and design project (see Figure 3.3). That is, there should be an evaluation of the proposals accompanying the

1. goal statement.
2. current system analysis.
3. information-system design.
4. data-system design.
5. system implementation.
6. system operation.

The goal statement evaluation is the feasibility analysis, discussed in Chapter 4. In this evaluation, exact cost figures will not be available, since the specifics of a system that will satisfy the goal statement have yet to be determined. However, it is possible to make reasonably realistic estimates by comparing the requirements with similar systems, within the organization or in comparable organizations, and using the costs of these systems. For the same reason, the value of expected benefits must also be estimated. Comparison with similar systems should also indicate the dimensions of expected benefits, although the specific organizational functions will have a greater influence on the benefits that can be achieved.

The evaluation of the current system is most important, as it is against this evaluation that system comparisons are to be made. The current system exists. The costs are for its operation, plus any losses resulting from the information problems detected during problem analysis. The benefits include the value of the current work load and the value of maintaining the status quo and not changing established work patterns.

Each alternative information-system design must be evaluated and then compared with the current system and with the other alternatives. On the cost side are the anticipated development and operational costs. Benefits include improved information flow and increased work load. The best system design alternative is the one that provides the most improvements, while keeping development and operational costs within the organizational constraints.

Similarly, each alternative data-system design must be evaluated. Costs include estimates of development, training, and operational costs. Benefits include response time improvements and adaptability to changing requirements.

After system implementation, it is important to answer the question, "How much did the development of this system cost?" This information is important for evaluation of future CBIS projects. One benefit should be an evaluation of the experience of developing or acquiring the new system.

After the new system has been in operation for some time, its benefits should be established. The motivating question is, "Does the system deliver the anticipated benefits?"

Evaluations performed early in the system's life cycle will be speculative in nature, as exact design proposals are not yet available. These evaluations must be based on estimates of anticipated benefits and costs or on similarities between the proposed system and others known to the analyst and/or organization. Nonetheless, early evaluations are important in establishing requirement priorities and organizational constraints.

In the following sections, evaluation criteria and procedures as they apply to the system analysis and design phases will be discussed.

EVALUATION CRITERIA

The purpose of an information system is to facilitate communication among the individuals within an organization. Therefore, the primary objective of an evaluation of a system is to determine the extent to which the system and/or proposed changes to it fulfill the goal statement. In addition, the system's expected benefits and costs and its legality and operability within the organization must be evaluated.

The financial resources available for an information system will always be limited. It is the task of the system analyst to ensure that the organization gets the best possible information system at a cost within the financial limits.

Setting Priorities

Before a system evaluation is performed, the goal statement must be analyzed and ordered by priority, as indicated by the goal analysis (see Chapter 4, Figures 4.4 and 4.5). Generally, setting priorities for the separate functions of an information system is the job of management. The direct users are too close to their own functions and will tend to give these highest priority. The system analyst is generally too distant from the organizational goals to be able to set true function priorities.

It should be possible to order the goals into at least three categories: necessary, desirable, and supplementary. If possible, priorities within these general categories should also be set for each of the goals, routines, and/or functions. A system evaluation must demonstrate that the necessary goals are met and that the system is affordable. Not all the desirable and supplementary goals may be feasible, and these should be expendable without damaging the structure of the system design.

The minimum facility requirements, personnel, space, and technical and financial resources, must be established for each goal group. These form the basis for the cost analysis.

Requirements for services to the organization, such as number of user groups served and types of information and information processes, should be established for each goal group. This forms the basis for the benefit analysis.

Requirements for processing speed and accuracy and the level of information quality should be established for a complete system, a system that includes only the necessary goals, and a system that includes the necessary goals plus some of the desirable and supplementary goals. These system attributes may be adjusted during system design to construct an affordable system.

The system features just given form the framework for the system evaluation. A number of system structures should be evaluated in order to determine which structure best suits the organizational requirements. The current system must always be included in a comparative evaluation, both to establish what improvement is expected and to allow the current system to be maintained should it prove to be the best system available given the organizational constraints.

Evaluation Categories

In addition to the traditional economic evaluation, a system must be evaluated for its adherence to legal, social, technical, and operational constraints. These constraints tend to be evaluated on a pass/fail basis. That is, the system or subsystem function either complies with the constraints as stated for the organization or does not comply.

Legal constraints generally involve the application to an organization and its information systems of national, state, and local laws intended to protect industry and individual privacy. Most industrial countries today have data privacy laws in effect. Other countries are considering such laws. These laws apply to collections of data describing individuals or organizations and their relationships to the data collecting organization. Since most information systems contain such a collection of data, the system analyst must make sure that the data collected conform to these legal restrictions. Most of these laws allow the individuals or organizations described to have access to the data and to correct it, if necessary. Information-system facilities must be designed to allow such access.

Social constraints on an information system involve its interaction with the people who are expected to work with it or otherwise be involved with it. These constraints may affect the type of terminal equipment to be used, the EDP expertise that the users can be expected to have, the type of operator-machine dialog to be included in the system design, the number and geographic dispersal of the user community, the response times required for each user group, and so on.

Technical constraints reflect the degree of technological support available to the information system. Technical support includes existing and planned computer hardware and software (see Chapter 10), EDP personnel available to develop and support the system, the budget for adding new EDP personnel, plans and budget for training the system users, and, importantly, the current level of EDP expertise within the organization.

Operational constraints are those involving the operational environment—human, physical, monetary, and time—for the information system. In particular,

- What persons are available to run the system?
- How much room, in the computer and within the data network, is there for the new system?
- What are the operational budget limits?
- When must the system be available?

The economic evaluation attempts to put monetary values on the facilities and services of the actual or proposed information system. The system's costs and benefits, both tangible and intangible, are listed and an evaluation of each is made. A system proposal must have a positive economic evaluation. That is, to be implemented, a system must be economically feasible; its expected benefits must exceed its anticipated costs. The only possible exception to this general rule would be a system mandated by law, although even here, the system design should be one that is economically feasible.

Evaluation Measures

Depending on the system characteristics being evaluated, a number of separate measures may be used. The most common is a monetary measurement, giving each system characteristic a price or dollar value. Other measures used in system evaluation include processing times, counts of goals served or users supported, and assignment of scores of subsystem quality.

The primary measure, and from a business point of view the optimal one, is monetary. That is, a monetary value is determined for each system characteristic to be evaluated. These values are then summed to determine a monetary value for the system. Though this is the measurement that enables a system's expected profitability to be determined, it is exceedingly difficult to assign monetary values to intangible costs and benefits (see next section). For these characteristics, other measurements must be used.

The processing times required for separate business functions may also be used as an evaluation measure. This measure is most useful in evaluating a system whose principal problems involve slow or inefficient work throughput. Normally, the time requirements for the individual processes within the current system are determined and system improvement proposals are evaluated in terms of improvement in processing or throughput times. Improvement in throughput is assumed to translate into profit by increasing the number of transactions that can be processed per time unit without increasing the size of the processing staff.

Counts of goals achieved or users supported may be used in an initial or partial evaluation of a new or significantly enhanced system for which there is little specific information on monetary costs and benefits or throughput measurements. Identifying the information services to be provided and the user community to be served may provide sufficient justification for developing a pilot or experimental system. Development of the pilot system into a full-scale system would require an evaluation that included monetary and/or performance measurements.

Quality scores may be assigned to the individual characteristics of the system and proposals for improving them. This measure is particularly useful for evaluating intangible benefits and costs. The score should represent a user community consensus concerning the quality of the system characteristic. Generally, such a subjective evaluation should be made on a scale with not more than 6 to 10 values ranging from nonexistent and poor to very good and excellent. System quality can then be stated as the sum of the individual characteristic values. Since the scores will not represent true numeric intervals, this evaluation method will only indicate the best system in the opinion of the intended users; it will not measure the relative quality of alternative systems.

The evaluation measure chosen will determine the measure used to state the organization's constraint framework. Clearly, system characteristics that are evaluated as exceeding the constraints will need to be changed or eliminated. A full system evaluation will commonly use several types of measurements for each system or system proposal evaluated. The relevant constraints must then be stated in terms comparable to the evaluation measure used for the characteristic set.

Performance Measuring

An evaluation of an operating system's performance is a necessary part of deciding whether or not to upgrade the system in some way. The evaluation is frequently limited to the supporting data system or even to the computerized subsystem(s). This evaluation is performed at the first or last stage of a system analysis and design project to either document the system once it has been implemented or characterize the system currently being used as the basis for a new analysis. See the information-system life cycle, Figure 3.1.

The performance evaluation has two goals: to determine the performance characteristics of the system and to determine how successful the user community perceives the system to be.

Performance characteristics measured include processing speed, accuracy of data manipulation, and completeness and relevance of the data base. Other performance characteristics measure utilization of the technological support system, i.e., computational efficiency, data network utilization, data storage and access utilization. System performance can often be improved by improving one or more of the utilization factors; this involves either improving the processing algorithms used or upgrading the level of technology used.

System success is an elusive measure, as it depends on the perceptions of the system's user community. Principal measures used attempt to assess the ease of use of system facilities and services and the degree of system use within the user community, e.g., how many users are there, how often or how long do they use the system, and so on. The success or failure of a system may actually be determined by factors other than system characteristics, such as its being the only system available, a prestigious system, a step toward job advancement, a well-sold system, or some other such factor.

A system's performance, both technical and social, is continually being evaluated. The goal is to constantly provide the best and most acceptable system possible given the constraints of the organization.

SYSTEM COSTS AND BENEFITS

Establishing and operating an information system entails costs, which must be offset by the benefits that can be attributed to the system. Though this is generally true, it becomes particularly important when an organization is considering an investment in a new computer-based information system for which new, and frequently expensive, equipment must be acquired. An information system has costs and benefits as it is being developed, during its operative life, and when it is replaced. All these costs and benefits should be included in an evaluation of a new system proposal. Figure 6.1 illustrates the general categories of costs and benefits as they occur over the system's life span.

Both costs and benefits have directly measurable or tangible components as well as intangible ones. Generally, tangible costs and benefits are those with a direct monetary value, such as computer equipment, consultant fees, salaries, or office space rent. However, these costs may be counted as benefits if they are lower than the comparable costs in the information system being replaced.

Intangible costs and benefits generally arise during system operation and as a result of changes in service levels, knowledge, public relations, or user satisfaction. Although it is difficult to calculate a monetary

Figure 6.1 System Costs and Benefits

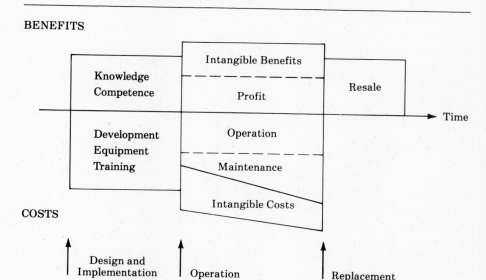

value for these characteristics, they can determine the success or failure of the new or modified system.

Next we will discuss some of the most important costs and benefits generally considered for information systems.

System Benefits

We assume that improving the processing capabilities of the information system will increase the organization's profits. In particular, we assume that improvements in processing speed and accuracy will lead to reductions in transaction-processing costs and improved decision-making capabilities.

Information-system benefits, then, are those results that contribute to the organization's profits. An information-system benefit also results when a system improvement reduces information-processing costs.

Tangible Benefits

Tangible benefits can usually be measured in monetary terms. These benefits are not necessarily direct; for example, information-system improvements that speed up the flow of information or increase its accuracy and timeliness tend to reduce the time required to process a single transaction. The measurable benefit comes from the ability to increase the number of transactions processed without increasing total processing costs.

Tangible benefits, and also indirect benefits, are most easily found and measured in the data system that supports the information system. Our list of expected benefits reflects this observation. Box 6.1 lists the tangible benefits most commonly claimed for information-system improvements.

Intangible Benefits

Intangible benefits are difficult or impossible to measure objectively. By nature, an information system is to a large extent an intangible entity, since it incorporates people's ideas and understandings. Thus, it should not be surprising that most intangible benefits can be classified as benefits in the information system external to the data system proper.

Box 6.2 lists the most common intangible benefits claimed for information systems.

Box 6.1

TANGIBLE BENEFITS

In the Information System:

During operation:
- Increased work throughput
- Increased accuracy
- Reduction or stabilization of staff size

In the Data System:

During operation:
- Increased processing speed
- Reduction of redundancy
- Reduction of data processing investment
- Reduction of data processing maintenance
- Reduction of data processing space requirements

Box 6.2

INTANGIBLE BENEFITS

In the Information System:

During system development:
- Increased knowledge and understanding of the organization
- Increased competence in information processing

During system operation:
- Improved control
- Reduction in routine decision making
- Improved information for decision making
- Expansion of profitable activities
- Improved employee morale
- Improved public relations

In the Data System:

- Increased operating efficiency

System Costs

System costs occur in two areas, as shown in Figure 6.1: the investment costs required to develop the system, and the recurring costs required to operate the system. There are both tangible and intangible costs associated with establishing and operating an information system, and both must be considered in the system evaluation.

Like system benefits, system costs are better measured in monetary terms, although some costs, particularly indirect costs, may need to be evaluated on a subjective scale. In this instance, care must be taken to chose a scale and evaluation as close as possible to the scale used to quantify the intangible system benefits.

The following sections discuss the most common costs associated with computer-based information systems. Like system benefits, system costs tend to be tangible in the data system and intangible in the information system. Note that not all of these costs, nor all of the benefits discussed, are associated with every system evaluated.

Tangible Costs

The tangible costs, or direct monetary outlays for a system, are typically measured by the direct cash outlays required to develop and operate the system. These include costs of personnel, materials, space, and services. For computer-based information systems, the costs of automation tend to be dominant, and they are concentrated in the data system in the areas of program development and technical equipment. However, there are also costs in the information system, principally those associated with the human information processors.

Box 6.3 lists costs commonly associated with the development and operation of an information system. Note that some costs may be moved from the information system to the data system if a different level of automation is chosen for the system structure.

Intangible Costs

Although they are more difficult to evaluate, the intangible costs resulting from slow or inefficient operations, tie-up of personnel, or negative public relations are important. Like intangible benefits, these costs are commonly found in the information system, and to some extent in the organizational system itself.

Reduction in intangible costs can frequently be classified as an intangible benefit. For example, if customers complain of difficulty in

Box 6.3

TANGIBLE COSTS

In the Information System:

During development:
- Personnal training
- System specification

During operation:
- Manual pre- and post-processing
- Staff salaries for information processors

In the Data System:

During development:
- System analysis
- System implementation, programming, and file or data-base generation
- Space preparation
- Purchase of equipment

During operation:
- Equipment costs
- System operators
- Materials, forms
- System maintenance

---

correcting "simple" data such as addresses, this may be perceived as a source of a system cost in public relations that is believed to result in a lower rate of increase in new customers. Improving system performance in this area would, it is hoped, lead to an improved perception of the organization and thus to an increase in the number of new customers.

Box 6.4 lists intangible costs commonly associated with computer-based information systems.

Cost/Benefit Analysis

A cost/benefit analysis is performed to determine the relationship between the expected costs and benefits to be derived from the system. Such an analysis should be made at each stage of the system development cycle as part of the project evaluation. When this is not feasible, the most critical points for a cost/benefit analysis are:

Box 6.4

INTANGIBLE COSTS

In the Information System:

During development:
- Work time during system change
- Employee morale

During operation:
- Customer service
- Negative public relations
- Loss of control

In the Data System:

During development:
- Unfamiliarity with new techniques

During operation:
- Existence of errors
- Insufficient processing capabilities

- In the feasibility analysis for the goal statement, to ensure that the goals being set for the system are feasible, i.e., within the constraints set by the organization.
- During analysis of the current system, to document the status of the current system and to form a basis for evaluating proposals for improving or replacing the system.
- In information-system design, where at least one and preferably two alternative system proposals should be analyzed to make possible the selection of a "best" system for implementation.

During system analysis, proposals for changes to the current system that are intended to improve system performance will be made. A cost/benefit analysis is the major tool for comparison of and selection among alternative system structure proposals.

Cost/Benefit Framework

A cost/benefit analysis for an information system should contain three sections, as illustrated in Figure 6.2:

Figure 6.2 Evaluation Framework

System Characteristics	Evaluation
I. System Description	
A. Process	Binary statement:
P-1	exists
P-2	does not exist
.	
.	
B. Processing Characteristics	Numeric description
Number of users	
Response time	
Number of terminals	
Data-base size	
.	
.	
II. Tangible Costs and Benefits	Monetary evaluation
Personnel	
Space	
Materials	
Technical equipment	
.	
.	
III. Intangible Costs and Benefits	Subjective evaluation
User satisfaction	
Ease of use	
Adaptability	
.	
.	

1. A system description, consisting of a priority-ordered list of the information processes and processing characteristics required of the system (from the goal statement)
2. Tangible costs and benefits, giving the resources required for both system development and operation, including personnel, space, technical support, and materials
3. Intangible costs and benefits

The system description section of the evaluation compares the existing or proposed system facilities with the information service requirements (the goal statement). It is possible (or even probable) that some of the information processes and services included in the goal statement are not included or only partially included in the current system. This must be stated clearly. Processing characteristics related to speed and information timeliness and accuracy must also be described.

All system costs must then be stated. These include the resources required for implementation and operation, including the costs of the people required to specify, develop, and operate the system; the space requirements for staff and equipment; and materials and equipment for operation and backup.

Finally, all expected system benefits are listed, including such subsidiary benefits as ease of use, acceptability within the organization, and growth prospects.

Cost/Benefit Measurements

Each section of the analysis will require different measurements:

1. A numeric statement for the system description
2. A monetary evaluation for the tangible costs and benefits
3. A subjective evaluation for the intangible benefits

The system description for a cost/benefit analysis includes, wherever possible, a numeric description of the characteristics of the system or system proposal. A binary evaluation (exists/does not exist) followed by a goal count is sufficient for comparing the system facilities against the goal statement. Numeric values should be given for such system processing characteristics as number of transactions per time period, number of data records kept, response times, and number of users served. Figure 6.3 illustrates this evaluation for the student administration model.

The tangible costs and benefits of the system, and as many of the intangibles as can be assigned a monetary value, should be listed with their monetary values. Wherever possible, the monetary evaluations should be stated exactly; for example, expected costs as given by equipment vendors and known costs of staff salaries.

When estimating monetary values for costs and benefits, one should provide three estimates:

1. A conservative estimate, which one is relatively certain can be attained
2. A moderate estimate, which is attainable if the system performs as expected and external variables have been correctly accounted for

Figure 6.3 Numeric Description: Student Administration Example

System Characteristics	Evaluation

I. System Description

  A. Processes

	Status*	Comment
P-1: Record grades	1	OK
P-2: Compile class statistics	0	required
P-3: Compile student transcript	1	OK
P-4: Respond to student queries	0	desired
Sum (of available processes) =	2	

  B. Processing Characteristics

Data-base size	500,000 characters
Data access	Sequential
Response time	1 day
Number of terminals	0

*1 = facility exists in the system.
 0 = facility does not exist.

3. An optimistic estimate, which requires full use of the system and few unexpected costs

The moderate estimate should be used for relatively standard system proposals, and the conservative estimate for a new system. This will allow for a more realistic statement about system characteristics and should reduce the tendency to expect more than can be delivered given the resources available.

A single monetary estimate can be calculated from the three estimates, conservative (C), moderate (M), and optimistic (O), using the following formula:

$$\frac{C + 4 \times M + O}{6} \tag{6.1}$$

This formula weights the moderate and most likely estimate, then adjusts it for the conservative and optimistic estimates.

Figure 6.4 illustrates the monetary evaluation for a portion of the student administration model as it exists. In this case the monetary values are known.

The scale used for subjective evaluation of the intangible costs and benefits should not have more than 6 elements; for example, the

Figure 6.4 Cost Statement: Student Administration Example

System Characteristics[b]	Evaluation		
	Units	$/Unit	Total
II. Tangible Costs and Benefits			
Personnel:[a]			
Operation	6mm	$2000.00	$12,000.00
Space (Regular office)	0		
Materials (Regular office)	0		
Technical Equipment:			
Computational expenses			$ 500.00
Total Costs			$12,500.00

a. mm = man-month (one person working full time for one month). This system is predominantly manual and requires 6/12 of a job that pays $2000/month.
b. System description is given in Figure 6.3.

Figure 6.5 Benefit Analysis: Student Administration Example

System Characteristics[b]	Evaluation	
	Score[a]	Comment
III. Intangible Costs and Benefits		
User satisfaction	1	Recorder only
Ease of Use	3	Poor documentation
Adaptability	1	
Accuracy	4	
Timeliness	2	Slow response

a. Scores: 0 = Nonexistent
1 = Poor
2 = Fair
3 = Acceptable
4 = Good
5 = Excellent
b. System description appears in Figure 6.3.

numbers 0 to 5 might represent gradations from nonexistent to very good. Psychological studies have determined that evaluations using a more finely graded scale tend to converge either on the center six values or on the top values, leaving the center value, "acceptable," uncertainly defined. Wherever possible, the subjective evaluation should be a consensus of several individual evaluations.

Figure 6.5 illustrates a subjective evaluation of the student administration model using several of the intangibles most commonly used to evaluate information systems.

The final evaluation will present the following information:

1. A numeric description of the system
2. A monetary statement of the costs and benefits
3. A subjective statement of system benefits and costs

Should the monetary evaluation be negative, i.e., should costs exceed benefits, the system proposal must score very high on the subjective evaluation to be considered further for implementation or use.

SYSTEM ALTERNATIVES

A system evaluation will normally lead to proposals for changes in the system being analyzed. This is because the evaluation will highlight the weak points of the system or system proposal, and most analysts will be quick to offer to improve the effectiveness of the system they are working with. Indeed, this trait is one of the most likely causes of system development project overruns.

In the context of computer-based information systems, alternative system proposals normally include an increased use of automation. The principal benefits anticipated are increased processing speed, improved accuracy, improved timeliness of information, and improved scope of information. All except possibly the first of these benefits are difficult to quantify; however, the assumption is that these benefits will improve the foundation for organizational decision making and thus improve organizational operations and increase profits. The principal costs are for computer equipment, technical personnel, training, and operation materials. Quantifying these costs is relatively straightforward.

One way to generate alternatives is to consider different degrees of automation: a core set of automated processes, a moderate set, and a fully automated system. Along with the current system, these alternatives should present a suggested path for gradually increasing the level of automation within the information system as needs and resources allow.

Each of the alternative system proposals must be evaluated against the system requirements, the goal statement, in order to ensure that

Figure 6.6 Presenting System Alternatives

System Characteristics	Current System	Alternatives 1	2	...	n	Evaluation Technique
I. System Description						
A. System Facilities						Binary statement
·						
Sum of Facilities =						
B. Processing Characteristics						Numeric description
·						
II. Tangible Costs and Benefits						Monetary evaluation
A. Tangible Costs						
·						
Sum of Costs =						
B. Tangible Benefits						
·						
Sum of Benefits =						
C. Benefits − Costs =						− −
III. Intangible Costs and Benefits						Subjective evaluation
Costs and Benefits						
·						
Sum of Scores =						

the alternative will really improve the situation while staying within the constraints set by the organization. If there has been a complete evaluation of the current system, evaluation of the alternatives need be no more complicated than an evaluation of the changes.

Evaluations of the alternative system proposals should be presented with the evaluation of the current system in order to emphasize the effects of the changes. Figure 6.6 illustrates one way of doing this. Note that each section of the evaluation should present a summation of the facilities included (normally the number of processes automated), the tangible costs and benefits, and the quality scores.

SYSTEM SELECTION

Before an alternative system structure is selected for implementation, at least two additional proposals (preferably three for a new automated system) should be developed. This is to give the decision maker a chance to see what possible alternatives there are and what the expected impact of different system structures could be. A presentation of only one alternative is really a go/no-go situation, and since the analysis was requested, there is great pressure to go with the alternative presented without truly considering its real benefits.

If the system alternatives represent a progression from an automated core system to a fully automated system, the decision maker can evaluate the organization's readiness and ability to handle each different level of technical sophistication. One would expect the automated core system to be the least expensive and also to give the fewest benefits. However, from this system one could, over time, develop the full system in graduated and controlled stages as resources and expertise become available. For an organization new to automation, the core system is absolutely preferable, assuming, of course, that it is an improvement over the current system.

Evaluating Alternatives

A system evaluation has three components: the numeric description, the monetary evaluation, and the subjective evaluation. When the alternative system proposals are compared, the characteristics of each component must be evaluated separately and then collectively for each of the alternative proposals. The organization must place a priority on each of the many separate system requirements. These priorities should be translated into weights in the evaluation in order to assure proper treatment of the requirements.

Since the separate evaluation components use incompatible measures, the results must be translated into some common measure for further comparison. A system evaluation can be presented using a weighted scoring model, in which the primary system characteristics are given importance weights, with each system facility in each alternative assigned a fulfillment score. The weight and score are multiplied to give a weighted score for the system component for the system alternative. The weighted scores can then be summed to give a single value for each system alternative.

Figure 6.7 illustrates a weighted scoring model for system comparison and selection. In this method, the "best," or preferred, system would be the one that has the highest composite score.

Figure 6.7 System Selection: Scoring Model

System Characteristics	Weight	Score			Weighted Score[a]		
		S-0	S-1	S-2	S-0	S-1	S-2

I. System Description
  A. Processes
  B. Processing character-
    istics
II. System Costs
III. System Benefits							

Sum of Weighted Scores =							

a. Weights, on a scale from 1 to 10 indicating priority, are multiplied by the system characteristic score, measured on a scale of 0 to 5 (nonexistent to very good).

Note that the scores, weighted scores, and sums do not measure equal increments of value, so that a system with a composite score twice that of another alternative is not necessarily twice as good a system.

Another advantage of the weighted score model, in addition to allowing comparison of noncomparable evaluations, is that the system choice can be tested for robustness by changing the requirement weights and recalculating the system weight scores. If the originally preferred alternative continues to be judged best, one can be relatively secure in selecting this alternative for implementation.

Sample Evaluation

We will continue using the student administrative system model to illustrate the use of the scoring model for evaluating system alternatives. The problem analysis, illustrated in Table 4.1, shows that most problems involve grade administration. As an example, we will show a simplified evaluation of three alternative grade administration systems:

- Alternative S-0 represents the current manual system for the administration of student grades.
- Alternative S-1 represents a semiautomated, batch-processing system (Chapter 10 discusses system processing characteristics) in which grades are sent to the administration, as in the current system, where they are then recorded on a computer file from which the transcript and class statistics can be automatically generated.

- Alternative S-2 represents a fully automated, on-line system in which faculty members use the grade recording program to record the grades. The transcript and class statistics are automatically generated as in alternative 2. A query processor is added to answer administration, faculty, and student queries to the grade register.

Figure 6.8 illustrates a scoring model for evaluating these three alternatives.

In this example, top priority, 10, is given to producing grades and transcripts, and high priority, 9, is placed on class statistics, whereas rather medium priority is given to support of user queries. These priorities are given by the users, or more accurately by the management responsible for the total system. Highest priority is also given to the number of users supported and to the ease of system use. Note that other priorities could change the determination of the best system for this university.

Figures 6.3, 6.4, and 6.5 give the evaluations of the current system. These values are converted to a score ranging from 0 to 5; this indicates nonexistence to very good service for subjective evaluations, and very expensive to inexpensive for monetary evaluations. Note that this gives the current system a very good evaluation, 5, for development and for the maintenance of computer equipment, as it has no expense for these activities.

The evaluations for alternatives S-1 and S-2 are estimates, as at this point (the final report for the system analysis phase) the detailed design specifications for these alternatives have not been made.

The best system, according to this evaluation, is alternative S-2, the fully automated system. This is not surprising given that the highest-priority benefits emphasize easy access to the system for all users, which is the usual goal of an on-line system. Also, system costs were given a rather low weight compared with the benefits. This will tend to encourage more advanced (and more expensive) solutions to the information problems.

SUMMARY

In this chapter we have discussed evaluating the tangible and intangible costs and benefits that can be attributed to an information system. Intangible costs and benefits, i.e., those to which it is difficult or impossible to assign a monetary value, are important characteristics of a system, as they may influence the system's acceptability and thus its success.

Tangible costs and benefits can normally be assigned monetary values. However, intangible costs and benefits must normally be evaluated on

Figure 6.8 Alternative Evaluation: Student AIS Example

System Characteristics	Weight[d]	Score[e]			Weighted Score		
		S-0	S-1	S-2	S-0	S-1	S-2
I. System Description[a]							
A. Processes							
P-1	10	3	3	4	30	30	40
P-2	9	0	5	5	0	45	45
P-3	10	3	5	5	30	50	50
P-4	6	0	2	4	0	12	24
					60	137	159
B. Processing Characteristics							
Data-base size	6	4	4	3	24	24	18
Data access	8	2	4	5	16	32	40
Response time	8	2	4	5	16	32	40
					56	88	98
II. System Costs[b]							
Development	8	5	3	2	40	24	16
Staff size	5	3	3	4	15	15	20
Space	3	3	3	3	9	9	9
Materials	5	3	2	2	15	10	10
Technical equipment	5	5	3	1	25	15	5
					104	73	60
III. System Benefits[c]							
Users served	10	2	2	5	20	20	50
Transactions per hour	8	2	4	4	16	32	32
Ease of use	10	1	2	4	10	20	40
Adaptability	9	1	2	4	9	18	36
Accuracy	9	2	4	4	18	36	36
Timeliness	8	2	4	4	16	32	32
					89	158	226
Sum of Weighted Scores =					309	456	543

a. Definitions in Figure 6.3.
b. See Figure 6.4.
c. See Figure 6.5.
d. Weights: 0 not important, 10 most important.
e. Scale of 0 to 5 indicating nonexistent to very good.

some subjective scale. We have proposed using a scoring model to quantify subjective opinions about system characteristics. Whenever the actual costs and benefits of a system cannot be ascertained, for example, when the system has not yet been designed, estimates must be used. Estimates should be obtained from at least three sources and should include conservative, moderate, and optimistic estimates of the system characteristic, cost, or benefit.

KEY CONCEPTS

Cost/benefit analysis
Evaluation categories
Evaluation measures
Intangible benefits
Intangible costs

Scoring models
System benefits
System costs
Tangible benefits
Tangible costs

DISCUSSION QUESTIONS

1. Define, set in context, and give an illustration for each of the key concepts.
2. When should a system evaluation take place? Why? Discuss the use of system evaluations in project management.
3. What system characteristics should be assigned priorities for a system evaluation? Who should set these priorities? How are the priorities used in the evaluation?
4. What are the nonmonetary considerations that must be looked at during a system evaluation? Discuss each, giving examples of situations in which such a consideration could cause termination of further system development.
5. What measures are used during a system evaluation? Why is it necessary to use measures other than dollar values? What system characteristics require a nonmonetary evaluation? How is this done?
6. What are the principal cost areas expected during system development?
7. What are the principal benefits expected from computer-based information systems? How are these measured?
8. When preparing proposals for alternative systems, why should more than one alternative be developed? What should be the general characteristics of the alternative set?
9. What is a scoring model? How can it be used in system evaluation?

PROJECT

1. Assume that the text example is a totally manual system. Prepare two or three alternative system structures that use different degrees of automation. Set up the evaluation and selection models for your three (four) systems.
2. Use the same evaluation framework for a system of your choice.

RECOMMENDED READING

Couger, J. P. and R. Knapp, eds. *System Analysis Techniques*. New York : John Wiley & Sons, 1974.

  This includes six papers on system evaluation theory, techniques, and their application, by Couger, J. Emery, Boyd and Krasnow, Sharpe, and Fried.

Layard, R., ed. *Cost-Benefit Analysis*. Harmondsworth, Middlesex, England : Penguin Books, 1972.

  This is a book of selected readings on the general theory and application of cost/benefit analysis.

Chapter 7
Information-System Design

INTRODUCTION

At this point in a system analysis and design project, the analysis of the current system, its user environment, and its problems is complete and an alternative system has been accepted by, as applicable, the system owners, users, subjects (those described by the system), and society (government). In addition, the proposed change has been accepted as feasible by the system designers, implementors, and component vendors.

The selected alternative gives the system requirements for a new or modified information system and indicates the locations within the current system where changes will be required. The alternative selected was the one considered most feasible given the constraints of the organization and the one promising the best cost/benefit ratio. These system requirements will form the framework for the design of the new or modified system.

The task of system design is to prepare the detailed system specifications that will be the basis for implementing the new or modified system that will provide the required information services.

Information-system design entails the development of specifications for the following system components:

1. Information processes and procedures, a subset of which will belong to the data system
2. Information archive, a subset of which will belong to the data system
3. Communication forms for transferring information and data to and from the system
4. Security requirements for both the information or data and the processes of the system

The formal components of the information system, which will require detailed design specifications, will form the new data system. A subset of this data system may be automated. The design specifications for the automated data system will need to be given in special detail. The design requirements and specifications for automated data systems are discussed in Chapters 8 to 11. In this chapter we will discuss the design of the information-system components, processes and information, the communication interface for transfer of messages to and from the system, and system security.

SYSTEM COMPONENT DESIGN

The system analysis documents the system components, the information and processes, as they exist in the current system. We also have, in the goal statement, a list of the desired characteristics of the new system. The task of component design is to develop specifications for new or modified system components that will satisfy the goal statement requirements. The design specification documents will include

- The documentation, from the current system, for components that are to remain unchanged
- Specifications for modification of those components to be altered
- Specifications for new components

The design documents should be in the same form as the preceding system analysis. When the new system has been implemented, these documents will become part of the system documentation. The design documents can be considered an update of the documents that have been under development from the initial problem/goal analysis. These include the

- information dictionary
- process dictionary
- information graphs
- information matrix

Information Element Specification

The information graphs, matrix, and dictionary document the information elements contained in the information system. Specifically, these documents describe the entity types of concern to the organization and the attributes that the information system uses to describe these entities.

For review, the terms *entity* and *attribute* are defined here. (See also Chapter 4, Figure 4.3.)

Entity Something with separate and real existence that has a meaning for or role in the information processes.

Attributes Those characteristics that describe an entity.

We distinguish between an individual entity, such as a person, and an entity type, such as students, to which individual entities belong. An entity type is described by an attribute set, the values of which represent characteristics or properties of the individual entities of interest to the information system or its organization. For example, the entity type *student* may be described by the attributes

(name, student identification, major subject)

An individual entity, a student, could be described by the attribute values

(Jane Doe, 123–45–678, System Analysis and Design)

Each entity type, identified by an entity-type name, is assumed to consist of a set of individual entities that can be described by the attributes of the entity type. It is possible for an individual entity to belong to several entity types if that entity exists in several roles or contexts within the organization. For example, a person could belong to both the entity types *student* and *teacher* if this is a possibility in the particular university. Within the information system, this person would be described as two entities: as a teacher and as a student.

Entity types can describe both a "natural" entity, i.e., one that has a physical existence, such as a person or a thing, and a relationship between natural entities, such as a contract between two persons or organizations or an order from a person for a product.

Defining entity types is one technique for organizing information for information-processing activities within an information system. The entity attributes have been identified during problem and system analysis as those attributes required for one or more information processes. The attributes of interest to the system have been recorded as elements of the information matrix. Entity definition is done in part by the system designer, who identifies the group of attributes that is most logical in the context of the information system under consideration. For example, it is quite possible for the system designer to define a number of student entity types; e.g., *academic-student* could consist of the academic attributes of the student, *financial-student* could consist of the financial attributes of the student, and so on.

The definition of a system's entity types is of particular importance for the data-system design, as the entity types become the basis for the definition of the file or data-base system. (See Chapter 9.)

The information-system designer must take the documentation of the information stored in the current system, the entity and attribute types, and supplement it with the new information elements, entity and/or attribute types, that must be added to satisfy the requirements of the goal statement.

The new specifications for the information archive must then be analyzed for coherence. That is, the entity-type definitions must be checked to ensure that the users can get information that describes the entities of concern to them.

The results of the information archive design will be an updated version of the information dictionary, graphs, and matrix.

Process Specification

The process dictionary, with the information graphs and matrix, describes the processes of the current system. The system evaluation has identified those processes that need modification and those goals from the goal statement that are not supported in the current system. The system designer's task is to design specifications for upgrading "problem" processes and for any new processes.

The new and modified process specifications, once implemented, should be added to the process dictionary and to the information graphs and matrix to form the new system documentation. A process specification must include a clear statement of the objective of the process, the major algorithm(s) to be used, the frequency of expected use, the data required, and the type(s) of data access required. (See also the definition of the process dictionary in Chapter 4.)

Process specifications at the information-system-design level are basically verbal descriptions of procedure, documented by the information graph and matrix. These procedures may be implemented as manual, semiautomated, or fully automated processes. The subset of the information processes that will become part of the automated data system will need further detailed specification, as discussed in Chapter 10.

THE SYSTEM INTERFACE

Until now we have been concentrating on the analysis and design of the content of the information system. However, there is more to making a successful system than good content. The system must also communicate well with its users, i.e., it must be easy to use and must give good products. More explicitly, the system must be perceived as easy to learn and to use. It must also present its output in clear and easily usable formats.

The communication routines between the user and the automated system are responsible for transmitting user requests and presenting system outputs. These routines make up the *system interface*. The system interface is characterized by the manner in which the users activate the system, present their service requests, and receive system responses. The method of communication is commonly called the *communication language*.

Constructing the specifications for the system interface, its communication language and report formats, is an important task of the system designer. The criteria for the communication language and report layouts must come from the system users, as it is they who need the information contained within the system.

Programmers should not be the ones to design the input/output forms of the system interface, primarily because they will not be the system users. Their design would probably make the programming easier and would possibly make the automated processing more efficient. However, the system interface is the users' contact with the system, and it will influence their acceptance and use of the system and thus its success.

System Input

System input specifications define all the input messages that the system is to receive: data, requests for information, and requests for information services (processing). There are several ways in which users can communicate with an information system. The designer must select those means of communication that best match the users and/or user groups with the information services they need. Note that an information system may well have a number of forms of communication, sometimes called communication languages, providing different user groups with different system services.

System users can be viewed, for input design purposes, as belonging to one of two groups: constant users and casual users.

Constant users are those who will use the system daily or very frequently. These users can learn and remember the specifics of relatively complex, detailed communication forms, which may include cryptic codes. An abbreviated communication form tends to reduce input time, thus allowing a greater volume of system communication. Users also consider the abbreviated form less tiring once they have learned it.

Casual users are those who use the system infrequently, but who know that it is available and that it contains information and services that are useful to them. These users will not be active enough to remember the details of a cryptic language. They will need help from the system in formulating their input messages if the system communicates in other than normal conversational English (or French, German, Norwegian, Spanish, or some other language).

Individual users of an information system need not remain permanently in either category. Some may be truly casual users. Others may progress from casual to constant users as they become familiar with the services the system provides. The input form design should encourage greater use of the system.

Generally, system input, when considering any one input message, will be one of the following types:

- Information/data for storage within the system
- Information/data describing an object-system transaction
- A request for information from the system

The form, or communication language, used for presenting system input should be designed for the intended user category as well as the type of input. The principal language types used are outlined here.

1. Parametric languages are languages whose sentence form is a list of data terms, or sometimes a list of data terms identified by attribute names. For example, if we wish to enter the fact that a student named John Doe has received a grade of A, we could express this in a parametric form as:

    1. JOHN DOE, A

    2. STUDENT-NAME=JOHN DOE, GRADE=A

2. Restricted English (or some other natural language) consists of stylized sentences, the grammar of which is a subset of the natural language. Typically the verb, representing the requested system service, begins the sentence and is followed by the data describing the input. Thus, the given statement could be expressed as:

    STORE GRADE=A FOR JOHN DOE.

3. Natural language allows the user to converse "naturally" with the system. For example, we could make a conditional request as:

    IF JOHN DOE IS AN "A" STUDENT,
    SEND HIS TRANSCRIPT TO ME.

Though much effort has been directed toward constructing natural language interfaces, at present there is no true natural language system for administrative data processing applications commercially available. The problem is primarily that a natural language is imprecise in its usage, leading to interpretation problems. Also, most administrative data processing does not really require this flexibility of expression.

The most frequently used processes in an AIS are those for data entry and transaction processing at the operational level. These processes are initiated by information clerks who use the system every day.

The most important criterion for a communication language supporting data entry would be assuring data accuracy. Traditionally, data has been entered using a parametric language, giving only the data values in some prescribed sequence. CRT terminals allow the use of preformatted screens that give the operator a clear form to complete with the required data. This allows the operator to check for correctness visually, as well as prompting for completeness. The screen forms should be designed with the operators who will be using them. An example of a completed screen form is given in Figure 7.1. Here the form is presented in capital letters, the data to be entered, in small letters.

Figure 7.1 CRT Form for Data Entry

```
    GRADE REGISTRATION - DATA ENTRY FORM

COURSE NAME: System Analysis and Design
COURSE IDENTIFICATION: B20.2312.1
SEMESTER: spring 1982

INSTRUCTOR'S NAME: JC Nordbotten
INSTRUCTOR'S IDENTIFICATION: 987-65-432

MULTIPLE ENTRIES? yes

STUDENT NAME: John Doe
STUDENT IDENTIFICATION NUMBER: 123-45-678
GRADE: A

END OF GRADES FOR THIS COURSE? no
END.
```

Traditionally, transactions have been presented to a TPS for processing using a parametric language. The general format is (transaction-code, param-1,param-2, . . .), where the transaction code signals to the AIS the processing routine required and the parameters provide the data values necessary for execution of the routine. The following example illustrates two variants (as previously discussed) of a parametric language statement activating a transaction to record an A grade for a student, with an identification code of 123-45-678, for the course "Systems Analysis and Design." (Note that the transaction code used here, T632A, is the reference name of the process for producing grades given in Figure 5.10.)

> T632A,123-45-678,SYS-ANA-DSN,A
> STORE S-ID=123-45-678 C-ID=SYS-ANA-DSN GRADE=A.

Though the parametric language form is easy to program and easy for constant users to learn, its specifics are quickly forgotten and it is generally illegible to anyone but a constant user, e.g., to a system auditor.

A preferable form would be a coded English structure. This input form is legible, reasonably easy to use, and not unduly difficult to program. The example could be formulated in restricted English as:

STORE AN A FOR STUDENT=123-45-678

FOR COURSE=SYS-ANA-DSN.

Both the parametric and restricted-English language forms must be learned and used constantly if the language details are to be remembered. The casual user, by definition, will not use the system often enough to learn this language level and thus make use of the system. Since natural language communication is still too inefficient for practical use, another system interface must be provided if the casual user is to be accommodated.

All users of a system can use menu communication. However, it may be most helpful for the casual user, since no learning process is required.

Figure 7.2 Process Selection by Menu, An Example: Initial Level Menu

```
        STUDENT ADMINISTRATION ASSISTANT

THE FOLLOWING FUNCTIONS ARE AVAILABLE:

    1. REGISTRATION OF FACULTY INFORMATION
    2. CATALOG UPDATE
    3. STUDENT APPLICATIONS
    4. CURRICULUM DEVELOPMENT
    5. STUDENT REGISTRATIONS
    6. CLASS ADMINISTRATION

WHAT FUNCTION DO YOU WANT TO WORK WITH? ..
```

Note: The menu set of Figures 7.2 through 7.4 could be used with the system described in Figures 5.7 through 5.10.

The menu-driven system presents the user with a list of options from which to choose. The choice may lead to another, more topic-oriented list from which another choice is made. This is repeated until the system knows what the user wants performed and does it. The menu set is constructed as a hierarchy, the depth of which is limited only by the user's patience. Figures 7.2, 7.3, and 7.4 show a three-level menu set. These menus could be used with the student AIS defined in Figures 5.7 to 5.10.

Most menu-driven systems allow the constant user to skip menus and present input in a parametric form. Using the example set of Figure 7.2, it should be possible to respond to the first menu with 633, which would be interpreted as option 6 of this menu, 3 of the next level, and 3 of the third level, or preparation of the grade sheet.

The option to switch from menu to parametric input should be reversible in the sense that the user can change from full menu format to parametric format and back again.

Figure 7.3 Process Selection by Menu, An Example: Second Level Menu

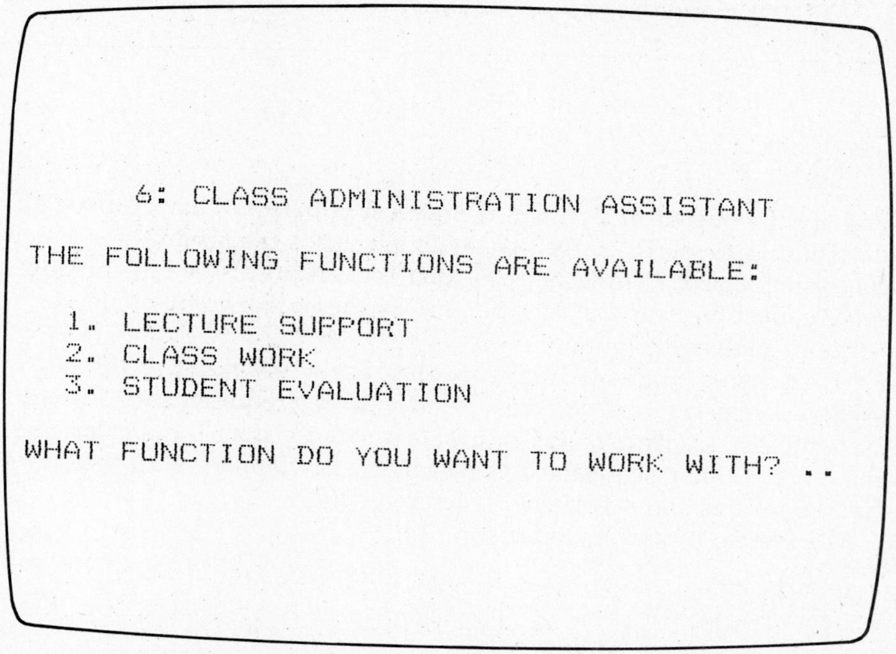

```
        6: CLASS ADMINISTRATION ASSISTANT

THE FOLLOWING FUNCTIONS ARE AVAILABLE:

    1. LECTURE SUPPORT
    2. CLASS WORK
    3. STUDENT EVALUATION

WHAT FUNCTION DO YOU WANT TO WORK WITH? ..
```

Figure 7.4 Process Selection by Menu, An Example: Third Level Menu

```
    63: STUDENT EVALUATION ASSISTANT

THE FOLLOWING FUNCTIONS ARE AVAILABLE:

    1. RECORD ASSIGNMENT AND EXAM GRADES
    2. CALCULATE GRADES
    3. PREPARE GRADE SHEET

WHAT FUNCTION DO YOU WANT TO WORK WITH? ..
```

System Output

Perhaps the output of a system is the most important characteristic in determining its ultimate success. After all, this is the product for which the system exists. It follows, then, that the output of the information system must be clearly intelligible, neatly presented, complete in its context, and easy to obtain.

The design of the output layouts must again be developed by the system designer, giving primary attention to the requirements of the system users. Generally, system programmers are poor output designers, since they cannot be assumed to be sufficiently familiar with the user's functional area and information requirements.

The system output includes:

- reports
- query responses
- receipt responses for data entry
- error messages

Reports can be quite long, and it is therefore paramount that the information details be easily located. Generally, a report should begin with a summary statement, taking no more than one page, followed by the supporting data. Data must be clearly identified by meaningful column and/or row titles and subtitles where applicable. The page format should be such that a row of data does not overrun several output lines. The page size should be such that the report will fit in the organization's manual files. The designer should use preprinted paper, on which line and column positions are indicated, for developing the report layout. The layout, with, if possible, sample reports, must be presented to the users for modification and final acceptance.

A system query typically asks a direct question about the status of some entity within the system. Query responses are usually quite short, usually one line, giving the requested information. When the action required by a query will take time (more than 5 seconds), there should be an initial response indicating that the input query has been received and interpreted as correct, and is being acted upon. The query response should then be presented in a legible form, preferably using common English (or other appropriate language). Cryptic or coded responses lead only to extra work for the user and possible interpretation errors.

Data entry typically entails providing quantities of data using a fairly rapid medium, e.g., tape or disk. The receiving program should contain input checks for data validity. An appropriate response for this is a record count, a print of the data received, a list of data found to be in error, and any cross sums that would facilitate accuracy control. Data entered through a terminal can be accumulated in the receiving program, with the control responses given at the end of the data entry session or at appropriate intervals.

Error messages are a necessary part of any system. They indicate any errors in input data or process performance that the system detects. The error message is sent to the system user, who must not be assumed to be familiar with the idiosyncrasies of the programming language or computer systems. Therefore the error message *must*:

- be presented in clear common English
- clearly identify the erroneous input data
- state the program that identified the error
- state what should be done to correct the error

An error message may include an error code whose translation can be found in the error description documents, which must be available to the users. Under no circumstances should a system just stop or stop with a message of the type: SYSTEM ERROR AB123. No one, not even the programmer, will be able to correct the error condition without leaving the work station for external aid in interpreting this message.

Input/Output Documentation

The input and output forms, including error messages, should be collected in a single system document that will be available to all users. The basic format for this document is:

> INPUT MESSAGE ⟨   ⟩:
> ⟨input example⟩
>
> ACTIVATES: Process ⟨p-1, p-2, ... p-i⟩
> MODIFIES (STORED) DATA: Elements ⟨e-1, e-2, ... e-n⟩
> PRODUCES OUTPUT:
> ⟨output example⟩
>
> POSSIBLE ERROR MESSAGES:
> ⟨er-1⟩: recovery action
> ⟨er-2⟩: recovery action
> •

THE CONTROL SYSTEM

System controls are designed to protect the security, integrity, and privacy of the information system, particularly its components: its data, processes, and supporting hardware. There are many texts that discuss techniques for providing information- and data-system security. (See in particular Martin, 1973, for an extensive discussion of security-related problems.) In the literature, the terms *security*, *integrity*, and *privacy* have been given somewhat overlapping and conflicting definitions. For the following discussion, the terms security, integrity, and privacy control are defined as follows:

Security Control The maintenance of control of physical access to the components of the information and data system.

Integrity Control The maintenance of correct, consistent data and programs within the information and data system.

Privacy Control The assurance that only required and legal data, describing persons or organizations, is maintained and made available by the system.

The security control problem can be viewed as a contest between the system, which needs to protect itself from elements of its environment, and persons or natural elements in the environment who can damage the system by physical attack or unauthorized use. The integrity control problem is concerned with maintaining correct and consistent data and functions within the system. The privacy problem involves the obligation of the organization that owns the system to respect and maintain the confidentiality of information about persons and organizations described within the system. These control areas are not mutually exclusive, and all involve protecting the system and its intended environment against misuse.

There are a number of areas in an information system where system controls can and should be applied. Principal control points are illustrated in Figure 7.5.

These control points represent the system areas that are activated by the system users, and thus are potential points for initiating misuse. Controls at these points can protect against and control for user-initiated violations of system security, integrity, and/or privacy. Specifically, these points are:

1. Human access to the system
2. Input interpretation
3. Data storage
4. Process selection
5. Processing
6. Data modification
7. Data base
8. Presentation
9. Recipient selection

User control, through identification and monitoring, is the principal function of the routines at points 1, 2, 4, 8, and 9. Control of human access requires that the identity and authorization of each user be checked. Some version of password control is usually used. The user control routines (1) generally rely on a list of authorized users, their password(s), and their authorized activities. Selection of processes (4), presentation of data for processing or storage (2), generation of reports and information from the system (8), and delivery of system output (9) can then all be restricted to authorized users.

Process control, at points 2, 4, 5, and 8, requires tests for data validity (2 and 4), monitoring of process selection (2 and 4), and monitoring of process activity (2, 5, and 8). Control over changes and additions to the processes is also important.

Data control, at points 2, 3, 6, 7, 8, and 9, requires monitoring of all data changes (2, 3, and 6), security control for the data base(s) (7), and recipient control (8 and 9).

To control the users (or misusers) and their system activities, procedures and automated routines for both manual and automated subsystems must be developed. The information system must be so designed

Figure 7.5 Information-System Control Points

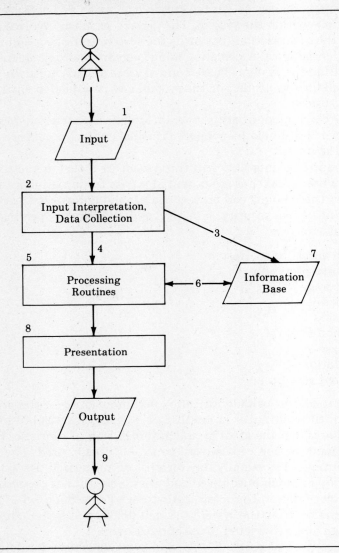

that appropriate system controls can be applied. This should be done before the system goes into the implementation phase.

The control points of Figure 7.5 are locations for routines whose primary concern is maintenance of security, integrity, or privacy control. The special considerations of security, integrity, and privacy control are discussed in the following sections.

Security Control

Security control includes those measures aimed at ensuring that no physical damage to the information system or any of its parts occurs. In addition to providing a secure environment for the information system, security controls may be required at the system input and output stations, processing routines, and data bases (points 1, 9, 5, and 7, respectively, in Figure 7.5).

Generally, security controls are concerned with securing the system against natural disasters and human mistreatment.

Physical Environment Control

The physical sections of the information system need environmental protection. These areas include the data storage files, both manual and automated, and the data processing equipment, particularly the computer, its input/output devices, and its communication lines.

Physical threats may come from:

- natural disasters, such as flood, wind, or earthquake
- human or technical error or failure, such as fire, building collapse, or electrical failure
- human aggression, such as revenge, war, or terrorism

Proper site preparation, building construction, and room location is the best protection against natural disasters and equipment failures. The computer location should be fireproof, or at least fire-resistant, protected from wind and from wind-blown dust or sand, and above the flood level. In an earthquake area, the building should be constructed to withstand "normal" tremors. Generally, the local weather must be taken into consideration when deciding where and how to locate computer equipment.

Electrical failure happens. There should be an in-house generator capable of providing electricity for a controlled power down, sometimes called a fail soft procedure.

Bomb threats happen. Particularly in our advanced societies, this seems to be a means of retaliating against alleged oppression by the owners of the computer installation. The best security is proper physical location of the computer installation and restricted access.

A necessary part of the physical security scheme, which will be activated in the event of a physical disaster, is to keep copies, called back-up copies, of all important data and processes. These copies can be kept on such machine-readable media as disks, floppy disks, or magnetic tape, or on external media such as microfiche or paper printouts. The choice of storage medium is determined by the need to reestablish computer files in the event of damage to the original set. Back-up copies should be stored in a location physically separate from the original set, such as another room or another building. A back-up installation for processing while recovery is in progress should be established.

Human Environment Control

Most CBIS users are real and honest members of the intended user community. However, where sensitive data or a possibility of economic gain exists, misusers should be expected and guarded against. Computer crime is growing with the increasing number of CBISs. Each year an increased number of cases are reported. Common misuse includes:

- unauthorized use of the computer resources, including private use of computer facilities and/or theft of software.
- alteration of data and/or programs, allowing theft of money by transfer of funds and/or theft of goods by decreasing or "moving" inventory quantities.
- tapping of sensitive data, such as trade secrets or medical records.

All areas of the information system must be protected against unauthorized access and use, particularly the data, the processes, and the computer resources.

A first-level security system to control human access is to provide physical barriers to the information-system area, particularly to the computers and their input/output stations. Such barriers could include guards and/or locked doors. To pass the guards or open the doors, a user would need a system access pass. More drastic, but necessary for highly sensitive systems, is to "hide" the system, for example under a mountain, as is done for certain military systems.

In addition to the physical security system, a password system, administered by the computer system's software, can be used to control general use of the computer system and access to the automated user files and program libraries. Basically, the password system functions in this way: A potential user must first provide the system with a valid password or code before any system services are allowed. A reasonably complete password system contains a file of valid users in which the data and data services (processes) to which each user is allowed access are described. The system may enter into a dialog with the user, requiring several correct responses, or passwords, before acceptance.

Relatively straightforward physical access and password systems are sufficient to guard against system use by people who are not part of the intended user community. However, once a person has gained access to the system, more sophisticated controls are required to monitor what the user is doing to prevent unauthorized changes to the data and/or programs. For complete protection, every requested change would have to be checked against a user privilege list before being made. Although possible, such extensive checking would be both time-consuming and expensive. It should be applied only in critical areas.

Data sent or received over a telecommunications network are susceptible to wire tapping. The traditional method of protecting against losing information in this way is to send only coded messages.

A well-publicized, strong security system will often deter the casually interested potential misuser. However, a determined misuser, particularly an authorized member of the intended user community, will be able to circumvent most of the common security systems by learning how the system functions and acquiring unauthorized access to the general modification password(s). Changing passwords frequently is one possible deterrent. Sensitive data should be machine-accessible for minimum periods of time. Sensitive programs could be burned onto read-only memory (ROM).

Misuse is commonly discovered after the fact during a general system audit. Unfortunately, the misuser may be gone by then.

Security Requirement Specification

Not all of a system's processes and data elements need the same level of protection. Part of the design of the security system will involve establishing a security level for each of the system components and an access authorization for each of the system users.

The user directory, begun during goal analysis, should be extended to include, in addition to the user identification, the password(s), a general security level, and access authority for each user. The directory must maintain a list of the procedures and processes each user can activate, the data that can be accessed, and how these data can be used (read only or modify). (See also Chapter 4, System Users, and Box 4.2, the User Directory.)

A security matrix can be constructed to define the process/information element interactions and the security requirements for the data and processes. This matrix, illustrated in Figure 7.6, gives the general security level for each information element, row 1 in the matrix. The right-hand columns give the security:usage level for each of the processes. In the figure, security levels are indicated on a 0 to 10 scale, where 0 indicates open information and 10 maximum security.

This type of security classification, assigning a security level to each data type and process, can limit access to attribute types within the information base. However, if partial access is required—for example, if a manager may have access to salary data for employees of his or her department only—this scheme will have to be extended.

Figure 7.6 Information Security Matrix

Information	Information Elements			Process
	Entity 1	Entity 2	. . .	Security[b]
Process	1 2 3 . . . n	1 2 3 . . . m		
Data Security	0 0 5 . . . Sn	0 0 6 . . . Sm[a]		
P-1	O O			0:W
P-2	I O			5:RW
P-3	I	O I		Sn:RW
.				
.		input/output		
.		indicators		
P-i				

a. Data security codes indicate security levels 0 to 10, representing no security to maximum security.
b. Process security is given as "security level:data operation," where operations are R:READ, W:WRITE.

A comparison of the user access authorities, from the user directory, and the security assignments, from the security matrix, will allow reasonable control of system use.

Integrity Control

Integrity control includes those measures taken to ensure that the system operates correctly and according to design. In particular, integrity control is concerned with ensuring that the system maintains, processes, and presents correct and consistent data.

Both internal and external integrity controls must be implemented. Internal controls, operative controls, function within the system to monitor activities as they happen. External controls, audits, check results after they are produced. The system designer should include procedures that will facilitate both types of integrity controls.

Integrity control is required for the major system components:

- Processing routines
- Content of the data base(s)
- Operative procedures

Using the system model given in Figure 7.5, the areas of primary concern for integrity control are those processes that can modify the data-base content, points 2 and 5, and the storage structures for the data base(s), point 7.

Operations Control

Those system processes performing data collection, storage, and manipulation change values within the data base(s). Controls must ensure that these changes are performed correctly and that the data base maintains a correct and consistent representation of the organization's situation. Principal techniques used for integrity control include:

- Design control
- Operating procedures
- Acceptance testing
- Input validation
- Concurrent processing control
- Back-up and regeneration procedures
- Auditing

The system design must include the routines necessary to ensure proper system functioning, i.e., maintenance of system integrity. The design elements concerned with integrity control must be reviewed by the organization and by both its internal and external auditors before general system implementation begins. Evaluation of these processes must consider the algorithms for each process and the interactions between processes. In many instances, a certain sequence of processes must be maintained to ensure correct functioning.

Operating procedures must be established and reviewed concurrently with integrity-control-system design. Primarily these procedures state (1) how system input is to be prepared, (2) the sequence of processes to be followed, (3) the action to be taken in the event of failure, and (4) how the system is to be modified. The procedures will cover actions of the primary system users, the information clerks, data entry personnel, EDP operators, and application programmers.

The acceptance of operative programs is vitally important to correct functioning. Operative versions of programs must be thoroughly tested before they are accepted into the system. The acceptance-test procedure should include execution of correct (not necessarily current) data as well as all possible variants of erroneous data. Procedures for operating in parallel with the preceding, operative version of the program should be used wherever feasible. (See also Chapters 12 and 13.) A single person should be given the responsibility for the operative version of the system, and only this person may alter the system content.

All input data presented for processing must be tested for validity. This can be done in a separate input validation program or by each of the processing programs. An automated data dictionary, containing valid data definitions, will facilitate this task.

If the operative environment allows parallel processing or if the information system is designed for multiprogramming, there must be procedures to prevent concurrent update. The problem here is that two or more processes from the information system could be attempting to update (change) data values for the same data record at the same time. This will lead to incorrect data unless the processes are properly coordinated. The problem arises most frequently in large, multiuser on-line environments. Controlling concurrent updates is a function of some operating systems and also of some data-base management systems. If the system requires parallel processing, the designer must ensure that control of concurrent update will be maintained.

Occasionally a poorly tested program or a machine failure will cause errors in the data. In this case, operative procedures for regeneration of the data base(s) must be put into effect. Data-base regeneration uses a back-up copy (a copy of an earlier version) of the data and logs of the input transactions or data changes that have occurred since the data-base copy was made. (For a more detailed discussion of data-base maintenance, see Chapter 13.)

Auditing

Auditing is an external (to the information system) examination of the processes and information of the system to establish the reliability of the system and its data. An audit is performed by someone outside the normal environment of the information system. The auditor may be a member of the organization (an internal auditor), or be from outside the organization, from an auditing firm or a government agency (an external auditor).

It is frequently advised that an auditor should participate in system design to ensure that the resulting system will be auditable. However, there is some concern that the auditor will thus lose his or her independence from the system. Whether or not an auditor is a member of the design team, the design must be checked to make sure that the resulting system will be auditable.

When performing an audit, the auditor may need special components that must be included in the system design. In particular, the auditor will be interested in the operating procedures which are set up for the system.

Privacy Control

Privacy controls aim to ensure that information describing individuals and organizations that may be kept within the information system is correct and relevant and that its confidentiality is maintained. Maintaining privacy controls are:

- the responsibility of the organization.
- the concern of the people described.
- governed by laws.

Many information systems contain data that describe the people within the system environment, such as the customers, suppliers, or employees of the organization. Typical data provide two types of description of the individuals:

1. An identification, giving name, address, telephone number(s), and account number(s)
2. A description of the relationship(s) with the organization, such as account balances, services or goods received, and so on

Information describing individuals and organizations is generally considered to be confidential, though the degree of confidentiality may vary depending on the attributes involved and the type of information system. For example, for many organizations, a list of the identification attributes of its customers may be relatively open information, while the status of these customer accounts is commonly considered confidential. In a medical system, patient diagnoses would be highly confidential, and even patient identifications are considered confidential. It is the organization's responsibility to ensure that its information is correct and relevant to the organization's business and that it is properly protected from misuse.

In many countries, the individuals described in an information system have the legal right to inspect the data about themselves and to influence the degree to which this information is disseminated to other organizations. The individual's inspection rights require information systems that contain information about persons or organizations to contain appropriate routines for informing the individual about the information collected and allowing for modifications of possible errors.

The general fear that uninhibited information collection could allow persons and/or organizations to intrude into the private lives of individuals has led to the enactment of national privacy laws. These laws have been established to protect individuals from uncontrolled information collection and possible misuse of the resulting data. In general, these laws allow for:

- individual inspection of data collected.
- the right to change or delete erroneous data.
- the right to restrict data dissemination to other organizations.
- the right to refuse to give information not deemed necessary for the business of the collecting organization.

The system designer and the owning organization must make sure that the information collected about individuals and organizations conforms to the letter and intent of the law. Further, security controls must be adequate to ensure the confidentiality of the data.

SUMMARY

This chapter has presented three important areas of stage 3 of an ISAD project, information-system design:

1. The design of the system components, the information archive, and information processes
2. The design of the system interface, input formats, menu layouts, and reports
3. The design of the security system

The design of the system components builds upon the documentation developed during system analysis, adding to it the specifications for new and modified information elements and processes. It is from these specifications that the data system is designed. The specifications for the system interface and control system can be implemented directly.

KEY CONCEPTS

Audit	Menu
Attribute	Parametric language
Communication language	Password
Concurrent update	Privacy
Entity	Security
Integrity	System interface

DISCUSSION QUESTIONS

1. Define and give an illustration of each of the key concepts.
2. Discuss the differences between system analysis and system design. Why must a system analysis precede system design?

3. What are the main considerations in information-system design? Why should a user-oriented system designer prepare the information-system design?
4. What role should the information and process dictionaries play in system design?
5. Give examples of an entity type, entity, attribute type, and property. Why is it important to differentiate among these concepts?
6. What is the system interface? Why is it important? Discuss how the definition of the user community can influence the design of the system interface.
7. Why are there different forms for system input? Discuss what types of forms are generally used, who is intended to use them, and for what.
8. How should the system handle errors?
9. Discuss the differences between security, integrity, and privacy controls. What techniques are available for constructing control systems for each of these areas?

PROJECTS

1. Prepare a detailed design of at least one new process requiring new data as determined in the goal analysis for your system.
2. Design the input and output forms for your system. Discuss why these forms will be good and who will be using them.
3. Design a control system for your information system. Include security, integrity, and privacy controls as required. Discuss the design alternatives and present the reasoning behind the controls selected for your project.

RECOMMENDED READINGS

Allen, B. "The Biggest Computer Frauds: Lessons for CPAs." *Journal of Accountancy*, 143, No. 5 (1977), 52-62.
    This article analyzes in some detail a number of different types of computer fraud, presents profiles of fraud perpetrators, and offers some measures for fraud prevention.
Bach, G. G. "Data Privacy—Critical Issues of the 80's." *Telecommunications*, 14, No. 5 (1980), 43-48.
    This article describes the need for security laws and briefly discusses the laws of the nine countries that have them. These countries include the U.S.A., Canada, Norway, Sweden, Denmark, U.K., and Germany.
Brabb, George J. *Computers and Information Systems in Business.* 2nd ed. Boston: Houghton Mifflin, 1980.
    The section "Auditing Electronic Accounting Systems" in Chapter 15 provides a concise discussion of the role of the auditor in the design and operation of automated information systems.

Kindred, Alton. *Data Systems and Management—An Introduction to Systems Analysis and Design*. 2nd ed. Englewood Cliffs, N.J.: Prentice-Hall, 1980.

Chapter 4, "Forms Design and Control," presents a good discussion of the design of input and output forms on cards, printouts, and display screens.

Martin, James. *Security, Accuracy, and Privacy in Computer Systems*. Englewood Cliffs, N.J.: Prentice-Hall, 1973.

This text discusses in detail the security problems that threaten computer-based information systems and the actions that can be taken to avert or reduce damage or loss of data and data services.

Whiteside, T. *Computer Capers: Tales of Electronic Thievery, Embezzlement, and Fraud*. New York: T. Y. Crowell, 1978.

A readable account of a wide variety of computer crimes.

PART III
DATA-SYSTEM DESIGN

Chapter 8
The Data Subsystem

INTRODUCTION

Data-system design is the activity in which the specifications for the manual and automated data subsystems of an information system are determined. We have defined a data system as those subsystems of an information system containing formal procedures and processes that utilize data. The objective of the data subsystem is to collect, store, process, transmit, and present relevant data to support the decisions and activities that make up the information system.

In the design of an information system, the goal analysis identifies the users, information, and processes that are to be included. The system analysis and evaluation determine the scope and type of data system required to support the information system and the portion of that data system that can feasibly be automated. The information-system design has, in addition to specifying the processes and information to be included in the information system, provided the specifications for the interface between the information system and the data system and the required controls.

The task of data-system design is to develop the specifications for a data system that will effectively and efficiently provide the required data services for the information system. A data system need not be automated, and many (or possibly most) are not. However, in this text we are interested in the design of at least partially automated systems, and the techniques presented here are appropriate for the design of such systems.

There are a number of interdependent subtasks in data-system design. The major subdivisions are the design of the processes and the design of the data structures. These subsystems must be designed in parallel because the data structures required are dependent on the processing requirements, which in turn are restricted in their options by the data structures. Unfortunately, our discussion must, by the nature of a book, be serial.

A basic tool for describing the "data world" of a data system is the data model, the specifics of which can be recorded in a data dictionary. This chapter discusses the development of a data model and data dictionary. Given a completed data model, the data dictionary, and the data usage specifications, the file or data-base system can be specified.

177

This process is the topic of Chapter 9. Development of the specifications for the processes will be discussed in Chapter 10.

The data collection maintained by the data system must include all the data that the existing and perceived data processes need. The data collection may be completely manual or partially or fully automated. If it is fully automated, then at least the data retrieval processes must also be automated. In addition to being complete, in the sense that all the required data are stored in it, the data collection must also be organized in such a way as to be easily accessible.

The design of the data collection structure must take into account both data completeness and the system's access requirements. An important design tool for the data collection is the data model. The data model provides the designer with a tool for describing the proposed data structure(s) and communicating with both the users and implementers of the system about the design.

DATA MODELS

The data collection of a data system represents the information known to the information system, and thus also indicates the way the organization that owns the information system perceives the world. In designing a data system that will give maximum support to the information-system activities, it is helpful to develop models of the information-system environment, information and data. Models can be developed at separate stages of the system design to provide

1. an object-system model, developed during system analysis, that identifies and describes the entities, their attributes, and their relationships to the environment of the information system which are of particular interest to the system being developed and/or analyzed.
2. an information model, developed during information-system design, that describes the information and/or data assumed by the information requirements.
3. a data model, developed during data-system design, that describes the data and data structures to be maintained by the system.

A number of techniques for developing these models have been proposed. Generally, these techniques can be classified according to the model type developed. The two basic model types used are tabular models and graphic models.

Tabular models provide a tool for describing the data at the attribute level. Interdata relationships are given by relationships within the table; that is, related elements are described in a single table. Tables are related by common columns. An important model type that uses this technique is the *relational model*.

Graphic models most commonly represent data at the entity level. Related entities are represented by connecting arcs. Important model types that use graphic techniques are the *hierarchic* and *network models*.

The design and use of data-base management systems (DBMS) has increased interest in data modeling and the development of data models. Initially the data model was used to describe the data to be maintained by the DBMS. However, the data model can be used at earlier system-design stages, and thus data modeling is a more generally applicable technique.

It is not necessary that models of the object, information, and data systems be of the same type, although this is advisable for continuity. So far there is no one model type that embodies all desirable system descriptive characteristics. The system designer should therefore choose the model type that is most familiar to the information-system environment, since the model is primarily a vehicle for communication between the designer, the users, and the implementers of the data system.

The literature on data-base management and data modeling suggests a number of model types that can be used to model the environment, information, and/or data that an information or data system is to maintain. The best known models are the network, hierarchic, and relational models. We will briefly describe each of these model types so that students may become familiar with these approaches and be able to assess other model types against them.

Network Models

The network model, first presented for data modeling by C. Bachman in 1969 (Bachman, 1969), gives the designer a tool for constructing a graphic model of entity types and interentity relationships. The model uses two graphic symbols:

　　　□　named rectangles to represent each entity type

and

　　　⟶　named directed arrows to represent relationships between entity types

Each symbol is given a reference name that represents a real-world entity type or relationship. For example, *student* and *courses taken* may be an entity type and a relationship, respectively, within a student AIS. (See Figure 8.1.)

Relationships may be singular (1:1), unidirectional (1:*N*), or bidirectional (*N*:*M*), and are to be interpreted as follows:

- *A* ——— *B*, a 1:1 relationship for which each entity *a* of type *A* is related to only one entity *b* of type *B*.
- *A* ——→ *B*, a 1:*N* relationship for which each entity *a* of type *A* is related to 0, 1, or more entities of type *B*, whereas each entity *b* of type *B* may be related to only one entity of type *A*.
- *A* ←——→ *B*, a *N*:*M* relationship in which each entity of type *A* may be related to 0, 1, or more entities of type *B* and each entity of type *B* may be related to 0, 1, or more entities of type *A*.

Figure 8.1 illustrates a network model for the student AIS. For purposes of discussion, the model illustrates four entity types, *student*, *course*, *teacher*, and *class*, and four relationships, a singular relationship between *teacher* and *class*, two unidirectional relationships between *teacher* and *course* and between *class* and *student*, and a bidirectional relationship between *student* and *course*. The model depicts a system in which the following relationships exist:

1. Each class has one and only one teacher, and each teacher has only one class.
2. Each teacher may teach one or more courses, but each course is taught by only one teacher.
3. Each student may take one or more courses, and each course is taken by one or more students.
4. Each class may have one or more students, but each student belongs to only one class.

The network model, as defined here, assumes that the attributes used to describe entities will be specified elsewhere. Another implicit assumption is that each entity has been defined by an exclusive set of attributes.

Figure 8.1 Network Model, Student AIS

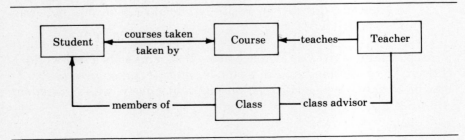

Entity definition is not generally considered an application area for the network data model.

Network data-base management systems (discussed in Chapter 9) usually allow only $1:N$ relationships to be represented. This is not a strong restriction, as a 1:1 relationship is a special case of the $1:N$ relationship and a $N:M$ relationship may be defined as two $1:N$ relationships to a common entity whose attributes describe the $N:M$ relationship. Figure 8.2 illustrates this reduction or normalization of the $N:M$ relationship between the entities *student* and *course* using the relationship entity *grade*.

Most often, when a $N:M$ relationship is important to the information system, there will also be important attributes that describe that relationship, such as the time at which the relationship was established and the current status of the relationship. In our example, the $N:M$ relationship between students and the courses they take can be described by at least two attributes: (1) the date of participation in the course and (2) the grade attained.

Figure 8.2 Normalized Network Model, Student AIS

General Network Model

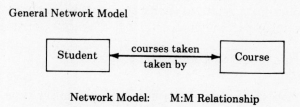

Network Model: M:M Relationship

Reduces to:

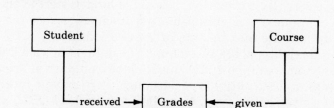

In general, any relationship between entities can be considered to be bidirectional. However, in designing a specific data system, it becomes important to select only those relationships that are required to support the activities of the information system.

Hierarchic Models

The hierarchic model became important as a data model when IBM's Information Management System (IMS) was introduced (IBM, 1975). It has since been used as the basic data model for many data-base management systems that are simpler than IMS. Although this model was initially designed to represent data storage structures and program-level records, it can also be used in earlier system-design stages to represent the objects and/or information constructs of interest to an information system.

The hierarchic model, like the network model, is a graphic model that allows entity types and interentity relationships to be represented. It is assumed that the attribute set that defines an entity is described elsewhere using other specification techniques.

We will assume that the graph nodes represent entity types that can be real-world objects, information constructs, data records as seen by users or programmers, or stored data records. Of course, in a given model, the nodes must relate to entity types of the same kind—real-world objects, information constructs, logical records, or storage records.

The hierarchic model uses two graphic symbols:

named rectangles to represent each entity type

and

_____   arcs, which may be directed and/or named, to represent the relationships

The arcs represent $1:N$ relationships directed toward the lower or rightmost entity. By convention, hierarchic models start at the top of a page and continue down, although some designers replace the arc with an arrow to indicate the direction of the relationship.

For this model type, the system must be defined in such a way that there is only one path, possibly consisting of a number of levels of $1:N$ relationships, *to* each entity type, although there may be more than one path *from* a given entity type. Using IMS terminology (IBM, 1975), there is one *root* entity type that initializes the structure and to which there is no path. The root entity is then "parent" to one or more "child" entity types, each of which may in turn be the parent to one or more child entity types and so on.

These constraints create a tree or hierarchic structure for the entity types. (See Figure 8.3.) Since there is only one path to a given entity type, its location within the system can be defined by naming its successive ancestors, making naming of the arcs unnecessary. For example, the "location" of the *student 1* entity type in the model of Figure 8.3 is (*teacher, course*).

Figure 8.3 presents a possible hierarchic model for the student AIS. The model assumes that the *teacher* entity type is most important in determining data access within the system. Each teacher is related to 0, 1, or more courses and to 0, 1, or more classes. Each course has a number of students, as does each class. The two *student* entity types have separate, possibly overlapping attribute sets, one describing the student as a participant in a course, the other describing the student as a member of a class. Like the network model, the hierarchic model assumes that the attribute sets that define entity types have been specified elsewhere.

The hierarchic model is a restricted form of the network model in that only a true tree structure is allowed, that is, any node that represents an entity type may be related to only one parent node. This restriction can lead to redundant definitions of entity types at the leaf level of the tree structure, for example, *student 1* and *student 2* in Figure 8.3. The model is also unable to represent $N:M$ relationships. In the example, the result of the hierarchic constraint on the $N:M$ relationship between students and courses will be the repetition of individual student records for each course they take.

Figure 8.3 Hierarchic Model, Student AIS

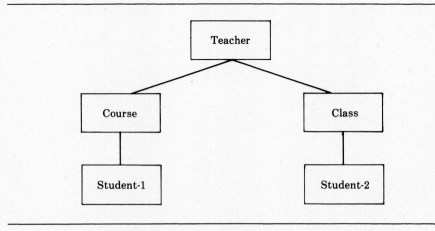

To reduce the redundancy caused by the hierarchic constraints, many hierarchic data-base management systems allow multiple tree structures with common entity (data record) types to be defined. The resulting hierarchic model actually consists of a number of tree structures. In the model set, different symbols indicate true placement and logical (desired) placement. The underlying hierarchic DBMS uses reference links (pointers, index tables, or other implementation techniques) to implement these "cross-tree" relationships.

Figure 8.4 illustrates an alternative hierarchic structure for our system using multiple trees. In this model, the actual entity placement is indicated by the solid rectangle, and logical hierarchic placement is indicated by a dotted rectangle with an arrow to the "real" entity.

In Figure 8.4, we have assumed that defining *student 1* and *student 2* separately was unnecessary. By defining a separate hierarchy for the consolidated student entity, we can preserve the two 1:N relationships to the *student* entity and the N:M relationship between the *student* and *course* entities. The two 1:N relationships, from the *course* and *class* entities, are implemented by reference links (or pointers) to the

Figure 8 4 Multiple-Tree Hierarchic Model, Student AIS

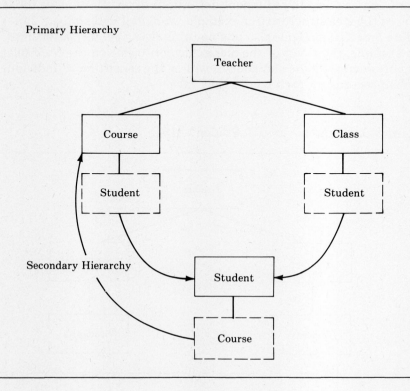

student entity. The 1:*N* relationship from *student* to *course* (normalization of the *N*:*M* relationship) is implemented by reference links to the *course* entity. Note that the attributes (date, grade) describing the *N*:*M* relationship between students and courses have not been separated out as an entity type in this example. (Compare Figure 8.4 with Figure 8.2.)

Relational Models

The relational model was introduced as a tool for data modeling in large systems by T. Codd (Codd, 1970) in a paper based on work by Childs (Childs, 1968). It differs from the network and hierarchic models in three fundamental aspects: First, it is a tabular model; second, it is concerned with the definition of attribute sets; and third, it defines both entities and interentity relationships using the single concept of a *relation*.

A relation is defined as follows:

Relation   Given the sets *D*-1, *D*-2, . . . , *D*-*n* (not necessarily distinct), *R* is a relation on these *n* sets if it is a set of *n*-tuples or simply tuples each of which has its first element from *D*-1, second element from *D*-2, and so on (Codd, 1970).

The sets *D*-1, . . . , *D*-*n* are called the *domains* of *R*. The number *n* is the *degree* of *R*, and the number of tuples in *R* is its *cardinality*. Figure 8.5 illustrates a relation, named *student*, of degree 3 and cardinality 5, since it is defined upon the three domains (attributes) S#, S–NAME, and ADDRESS and has 5 rows or tuples. Note that each row (tuple) represents an entity of the type defined by the relation.

A relational model consists of a list of the relations defined for the data system. The model is commonly illustrated by tables of example data for each relation. Figures 8.6 and 8.7 show a possible relational

Figure 8.5 A Student Relation, Student AIS

	Student	
S#	S–NAME	ADDRESS
82001	Tom Jones	Bergen
82002	Jane Doe	New York
82003	Peter Pan	Oslo
82004	Anne Olson	Bergen
82005	Jan Martin	Bergen

Figure 8.6 Relational Model, Student AIS

Student	⟨S#, S–NAME, CL–ID)
Course	⟨C#, C–NAME, CREDIT⟩
Teacher	⟨T#, T–NAME⟩
Class	⟨CL–ID, SIZE, T#⟩
Courses Taken	⟨S#, C#, GRADE, DATE⟩
Teaches	⟨T#, C#, DATE⟩

NOTE: The key attributes are indicated by the underlined attribute name.

model for the student AIS example. The list of relations in Figure 8.6 is sometimes referred to as a relational schema (Tsichritzis, 1982). Figure 8.7 shows a possible extension (Tsichritzis, 1982) of the relational model.

An entity type, representing an object type, is defined as a relation of strongly related attributes, or attributes that are functionally dependent (for their values) on the values of the key attribute(s). Functional dependency is defined as follows: one value, A, is functionally dependent on another, B, if the value of B determines the value of A. For example, if S# is a determinant (key) attribute, the key value "82001" determines the attribute values for S–NAME and ADDRESS as "Tom Jones" and "Bergen," respectively (according to the model in Figure 8.5).

The rules for the definition of relations are called rules for *normalization* (Codd, 1970). Basically these rules seek to guarantee the functional dependencies of the nonkey attributes. Much research has been done to determine how to define formal rules for the definition of relations. A practical synthesis of this work gives the following rules for defining relations representing entity types.

1. Each relation must have at least one *key*, consisting of one or more attributes, whose value defines exactly one tuple of the relation.
2. No attribute defined as part of the key can be removed without destroying the key's ability to identify unique tuples.
3. All attributes of a relation must be simple, i.e., defined on one domain.
4. All nonkey attributes in a relation must be functionally dependent on the key attribute; i.e., given the key attribute value, the value of each nonkey attribute is determined.

Interentity-type relationships can also be defined as relations in which, generally, the key attributes of the related entities are considered the composite key of the relationship relation, which may have nonkey descriptive attributes. A 1:1 relationship may be represented as a

Figure 8.7 Partial Relational Model Extension, Student AIS

Student

S#	S-NAME	ADDRESS
82001	Tom Jones	Bergen
82002	Jane Doe	New York
82003	Peter Pan	Oslo
82004	Anne Olson	Bergen
82005	Jan Martin	Bergen

Courses

C#	C-NAME	CREDIT
I-21	SYS-ANA	3
I-22	ADV-PROG	3
I-23	DATA-ADMIN	3
I-24	COMP-ARCH	3

Courses Taken

S#	C#	GRADE	DATE
82001	I-21	A	6/81
82001	I-22	B	6/81
82001	I-23	B	6/81
82001	I-24	C	6/81
82002	I-21	B	6/80
. . .			

separate relation, or as a "foreign key" attribute in one of the related entity relations. A foreign key is defined as an attribute in a relation that functions as a key in another relation. In our example (see Figure 8.6), the *class* relation includes the foreign key T# to implement the 1:1 relationship between *class* and *teacher*.

1:*N* relationships may also be represented as separate relations or through foreign key attributes in the multiple-entity end of the relationship. For example, the 1:*N* relationship between *class* and *student* can be represented by the foreign key *CL-ID* in the *student* relation. However, if there are attributes describing the relationship, as with our *teaches* relation, a separate relation should be defined. Note that the *teaches* relation can also represent a *N:M* relationship if we assume that different teachers may teach the same course.

N:M relationships are represented by separate relations with a composite key made up of the keys of the related entity relations. Relationship descriptive attributes are included in the relation definition; see the *courses taken* relation in the example.

The relational model is a particularly important data modeling tool, since it forces the user to pay attention to the definitions of the datasystem entities and their interrelationships. There are a number of relational data-base management systems that support data administration for data defined in accordance with this model.

Choosing a Model Type

Data modeling is a tool for clarifying the data and interdata relationships that are of concern to (are to be included in and maintained by) the data system. There are at least three groups for whom the data model is of value:

- System users or end users, those people in the system environment who need a model that describes the data available to support their activities
- Application programmers, who interpret and implement the data processing requirements of the end users
- Data-base designers and administrators, who implement the data administration tools

The data model should facilitate communication between these groups concerning the content of the data system. Ideally, a single data model should be sufficient to serve all the user groups; if it is, many misunderstandings about data interpretation can be avoided. However, it seldom happens that all users are familiar with the type of data model chosen. Also, the same model type may not serve the information requirements (about the data content of the data system) of each individual user group equally well.

The system designer must choose the model type that best fits the needs and preferences of the intended user of the model.

If the intended user is the system or end user, the designer must determine whether an entity-level model or an attribute-level model is more compatible with the way these users view their data requirements. Depending on the specific environment and the individual users, these people may prefer an entity-oriented model, such as the hierarchic or network models, or they may prefer an attribute-oriented model, such as the relational model. The individual end user is generally concerned only with those data that he or she needs. These data are typically described by attribute sets, making the relational model a good choice.

The application programmer is also concerned with only subsets of the data, those required for the program at hand. If the DBMS can support it, the relational model may provide the best data description. Otherwise, the programmer should have a data model that corresponds to the model used by the DBMS.

The data-base administrator is concerned with the total data base, not with its separate entities. Normally a model showing the storage files (entity types or record types) used should be sufficient, and an entity-level hierarchic or network model would be good. If a specific DBMS has been chosen, however, then the DBA model should be the one used by that system.

In practice, the designer is likely to choose the model type he or she is most familiar with or the model used by the DBMS. However, the designer should be able to represent this data model in several ways to ensure that all required attributes of the data system have been identified.

DATA DEFINITION

The data model is clearly part of the data definition. However, by itself it is not sufficient, since it is merely a definition of the entities, their attributes, and their interrelationships. The data definition for a system must also specify such data attributes as:

- data type (character, numeric, code, and so on)
- data-value domain and range
- storage and presentation formats
- data volume
- usage
- allowable users

Collection of these data descriptive attributes was begun during the initial system analysis. During data-system design, the data definition that the system users will need must be completed. Further implementation characteristics will be added as the system is implemented.

Because of the volume of data descriptive information, a data dictionary should be used for maintenance, organization, and control. This
dictionary is a natural extension of the information element definition
in the information dictionary as presented in Chapters 4 and 5. (See
particularly Boxes 4.3 and 5.1 and the accompanying text.)

To design efficient data storage structures, it is necessary to know
the intended use of the data. Again, collection of this information was
begun during the system analysis and design phases. Data-system design
includes making specific the usage data required by the processes to be
included in the data system. We will return to the application of the
usage data for the design of storage structures in Chapter 9.

The Data Dictionary

A data dictionary contains a complete data description of each data element in the system. Box 8.1 lists the minimum data characteristics.
Note that these are an extension of the characteristics of the information dictionary. (See Chapter 4.) Indeed, it is advisable to append the
data characteristics to the entries of the information dictionary, thus
converting the information dictionary into a data dictionary. The data
dictionary will then define all the information and data items of the
information system, including those that are not to be represented
formally in the data system.

Entries in the data dictionary should be ordered by their data name.
It is possible to enforce data naming conventions and standards at this
point. However, if more than one name is to be allowed for a data item,
the legal synonyms must be recorded. All of the reference names for
the data item that are used in the design documents and programs
should be included.

Normally, the data definition or interpretation for the corresponding
information element will have been included. However, if the data item
is a part or aggregate of an information element, the other data and/or
information items must be identified. Interdata relationships must also
be defined, giving (1) the data items to be grouped into each record
type and (2) the record types to be linked together.

The acceptable values for each data item must be defined, including
the data type (character, numeric, code with code interpretation, and
so on), value range, and length. Further, the storage format and all
presentation formats must be specified. For example, a data item
representing a monetary value may be stored as a four-place decimal
number, 999999.9999, to assure correct calculation, while its output
format may be defined as $99999.99. Expected volumes of data should
also be recorded. For example, it is important for file design to know

Box 8.1

DATA DICTIONARY COMPONENTS

1. Identification, giving:
   - standard name
   - name of corresponding information element
   - synonym names from programs and design documentation

2. Definition, or interpretation, giving:
   - definition as part (or aggregate) of information element(s)
   - type of data item: item, record, file, or relationship

3. Type of data represented:
   - character or text
   - numeric with type: real, integer, decimal, and so on
   - code with code interpretation
   - allowable values

4. Format, giving:
   - sequence of fields in a record and records in a file
   - field, record length, file size
   - storage format (data type)
   - presentation format for input and output

5. Usage:
   - unique record (entity) identifier
   - group selector
   - read only or modify

6. Users, both people and programs, and their authorized usage

---

whether the file structure should be able to accommodate 100 or 1,000,000 records.

The acceptable and expected usages should be defined for each attribute, giving usage as a key, as a group selector, allowable modifying programs, and so on. Finally, the authorized users, people and programs, must be defined.

The data dictionary information should be collected in a common file, which may be either manual or automated for the total system. There are commercially available, automated data dictionary systems (DDS) that allow some or most of the data characteristics indicated in Box 8.1 to be registered. Some of these systems are oriented toward use with a specific DBMS package. Others are general-purpose systems. For large systems there should be a data-base administrator (DBA) who

is responsible for maintenance of the data collection, the data dictionary, and the programs used to maintain both. [See (Weldon, 1981) for a
review of data dictionary systems and a definition of the tasks of the
data administrator.]

Data-Usage Specification

During information-system design, an information matrix was developed
for the processes of the information system and their information requirements, identifying the information elements used as input, the elements produced, the frequency of execution of the process, the volume
of data processed, and the type of data access required. (See Chapter 5,
Figure 5.8 and the accompanying discussion.) In data-system design,
this matrix is extended to become the basis for data-usage specification.

The first step in preparing a data-usage matrix for an automated system is to extract from the information matrix those processes that are
to be included and their requirement specifications. The resulting
process set must be analyzed to determine which processes (if any) are
to be grouped into programs. Each row of the data-usage matrix will
then describe the data requirements for a program.

The data element usage specifications define the manner in which
each program uses the data. Here the I (input) and O (output) indicators from the information matrix are replaced with the following usage
codes (examples refer to Figure 8.5):

- K: Key, or primary key, indicates that this program uses this data
  element as the unique identifier for a set of elements, normally a
  record. For example, values of the data element S# are key
  values, or unique identifiers, for tuples in the *student* relation.

- S: Selector, or secondary key, is used to select those records for
  which this data element has a common, given value. For example,
  the data element *address* could be used as a secondary key to
  select those students (tuples) with a common value for this
  attribute, for example, *Bergen*.

- R: Retrieve indicates that the data element is used for input or
  read-only data.

- M: Modify indicates that this program changes the value of this data
  element.

- A: Add new value indicates that the program adds new occurrences
  of this value. For example, a program to record data about new
  students will *add* these data to the file containing data on old
  students.

- D: Delete indicates that the program deletes data values from the data set or file. For example, a program dealing with graduated students might delete such student records from the active student file(s).

Figure 8.8 shows a data-usage matrix for the student AIS. The data-usage requirements for three programs are described: P-1, new student registration; P-2, grade recording; and P-3, generation of class rosters. Note that P-1 and P-2 use the student identification, *s-id*, as the key for identification of the actual student being processed. P-3 uses no unique key, but rather uses the combined elements ⟨*course, date*⟩ as a secondary key to select students from a particular class.

Figure 8.8 Data-Usage Matrix, Student AIS

Program[a]	Data Elements[b] 1 2 3 4 5 6 7 . . .		Processing Requirements[c]	AC-3	AC-4	AC-6
P-1	K A A A A A			1	D	10 s
P-2	K R K M M			1	D	10 s
P-3	R R R S S			35	G	6 hr
.						
.						
.						
No. of Users	3 3 1 2 3 1 3					
Prime Usage	K R — R S M M					

a. Programs:
   P-1: New student registration
   P-2: Grade recording
   P-3: Generation of class rosters
b. Data Elements:
   1: s-id   student identification
   2: name   ⟨last name, first name⟩
   3: address   ⟨street, city, state, Zip code⟩
   4: faculty   of major field of study
   5: course   course identification
   6: grade   in course in element 5
   7: date   DDMMYY of grade assignment, element 6
c. Processing Requirements:
   AC-3: Volume of data required for one execution
   AC-4: Data access required
   AC-6: Response time from initiation to output
Note: AC-1, process priority; AC-2, processing frequency; and AC-5, processing type, are not included in this example.

The data elements in the matrix may be atomic, such as *s-id*, or compound, such as *name*. Compound elements should be treated as units or atomic elements in the programs in which they are used. The data elements in the matrix need not be in any particular sequence. However, grouping those elements that relate to common entities will make the matrix easier for the human reader to interpret.

Because of space limitations, Figure 8.8 shows only three processing characteristics. AC-3 and AC-4 are repeated from the information matrix shown in Figure 5.8; AC-6 is new. The processing characteristics are particularly important in file design. To repeat and expand, the required processing characteristics are:

- AC-1: Priority of the program among the programs of the system.
- AC-2: Frequency of execution of the program within some common time unit, for example, per day, week, or month.
- AC-3: Volume of data records used during one execution of the program.
- AC-4: Data access required by the program: D, direct access to one record given its unique key value; G, group access to a set of records with a common data value for the selector keys (secondary keys); or S, serial or sequential access to all records of a given kind.
- AC-5: Processing type: M, manual, or A, automated; this will always be A for programs.
- AC-6: Response time that the users require, measured from the time the program is initiated until its results, output, are available.

The data-usage matrix provides a total picture of the data that the programs of the data system require and how these data are used. Whenever more than one program accesses the same data, there is a possibility of conflicting usage requirements. The matrix allows the system designer to evaluate the effect of various designs on the program set. The design that is best for the system can then be chosen. Summing the data-usage characteristics indicates which elements are important, that is, most frequently used, and which could possibly be used as primary and secondary keys. This information is the basis of file design.

SUMMARY

The purpose of developing a data model is to give the system designer a tool with which to record the entities, their attributes, and their interrelationships. The model is first used to communicate between the designer and the users of the system, so that all elements can be determined and usages ascertained. Thereafter, the model provides the foundation for specification of record, file, and data-base structures (see Chapter 9).

We have presented the three most common model types, network, hierarchic, and relational. There are many others. The network and hierarchic models concentrate on modeling the entities and those inter-relationships that are important to the information system. These models must be supplemented with a data dictionary that defines the attributes (data elements). The relational model concentrates on modeling the relationships between the attributes of the system. This model could well be supplemented by some graphic presentation of the entities and relationships determined for the system.

Finally, the data-usage matrix is an important tool for presenting the usage characteristics necessary for determining appropriate file and/or data-base structures.

KEY CONCEPTS

Attribute
Data definition
Data dictionary
Data dictionary system (DDS)
Data model
Data processing characteristics
Data system
Data-usage matrix
Graphic model

Entity
Functional dependency
Hierarchic model
Network model
Normalization
Relation
Relational model
Relationship
Tabular Model

DISCUSSION QUESTIONS

1. Define and give an illustration of each of the key concepts.
2. Discuss the specific tasks of data modeling. What information from earlier system analysis and design steps is required? Why is data modeling important?
3. What is a data model? What exactly is being modeled? Why?
4. Discuss the differences between graphic and tabular data models. Give examples of each. When is each model type preferable?
5. Define and give examples of 1:1, 1:N, and N:M relationships. How are each of these represented in the hierarchic, network, and rela-tional data models?
6. Discuss the differences between and application areas for hierarchic, network, and relational models.
7. Normalization is given as a set of rules for defining relations. Discuss how these rules apply to data modeling using hierarchic and network models.

8. What should the selection criteria be for a data model type? Why?
9. Which data characteristics are not captured in the data models defined here? Why are these characteristics required? Where should they be recorded?
10. Discuss the components of the data-usage matrix. How can the information captured here be used?

PROJECTS

1. Prepare a hierarchic, network, *or* relational model for your system. Supplement the model with a data dictionary and a data-usage matrix.
2. Prepare hierarchic, network, *and* relational models for your data system. Which model type fits your application best? Why? What adaptations were necessary when converting from one model to another?

RECOMMENDED READINGS

Bachman, C. W. "Data Structure Diagrams." *Data Base*, 1 (1969).
    This paper is generally considered the foundation paper for data modeling. The proposed network model is the basis for the CODASYL DBTG proposals for data-base structures.
Childs, D. L. "Feasibility of a Set-Theoretic Data Structure—A General Structure Based on a Reconstituted Definition of Relation." *Proc. IFIP Congress.* 68, North-Holland Publishers, 1968.
    This paper presents the relation concept for use in data definition. A basic paper.
Codd, E. F. "A Relational Model of Data for Large Shared Data Banks." *CACM*, 13 (1970), 377–387.
    Codd's work on using relations to define data bases, data manipulation languages, and data-base management systems is fundamental for much of the data-base research and implementation being done today.
Tsichritzis, D. C. and F. H. Lochovsky. *Data Models.* Englewood Cliffs, N. J.: Prentice-Hall, 1982.
    This book presents a common theoretical framework and concise discussion of the modeling techniques that are most widely advocated at present, including the basic hierarchic, network, and relational models.
Weldon, J. L. *Data Base Administration.* New York: Plenum Press, 1981.
    This book describes the tasks and tools of data-base administration, including data-base design, implementation, and management. Several commercially available DBMSs and data dictionary systems are presented and compared.

Chapter 9
Data Structures

INTRODUCTION

The data model provides the information needed to design storage structures for the data collection. Primarily these storage structures must support efficient data access for the program set of the information system. They must also be flexible enough to allow the data system to grow and to support changes in the information system.

The file structures discussed in this chapter are general types, available or implementable on any computer system. However, details of terminology and implementation can and do vary among different software and hardware systems. At this point in system design, one is still looking for a design that is optimal for a user, but the user is now considered to be an application programmer who can convert the end users' information requirement into a program that uses the machine efficiently.

In the literature on data structure design, a number of different terms are used. This is mainly a result of the parallel work of researchers and the individual machine and software vendors. The terms used in this text are generally understood, if not always used, within the data-structuring community. The basic terms used in this chapter are defined as follows.

Data Element A single data value with a reference name and descriptive characteristics, such as type (character, number, code) and length in characters or digits.

Data Item The reference name and set characteristics for the data elements describing an attribute; for example, the data item *student identification* may be characterized as a four-digit number whose value must be between 1 and 1000.

Field A storage location for one data element; for example, the storage space for a student identification number.

Record Type A set of data items to be grouped together for processing, normally defined as a specific sequence of fields, with field names and data item names equivalent; for example, a *student* record type can be defined as the sequence of field names (data items)

⟨stud–id, stud–name, stud–address⟩

Record (Physical) A storage location, made up of a sequence of fields, that will contain the data elements that describe some entity; for example, the storage area needed to contain the identification number, name, and address of one student (when using the record type previously defined).

File

1. The set of records of a single type containing the data elements that describe a set of entities; for example, a student file would contain one record for each student in the system.
2. The storage area required to contain a file.

Data Access The manner in which a program accesses the physical records of a storage file.

Data Base The storage area reserved for a set of interrelated record types.

The drawing in Figure 9.1 illustrates the relationship between the terms *field*, *record*, and *file*. It is important to differentiate between *occurrences* of data and *types*, which provide only reference names and structure. A file type is described by a name and (usually) its structure; a record type is described by its name and the names, in sequence, of its fields; and a field type is described by its name and such characteristics as its length and the type of data to be stored, for example, character or numeric data. Occurrences are actual data, organized according to the pattern specified by the type. Figure 9.1 also shows a record type and an occurrence of the record type.

ACCESSING DATA

The data access requirements for the whole data system must be analyzed before the record and file structures are designed. Such an analysis is also required before selection of a particular type of data-base technology. In the following section, we will discuss the structuring options open to the system designer and the tools that are currently available to help with the design tasks.

The data-usage matrix, presented in Chapter 8, contains the data-access requirements for each program. There are only three access modes:

Figure 9.1 Fields/Records/File

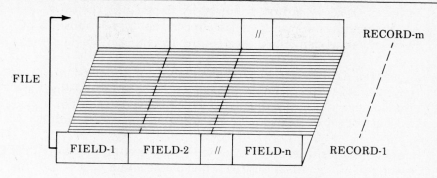

Field, Record, and File Relationships

<STUD-ID, STUD-NAME, STUD-ADDRESS>

Record Type: STUDENT

3331	TOM JONES	3 MAIN ST., BERGEN

Record Occurrence for Student 'Tom Jones'

- Serial or sequential access to *all* records, during which the program processes each record in some way
- Direct access to *one* record, where the processing program accesses only one record of the file
- Subset access to a related *group* of records, where the processing program accesses some subset of the data records, usually containing some common data value

Both direct access and subset access can be simulated through a serial search of the data. For a small volume of data, less than 1000 records, or an infrequently used, low-priority program, serial search may be the best strategy. The system designer must select file structures that support the data-access requirements of the most important, highest-priority programs.

Serial and Sequential Access

Serial and sequential access are two methods of accessing all the records of a file. We shall differentiate between serial and sequential access requirements as follows:

Serial Access Access to all the records of a file that has not been arranged in a predetermined order. The record that is physically first in the file is accessed first, followed by the second, the third, and so on. No assumptions can be made concerning the relationships between the data elements of one record and those of its neighbors.

Sequential Access Access to all the records of a file in some predetermined order. To maintain the sequential order, the records are arranged in a physical sequence in which the data values of a specified field or set of fields are in ascending or descending order.

Serial access is sufficient in cases in which "first-in, first-out" (FIFO) processing of all records is desired. Such a case could be an input file for the processing programs, or a data file kept in chronological order of receipt of data. Transactions to be charged to a set of accounts could be processed as a FIFO (serial) file.

Most statistical processing is independent of the sequence in which the data records are received. In the student AIS model, a program that calculates the average grade for all students would use serial access to the student file (assuming that grades are stored there).

Any file structure can be accessed serially.

Sequential access implies that the records of the file are ordered according to the ascending or descending values of some set of fields, called the sort key or sequence field(s). Processing programs can make use of this sequence during processing of the file.

Any file can be sorted into a sequential file. However, the file can only be sequential in terms of one sort key, which may be a composite key.

The telephone book is an example of a sequential file ordered by name. In our example, writing a program that would produce an alphabetical list of the student body would be simple if the student file were ordered alphabetically according to the last names of the students. If the file is not ordered in this way, a sequential file in the desired sequence must be prepared before the list can be printed.

Direct Access

Direct access implies that the processing program knows which record is required. Records that will be accessed directly usually contain a *key field* whose values can uniquely identify a single record. The processing program must then be able to recognize this key value and convert this knowledge into a record location within the file. Because names are not unique (there are pages of families named Smith in American telephone directories), an identification number is commonly added to the attributes recorded about entities so that specific individuals within the file set can be identified. Examples of such identifier attributes include Social Security numbers, policy numbers, account numbers, part numbers, and so on.

Special file structures that support direct access can be chosen. (See the section on direct-access file structures, pages 206–209.) Direct access can also be simulated, in small files, by using a serial search to locate the requested record.

Typical direct access queries would be, "What is the quantity of part #12345 on hand?" or "What is the balance in account #123-45-678?" In the student AIS model, a program to report the grades of a given student would preferably use direct access to the student file. The search key used should be a student attribute whose value is unique within the set of students. A suitable identifier could be a Social Security number (USA), a personal identification number (Scandinavia), or an enrollment number.

Subset Access

Subset access implies that the processing program requires only a subset of the records of a file and that there is some data value known to the program that identifies the group. The group identifier is normally an attribute of the entities that has a relatively small number of distinct values. Common group identifiers for persons include city or state of residence, age, profession, job type or department, education level, course participation, and so on. The processing program needs to know both the attribute(s) identifying the group and the desired value(s).

Special file structures that support subset access can be constructed. (See the section on subset file structures, pages 210–213.) The program may also simulate subset access by serially accessing each record and checking for membership in the group to be processed.

Examples of queries for subsets would be, "What parts are located in warehouse A?" or "Which accounts have a balance greater than $10,000?" An example of a program in the student AIS model that requires subset access would be one that calculates the average grade in a particular course. The course identification would be the group identifier attribute. If a grade record is defined as ⟨stud–id, course–id, grade, date⟩ (as in the *courses taken* relation in Figure 8.6), this program could calculate the average course grade by selecting those records that contain the correct course identification value.

RECORD STRUCTURES

A record type is given as a list of data items used to describe a set of similar entities, for example, students. A record structure is defined as the set of fields used to store the attribute values of a record type. (See Figure 9.1.)

Normally, there will be a direct mapping from a record type to its record structure; that is, there is one record structure per record type, with the record structure containing a single field for each data item of the record type. However, in some file types (for example, linked structures) or data bases, the record structures may contain fields for data other than the attribute values, such as pointers. (See page 211 and Figure 9.7.) It is also possible to define more than one record structure for the data items of a record type.

In most applications, a minimum record structure will consist of at least two fields: one that contains the identifier value for a single entity, and the other(s) that contain the descriptive attribute value(s).

Research in data structuring, particularly research in developing relational data models, points toward two basic principles for defining record structures:

1. Each record structure should contain at least one field for the data item each of whose values uniquely identifies one record occurrence. This data item and its field are termed the *primary key* for the record type and record structure, respectively.
2. All other fields for the data items of the record type should be such that their values are uniquely determined given the value of the key field; that is, if only the key field value is given, all other values for the record occurrence can be identified.

For example, we can define a record type and record structure to represent data about students. The primary key can be named *stud-id* with values of Social Security numbers, which are assumed to be unique within the population. Other data items describing a student could include name, address, age, height, and weight. These data items are dependent items, since the values of each can be determined for an individual if the primary key value is known. However, a grade data item will not be uniquely identified by the *stud-id* value alone, since, assuming that a student can receive many grades, it is also necessary to know the course id.

Using guideline 2 will ensure that each record type in a data system contains only those data items that describe one entity type in the object system. It has been shown (Codd, 1970) that this will help in maintaining data integrity within the data system. Using this principle, the student AIS will have separate record types, and thus separate files, to represent students, teachers, courses, grades, and so on. (See also the data models of Chapter 8.)

The data-usage matrix can be used as a tool for determining the record types and structures the system requires. The matrix identifies the data items required by each program and indicates all the data-item combinations (candidates for record structures) used in the system. As an illustration, Figure 9.2 repeats and expands the data-item usage section of the data-usage matrix of Figure 8.8.

Obtaining record structures from the data-usage matrix involves three steps:

1. Grouping related data items
2. Selecting primary keys
3. Reducing record structures to processing units

The first step is grouping related data items, those data items that describe the same entity. Some data items can describe more than one entity; for example, an address can be an attribute of a student, his or her house, or his or her school. The system designer must decide which record structures are to contain these items. One choice is to repeat the item in each of a number of record structures. This will cause data

Figure 9.2 Data-Usage Matrix—Data-Item Usage

Program[a]	Data Items[b]									
	1	2	3	4	5	6	7	8	. . .	
P-1	K	A	A	A	A		A			: K = Primary key
P-2	K	R			K	M	M			: S = Group key
P-3	R	R		R	S		S			: R = Retrieve
P-4	K	R	R	R	K	R	R	R		: A = Add
⋮										: M = Modify
No. of Users	4	4	2	3	4	2	4	1		
Prime Usage	K	R	R	R	K	M	M	R		

a. Programs:
  P-1 : New student registration
  P-2 : Grade recording
  P-3 : Generation of class rosters
  P-4 : List transcript for one student
b. Data items : (See also Appendix C)
  1 : stud–id   5 : course–id
  2 : s–name   6 : grade
  3 : s–address   7 : date (of grade assignment)
  4 : faculty   8 : c–name (name of course)

redundancy, or multiple copies of data values, and increase data maintenance for these values. An alternative is to define a separate record structure for the item(s) used more than once and add reference *links* or *pointers* from the other record structures to the common item.

The record structure placement for data items used more than once will depend on the extent to which their values are modified (indicated in the data-usage matrix). For infrequently modified items, data redundancy may be best. This will keep related data items together in each record structure, thus facilitating data access. For frequently modified items, a single location will facilitate the update procedures and tend to ensure data integrity.

Often, multiply owned data items are actually descriptors of a relationship between entity types; for example, the grade attribute of student and course actually describes the event that a student has taken, and receives a grade for, a given course. In this case, a separate record type should be defined to describe the relationship. The multiply used data item will then be a part of the relationship record structure.

In our example we can define three entities, students, courses, and grades, where the grade entity actually describes the $M:M$ relationship between students and courses. Figure 9.3 illustrates three possible record types for this system. Note that the data item *faculty* is used in the student record to describe the "faculty for major field of study" and in the course record to give the "faculty responsible for the course." The *grade* record type also contains repeated data items, *stud-id* and *course-id*. These are used as *links* to the student and course record types, respectively, for the student and the course for which the grade applies.

The second step in record structure definition is to determine which data item(s) can be used as the primary key. The first condition is that the item(s) be known to be an identifying attribute associated with the entity. For example, a name is such an externally known attribute, whereas weight is not. The data-usage matrix indicates those data items whose values are used by the programs to select record occurrences, that is, those data items with usage code K (selection of a single record occurrence) or S (selection of multiple record occurrences that contain the same value for the S attribute). These data items are possible key

Figure 9.3 Record Types for Student AIS Model

Student: ⟨stud-id, s-name, s-address, faculty⟩
Course: ⟨course-id, c-name, faculty⟩
Grade: ⟨stud-id, course-id, grade, date⟩

---

items. K access indicates that unique identification of a single record occurrence is required, and the data item is then a candidate for primary key.

In the case of records describing natural entities, such as people, organizations, or objects, there will usually be a unique identifier that can be used as the primary key; if not, one must be constructed. The primary key need not be a single data item, but should be the smallest possible set of data items whose values can uniquely identify a single entity as described by its record occurrence. The record types that describe interentity relationships will usually have a composite primary key made up of the primary keys of the related entities. The primary keys for our example are:

> Student: stud–id
> Course: course–id
> Grade: stud–id, course–id

Finally, the record structure must be analyzed for possible reduction into smaller units. In actual systems, there are often 100 or more data items of interest to the information system for record types that describe natural entities. However, the individual programs and their end users seldom require more than a small subset of these, perhaps only 5. To save transmission and processing time, as well as to reduce possibilities of error and misuse, it is important to determine whether the record type can be represented by multiple record structures made up of groups of fields that are used together. For example, in a full student administration system, defining a number of different types of students might be practical:

- academic, with data items describing academic status
- financial, with data items describing financial status
- sports, with data items describing participation in sports

FILES AND FILE STRUCTURES

A file contains the record occurrences of a single record type. The unit of access for a file is a record. A file structure is created by ordering the records of a file in a way that facilitates access. File structures may be simple, with only user data stored, or complex, with control data in the form of indexes and/or links embedded with the user data.

Many specific file structures have been developed for individual data systems or for general data processing types. These structures can be grouped into four types:

1. Serial and sequential structures
2. Direct access structures
3. Indexed structures
4. Subset structures

We will present each of these basic structures and discuss the types of data access for which it is most suitable. For a more extensive presentation of file structures, see Martin (Martin, 1977).

Serial and Sequential File Structures

Serial and sequential file structures may be used to support access requirements for all or a majority of the data in the file.

Serial file structures are the simplest structures available. The record order of the file is determined by the sequence in which the records were entered when the file was created. Once the file has been generated, there is no sequence implied by the order of the records.

In a serial file, the record that is physically first is accessed first, followed by the second, the third, and so on.

This structure is useful for any file for which chronological sequence is important, such as incoming messages, outgoing messages, transactions logs, or audit trails. The structure is also sufficient for data to be used in any statistical processing.

A serial file structure can be transformed into a *sequential* file structure by ordering the sequence of the records of the file according to ascending or descending values of one or more fields. The process of ordering the records is called *sorting*. The *sort key* is made up of the field(s) selected for determining the record sequence.

A sequential file is accessed the same way as a serial file, that is, the first physical record is accessed first, then the second, third, and so on. However, the program using the data can also use the fact that the records received are in some predetermined order.

The sequential file structure is used for ordered transaction input, reports, and multiple record updating programs.

Figure 9.4 illustrates a serial/sequential file. Note that the file is a sequential file for those programs that know that it is ordered by student name. For all other programs, there is no order, and the file must be processed as a serial file.

Direct-Access File Structures

Direct-access file structures are created to support direct data-access requirements, that is, the need to gain access to one particular record

Figure 9.4 Serial/Sequential File Structure

Rec.no.	< s-id,	name,	course,	other data ...>
1	1234	: ADAM	: SAD	:
2	5678	: BRUCE	: DB	:
3	9012	: CLARK	: SAD	:
4	3456	: DAVID	: DB	:
5	7890	: ERIK	: PLC	:

Serial structure according to primary key 's-id'.
Sequential structure according to sort-key 'name'.

in the file. Direct access is sometimes called *random access* to emphasize the fact that the requests for individual records are in no particular order.

In a direct-access file structure, each record is stored at a location calculated from the value of its primary key. All programs referencing the file must know this *transformation algorithm*, as it must be used to calculate the initial storage address and all reference addresses for the records.

The transformation algorithm takes each primary key value and converts (transforms) it into a relative record address (RRA). The RRA is a number between 1 and M, where M is the number of storage locations in the file. A direct-access file normally requires more storage space than the actual number of data records because:

1. Most primary key value sets are not sequential numbers from 1 to N, where N = number of data records.
2. There is no transformation algorithm that can make them into such a sequence set.

This implies that a direct-access file will require more storage area than a serial or sequential file to store the same data.

Another problem with the transformation algorithm is that it can produce the same RRA from two different primary key values. Records with a common RRA are called *synonyms*, and their storage requires the use of overflow areas, free (empty) areas within the direct file for the storage of new and/or synonym records. There are a number of strategies for storing synonym records, one of which must be selected and become part of the transformation algorithm.

Figure 9.5 illustrates a direct-access file structure. The transformation algorithm here takes the last digit of the primary key plus 1 as the RRA. Note that this results in all keys ending in 0, 1, 2, etc., becoming synonyms. Space for these synonyms can be allocated by multiplying the last digit by the number of keys expected to have common last digits. The synonym placement algorithm could then use the calculated RRA to start a serial search for the requested record or space for a new one.

To access a direct-access file, the user program must present the primary key value for the desired record to the transformation algorithm. Note that a direct-access file may also be accessed through a serial-access routine. This routine must test for empty records, that is, records with no valid data.

Figure 9.5 Direct-Access File Structure

Rec.no.	< s-id,	name,	course,	other data ...>
1	7890	: ERIK	: PLC	:
2				
3	9012	: CLARK	: SAD	:
4				
5	1234	: ADAM	: SAD	:
6				
7	3456	: DAVID	: DB	:
8				
9	5678	: BRUCE	: DB	:
10				

Transformation algorithm:
RRA = last digit of primary-key value plus 1.

Direct-access files are useful when only one record at a time is used for processing and when the key value for that record is known. On-line processing systems, such as bank account service systems, typically use this type of structure. To write reports from a direct-access file, the file must be processed the same way as a serial file.

Indexed File Structures

Indexed file structures are created to support both direct and sequential data-access requirements; that is, they support data processing systems in which the direct-access requirement and the sequential-access requirements have relatively equal priority.

An indexed file structure consists of two or three parts:

1. The prime data area, containing the user data ordered as a sequential file and divided into physical blocks with some constant number of records
2. The index area, containing an index to each of the data blocks in the prime data area
3. (optional) An overflow area, containing free space for storage of new (since the creation of the file) records

The data within the prime area blocks are kept in strict sequential order. The blocks themselves may be kept in sequential order or may be ordered through the index.

The index contains one entry (record) for each block. This entry contains the highest key value within the block and the block address within the prime data area.

New records may be introduced into the file in two ways. One way is to add the new record to the overflow area and indicate a block overflow in the index by adding the overflow address. Another, and preferable, way is to add the new record in its sequential place within the prime area block. If there is no room, a new block is taken from the overflow area, and the records of the original block plus the new record are divided between the two blocks. A new index entry is made for the new block.

Figure 9.6 illustrates an indexed file structure for which the prime data block size is two records. The index is built on the key *name.* Note that the indexed data item *must* also be the sort key for the sequence of the file.

To access the indexed file directly, the user program must present the primary key value of the desired record. The index is then searched sequentially for the entry that indicates the block in which the requested record is stored. This block is then searched sequentially for the desired record.

Figure 9.6 Indexed-Sequential File Structure

INDEX FILE		Rec.no.	DATA FILE			
Key	Address		< s-id,	name,	course,	...>
BRUCE :	1	1	1234	: ADAM	: SAD	:
DAVID :	3	2	5678	: BRUCE	: DB	:
ERIK :	5	3	9012	: CLARK	: SAD	:
		4	3456	: DAVID	: DB	:
		5	7890	: ERIK	: PLC	:

Index and Prime data area sequenced on sort-key 'name'.
Prime data area block size = 2 records.

Indexed access files are useful when both processing of one record at a time with known key value and sequential processing are required. On-line processing systems with major report generation requirements typically use indexed-sequential files.

Subset File Structures

Subset file structures are created to support group access requirements, where the group or record subsets are identified by a common data-item value. The group or subset identifier, referred to as a *secondary key*, is a data item or set of data items whose values occur repeatedly throughout the file. For example, the *city* data item of an address could be used to select subsets of persons by their city of residence.

There are two types of file structures that support group access:

1. Linked file structures, also called list, multi-list, or chained structures, in which control fields are added to the individual records of the file. A control field contains a *pointer* to the next record of the subset, thus linking records with common data values.
2. Inverted file structures, in which a separate directory is established. The directory is a file in which each record contains a list of pointers for each subset in the main data file.

Linked file structures append to the basic record structure, with a pointer area giving the record structure:

⟨⟨data-item list⟩⟨pointer area⟩⟩

A *pointer* is a field whose data value is an address—in our context, an address to a record within a file. Note that a pointer address is actually a relative record address like that used for direct-access files. In a linked file structure, the pointer addresses the next record containing the same value for the secondary key as the current record. Normally, there will be one pointer for each data item that is the basis for subset access.

For example, suppose that we have defined the student record as follows:

$$\langle\langle \text{stud--id, s--name, city, current-course}\rangle\langle \text{pt.1, pt.2}\rangle\rangle$$

We could use the pointer field *pt.1* for pointers joining student records with the same city value, and *pt.2* for pointers connecting students taking the same course.

Implementation of a linked file is illustrated in Figure 9.7. Here the secondary key is *course* and there are three groups or subsets illustrated: SAD, DB, and PLC, one for each value of the course data item. Remember, the pointer contains the address of the next group member. The last record of the group is indicated by a pointer with the value 0.

There are a number of variations of the linked file structure. First, there may be more than one pointer for the subsets of one data item. The second pointer for a group gives the address of the *prior* record in the group; this is useful when records are added to and deleted from the subset frequently. A third pointer can be introduced to point to the first record of the set. This is useful when there are many large sets with many member records and when processing requires that records that are members of multiple sets be identified. Alternatively, the last pointer of a chain may contain the address of the first record rather than 0, thus creating a ring structure.

Finally, the first record of a subset may not be a data record at all, but a control record whose data items describe the subset. The control record contains such data items as

        ⟨subset-data-item-name, subset-data-value,
        #records in subset,
        first-rec.address, last-rec.address.⟩.

For example (from Figure 9.7),

            ⟨course, SAD, 2, 1, 3⟩

The set of control records describing each of the subsets of the file are collected into a directory area, normally at the beginning of the

Figure 9.7 Subset File Structures

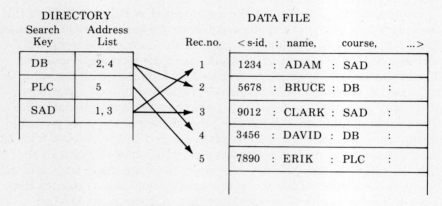

Rec.no.   < s-id,   name,   course,   ...> <pointers>

1	1234	: ADAM	: SAD	:	3
2	5678	: BRUCE	: DB	:	4
3	9012	: CLARK	: SAD	:	0
4	3456	: DAVID	: DB	:	0
5	7890	: ERIK	: PLC	:	0

Linked File Structure

DIRECTORY   DATA FILE

Search Key	Address List		Rec.no.	< s-id,	: name,	course,	...>
DB	2, 4		1	1234	: ADAM	: SAD	:
PLC	5		2	5678	: BRUCE	: DB	:
SAD	1, 3		3	9012	: CLARK	: SAD	:
			4	3456	: DAVID	: DB	:
			5	7890	: ERIK	: PLC	:

Inverted File Structure

Linked file: 3 chains on group key 'course'.
Inverted file: 3 directory entries for group key 'course'.

file. This directory will then be searched first to locate the start of the requested subset(s).

Inverted file structures extend the directory records of the linked file so that each record contains the pointers for the entire subset. This eliminates the need for *prior* and *first* pointers. It also eliminates the need to extend the data record structure definition. Note that this does not save space, as the pointers are merely moved to the directory records.

The inverted file structure is illustrated in Figure 9.7. There are actually two files in this structure type, the directory and data files. Each can be implemented with a separate structure. The data file is commonly implemented as a direct-access, serial file with access through the directory. This reduces directory maintenance when new records are added to the file. The directory file could be sequential on the search key values, or indexed-sequential if the number of values is large.

Accessing either the linked or the inverted file structure requires locating the first record of the requested subset. Each successive record is then retrieved using the subset pointer in the current record for a linked file, or the directory for an inverted file.

Both of these structures support group access requirements (selection of subsets of records based on some common data value). In both, access to a single record requires a serial search. Both require special maintenance routines for the pointer sets. The linked file structure has been preferred for systems whose subsets can be predetermined and predefined, and also for systems where the typical search query normally involves one key value: for example, "Find those students taking SAD."

The inverted file structure facilitates support of unpredictable queries, that is, those that are not known when the system is designed. The structure is also good for the type of data search for which multiple secondary keys are given: for example, "Find those students from Bergen who are taking the SAD course."

DATA BASES

In medium-sized data systems there are typically fifteen to twenty files representing multiple interrelated entity types. The application-program logic maintains the interentity relationships through knowledge of common data items stored in separate files. Experience has shown that such file systems contain large amounts of redundant data, are difficult to maintain, and are inflexible in terms of accommodating changes in the information-system requirements.

A main cause of these problems has been that there is usually no central data administration program for the file system. Thus the separate application programs have had to maintain the interrelationships and the file structures. When new data structures and/or data expansion (more data types) are required, it has been easier to create a new file, repeating existing data where necessary, than to update each of the application programs that use the affected file.

The objective of data-base management systems has been to create a data administration system that will alleviate these problems. The principal goals for a DBMS are:

1. to provide general data administration facilities separate from the application programs.
2. to provide data independence by freeing the application programs from knowledge of and responsibility for the physical structures of the data.
3. to reduce data redundancy by giving each data element a single location.

In our discussion, we will use the following definitions for a data base and a data-base management system. Data administration systems that do not recognize, implement, and maintain interfile (inter-record type) relationships are called *file management systems*.

Data Base (DB)   This contains the record occurrences and inter-record relationship links for multiple interrelated record types. It encompasses the multiple files of a file system, and contains inter-record-type linkages.

Data-Base Management System (DBMS)   A software system that provides data access and structure maintenance for a data base.

The actual physical structure of a data base is designed by a *data-base administrator* (DBA), taking into account the logical design for desired data structures and the structure possibilities supported by the DBMS. In a data base, linked file structure techniques are commonly used to connect records of the same type. Interrecord-type relationships can be implemented by linking records of differing types.

The system designer is responsible for providing the DBA with the preferred logical design for the data base. This logical design must indicate which record types and interrecord-type relationships are required by the users and should thus be supported in the data base. The logical design should be presented as a data model, network, hierarchic, or relational (see Chapter 8).

A data model can also be used to describe the physical structures of the data base. Commercial DBMSs assume a specific data model and use this model as a pattern for the layout of the data base. The model type used is reflected in the name of the DBMS; thus, there are network, hierarchic, and relational DBMSs. We will review the structures used in these DBMS types very briefly. Readers are encouraged to consult one of the many books on data-base management systems for a more detailed discussion and presentation of individual systems; for example, (Date, 1981; Martin, 1977; Tsichritzis, 1977).

Network Data Bases

The most common storage structure used for network data bases is the linked file. The occurrences of each record type are linked together. In addition, interrecord-type relationships, called *sets*, are named and implemented, using pointers in the related records. Figure 9.8 illustrates a storage structure that could be used for the student ⟷ course data. (See also Figure 8.2 and the discussion on network models in Chapter 8.)

Figure 9.8 Network Data Base, Student AIS Model

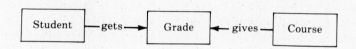

Network Model of Record Types

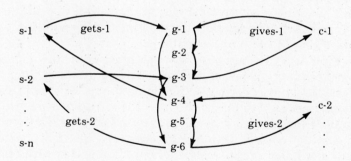

Network Model of Record Occurrences*

*Record Structures:

	Data	Pointers
STUDENT	<< s-id, . . . >	< next-s, first-grade >>
GRADE	<< grade, . . . >	< next-grade, next-for-s, next-for-c >>
COURSE	<< c-id, . . . >	< next-c, first-grade >>

A relationship between two record types is called a *set* and is represented graphically by an arrow. By convention, the record type at the base of the arrow is called the *owner* of the set. The record type at the point of the arrow is called the *member* of the set. Two sets, *gets* and *gives*, are illustrated in Figure 9.8. The record types *student* and *course* are owners of the sets *gets* and *gives*, respectively. The *grade* record type is a member of both these sets. There are no restrictions on the number of sets in which a record may participate.

There will be one set occurrence for each record occurrence of the owner record type. That is, there will be as many sets of type *gets* as there are students registered within the data base. Each set may have 0, 1, or many members. A set occurrence is *empty* if there are no member record occurrences. In our example, the record describing a new student would be the owner of an empty *gets* set, since presumably no grades would have been given at initial registration time.

Two set occurrences for each of the set types *gets* and *gives* are illustrated in Figure 9.8. Here course *c-1* has given the grades *g-1*, *g-2*, and *g-3*. These four records constitute the set occurrence *gives-1*. Also, student *s-1* has received the grades *g-1* and *g-4*. These three records constitute the set occurrence *gets-1*.

Note that there will be one set of pointers for each relationship in which a record participates, in addition to the pointers that link records of the same type. Thus, each of the grade records will have two pointer sets to represent the sets *gets* and *gives*. In the network model of record occurrences in Figure 9.8, the pointers to "next of same kind" have been omitted for clarity. As with linked file structures, a pointer set for a relationship may include, in addition to a *next* pointer, a *prior* and/or an *owner* pointer.

To access a network data base, the user must know the names of the records and relationships represented in the DB. The user then navigates to the desired record occurrence by naming the records, sets, and data-item values connected to (along the path to) the desired record(s). A network DBMS provides a data manipulation language (DML) that the user can employ to state his or her data requests. The DML generally consists of a number of statements designed to be used with (embedded in) a host programming language such as COBOL or PL/1. The basic DML statements allow access to one record at a time; the next record may be of the same type or a related record accessed via a named set.

The CODASYL committee (CODASYL, 1971, 1978) developed specifications for a network DBMS, which have been used in the development of most commercially available DBMSs.

Hierarchic Data Bases

The principal hierarchic data-base structure is a *tree*, defined as those records related to one root record occurrence. Within a tree, the records are ordered according to their defined hierarchic sequence. There will be one DB tree for each root record occurrence. The full DB is the collection of all trees.

Hierarchic sequence is defined by the tree nodes from top to bottom and from left to right. Maintaining this hierarchic sequence is the goal of the storage structure. Figure 9.9 illustrates the hierarchic sequence for the tree defined by the root node A. Here, A has three second-level components, B, C, and D. The B node has a subtree consisting of E and F; the C node has one subcomponent, G. The hierarchic sequence for this tree is $\langle A, B, E, F, C, G, D \rangle$.

In the simplest hierarchic data bases, sequential structuring techniques are used to maintain the hierarchic sequence. Each tree is considered to be a data-base record and contains all the records directly related to one root record occurrence. These are ordered in strict hierarchic sequence, as illustrated in Figure 9.10. This figure illustrates a storage structure that could be used for the data modeled in Figure 8.3.

Hierarchic sequential storage structures are effective when the processing requirements are for whole trees. However, this structure cannot support efficient processing of any other access type. A number of techniques are used to improve support for different access requirements. Most common is the generation of a DB index of pointers to the data records. These index pointers are kept in hierarchic sequence, thus

Figure 9.9 Hierarchic Sequence

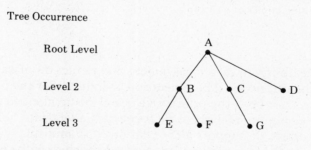

Tree Occurrence

Root Level

Level 2

Level 3

Hierarchic Sequence: A, B, E, F, C, G, D

Figure 9.10 Hierarchic Data Base, Student AIS Model

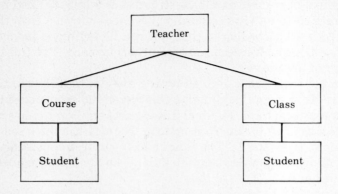

Hierarchic Model of Record Types

T-1	c-1	s-1	s-2	—	s-j
	c-2	s-k	s-1	—	s-m
	cl-1	s-r	s-s	—	s-t
T-2	—				

Hierarchic Model of Record Occurrences

NOTE: Hierarchy implemented by physical adjacency.
The student record sets *s-1* to *s-j*, *s-k* to *s-m*, and *s-r* to *s-t* may overlap, or contain repeated copies of a record.

allowing flexibility in record placement and reduction of data redundancy at the leaf nodes. The generation of indexes for the individual record types, for both the primary keys and group identifiers, allows individual and group records to be processed independent of the hierarchic structure. To support $M:M$ relationships, multiple hierarchic data bases with the possibility for cross-referencing can be established. (Refer to Figure 8.4.)

The simple hierarchic structure, with sequential storage of the data records, requires little system-generated data for pointers and/or indexes. As the hierarchic structures are elaborated to support multiple access requirements, their complexity and the quantity of control data required increases. A hierarchic DB with maximum flexibility will require control data comparable to those of a network DB.

To access the hierarchic data base, the user must know the placement of the desired record type(s) within the defined hierarchy. The access path is defined as the sequence of *owner* records from the root record to the desired one. Hierarchic DBMSs offer the user a DML for expressing access requirements similar to that of the network DBMS.

IBM's IMS is a complex hierarchic DBMS and one of the major systems on the market. There are also a number of other simpler hierarchical DBMSs available for both IBM and competitors' equipment. The major criticism of hierarchic DBMSs is their difficulty in supporting or total lack of support for $M:M$ relationships. IMS meets this criticism by supporting multiple interrelated DBs.

Relational Data Bases

The most common storage structure used for relational data bases is a set of direct files, one for each relation. The storage location of the tuples (occurrences) of each relation (record type) is calculated from the primary key. Interrelation (interrecord-type) relationships, actually also relations, are represented through the key values of the related relations. These values may be stored as attributes of one of the relations, or a separate relation may be implemented. Pointers, as used in linked file structures, are not used. However, most systems allow indexes of the type used with inverted file structures to be constructed to facilitate subgroup selection. Figure 8.7 illustrates a possible storage structure for the student ⟷ course model. There would be three direct-access files, and there could be secondary indexes for *address* and *grade*.

There is no requirement that the relational DB be implemented as a set of direct files, one for each of the relations of the relational model. Another storage technique is to create a file for each of the columns of the relations. The order of the records (actually the attribute values) is maintained so that the individual tuples of the relation can be reconstructed. This storage strategy is called *transposed files*. It is very efficient for relations with many attributes (more than 15) and individual user requirements for only a few of these attributes (fewer than 5). A somewhat more flexible variant of this method is to construct binary tuples, where the relation key is stored with the attribute.

To access a relational data base, the user must know the names of the attributes and relations in the DB. The user then specifies the desired relation by identifying a combination of attributes, or giving the relation name if it has been previously defined. A table of tuples for the defined relation is returned to the user for processing. A relational

DBMS provides a data manipulation language through which the user can state data requests. Statements in this language allow for definition of the relation to be processed and processing specifications for operations on the whole table or some subset of it. The relational DML may be designed to be used with (embedded in) a host programming language such as COBOL or PL/1, or it may be a complete language in its own right.

A number of relational DBMSs are available. The one illustrated here is System-R from IBM.

DATA STRUCTURE DESIGN TOOLS

The design or selection of appropriate storage structures for a data system involves matching the processing requirements with the file or data-base access support. A great deal of research has been done on determining the characteristics of file structures and developing algorithms that will match access requirements with storage structures.

As of 1982, there were commercially available a relatively small number of automated systems for evaluating processing requirements and proposing data structures. The best of these are those data dictionary/directory (DD/D) systems that collect the data required for designing physical data bases and produce a DBMS schema. Unfortunately, much of the logical design process is still left to the system designer, with no tools other than a particular design methodology.

The designer must decide whether to select a file or data-base system. This decision must be made on the basis of the complexity of the data requirements. Some guidelines:

- A system with fewer than 5 loosely related entity types and a low level of concurrent processing can normally be well served by a file system.
- Systems with many (more than 50) programs or queries to the data where data access is varied and complex (with multiple selection criteria used) and many (more than 10) entity types will be best served by a DBMS.
- Systems where the number of users, applications, and data types is expected to grow will be best served by a DBMS.

Selecting a File Structure

Each of the file structures outlined provides access support for one or possibly two access types. Usually a data system will require all types of data access: sequential, direct, and group. Selecting one file structure for the data means giving preference to that (those) program(s) with a data access requirement that is supported by that file structure. Remember that both direct and group access can be simulated by a serial or sequential search of the file. This "only" costs time.

Table 9.1 rates the file structures on a number of data processing characteristics. Once the designer knows the processing requirements, indicated by the data-usage matrix, this table should help him or her to select an appropriate file structure. The grades given in the table indicate the relative support for the processing requirement within the file structure. A structure rated A is better than one rated B. A rating of D indicates that the facility is not supported or is very difficult and/or time-consuming.

Selecting a DBMS

Although there are many DBMSs available, one major constraint may reduce and/or eliminate the choice. The system must function on the available computer.

All DBMSs (as previously defined) can administer interrelated data. Therefore, the choice should depend not so much on the model type as on the user interface provided. The designer should give preference to the DBMS that best supports the application and the intended users.

If the immediate DB users are application programmers, a DBMS with a programming language DML may be the best choice. Most network and hierarchic DBMSs that have been developed can use host programming languages. In general, a network DBMS will be more flexible (and easier to use) than a hierarchic DBMS.

If the intended users are not programmers, the DBMS must have an interactive DML through which the data processing requirements can be completely defined. Most relational DBMSs have been developed for this user group. Note, however, that some network and hierarchical DBMSs also have interactive languages for the casual user.

SUMMARY

We have introduced, briefly, the extended topic of data, record, file, and data-base structures. The system analyst must understand the implementation alternatives available for the data of the system being developed. Basic design guidelines include:

- Describe no more than one entity in a single record structure; provide a separate record structure for repeating groups.
- Define separate files for each record structure.

Table 9.1 File Characteristics

Processing Characteristics		File Structures				
	Serial	Sequential	Direct	Indexed Sequential	Linked	Inverted
1. Storage Media[1]	Tape	Tape	DASD	DASD	DASD	DASD
2. File Size[2]	N	N	$1.2N$	$1.2N$	$1.5N$	$1.5N$
3. Overflow Area	none	none	yes	yes	none	none
4. Single Record Access (avg.)	$N/2$	$\log(n)$	1	2	$N/2$	$N/2$
5. Group Access[3]	N	N	N	N	$M+1$	$M+1$
6. Single Record[4]	D	C	A	B	C	D
7. Group Access	D	D	D	D	B	A
8. Serial Access	A	A	B	A	B	A
9. Sequential Access	D	A	D	A	B	D
10. Key Modify	A	D	B	D	C	A
11. Data Modify	B	B	A	A	C	C
12. Addition	A	C	A	C	C	C
13. Deletion	B	C	A	C	C	C
14. Reorganization[5]	n.a.	B	n.a.	C	D	n.a.
15. Generation	A	B	B	C	D	D

1. DASD: direct access storage device.
2. N = number of data records in file. Actual file size = $N \times$ record length.
3. M = number of records in the group, commonly $.01N$.
4. Evaluations range from: A, file structure handles operation very well, to D, file structure handles operation poorly or with difficulty.
5. n.a.: not applicable for this file structure.

- For systems with few (less than 5) loosely or disconnected files, use a file management system for data administration.
- For systems with many (more than 5) interconnected record types, use a data-base management system for data administration.

KEY CONCEPTS

Data base (DB)
Data-base management system (DBMS)
Data element
Data item
Direct access
Direct file structure
Field
File
File structure
Hierarchic data base
Indexed-sequential file structure
Inverted file structure

Linked file structure
Network data base
Pointer
Primary key
Record
Record structure
Record type
Relational data base
Secondary key
Serial file structure
Sequential file structure
Transposed file structure

DISCUSSION QUESTIONS

1. Define and give an illustration or example of each of the key concepts.
2. What is the role of the data model in the design of data structures? How is the data-usage matrix used in structure design?
3. What types of data access are there? What structural features are required to support efficient access for each type?
4. Discuss the guidelines for construction of record types. What function does the primary key have? What other elements should be part of a record type?
5. Table 9.1 rates a number of characteristics of file structures. Discuss these ratings.
6. Describe the differences between hierarchic and network data bases; between network and relational data bases.
7. What criteria should be included in the choice of a DBMS?

PROJECTS

1. Design a file system for your project. Defend the selection of file structures. What improvements can be expected from use of a DBMS for your project?

2. Select one entity type from your project system. Describe the data accessing algorithms your processes require if the data are structured as a sequential, direct, indexed-sequential, linked, and inverted file.
3. Construct an instance-level model of a network data base for your system.

RECOMMENDED READINGS

Date, C. J. *An Introduction to Database Systems*. 3rd ed. Reading, Mass.: Addison-Wesley, 1981.
   Date gives a detailed discussion of two relational DBMSs, System R and Query by Example; IBM's hierarchical DBMS, IMS; and CODASYL's network DBMS proposal.
Martin, J. *Computer Data-Base Organization*. 2nd ed. Englewood Cliffs, N.J.: Prentice-Hall, 1977.
   Part II of this book, chapters 17 to 35, gives an extensive discussion of the physical storage structures available for computerized data.
Tsichritzis, D. *Data Base Management Systems*. New York: Academic Press, 1977.
   This book presents a number of central concepts and facilities of DBMSs, a general discussion of the three major system types (network, hierarchic, and relational), and a presentation of five commercially available systems.

Chapter 10
Process Specification

INTRODUCTION

The processing component of a data system consists of the formal processes and procedures that support or represent the information services and activities of the parent information system. A data system can be considered a functioning model of real-world activities. Our task is to ensure that this model, the data system, is as efficient and effective as possible.

In discussing the development of process specifications, we will use the following definitions of the terms *procedure*, *process*, and *program*.

Procedure A specified sequence of processes required to perform some information-system activity.

Process Those operations required to perform some unit of work, normally a subtask of an information-system activity.

Program An automated process or set of processes.

We assume that an information-system activity consists of some number of processes and that ordering these processes so that the activity can be executed satisfactorily is an information-system procedure. Within the data system, a procedure will typically define the sequence of processes and/or programs required to produce a response to an information processing request, for example, to generate the monthly payroll.

In nonautomated information systems, all procedures and processes are manually executed by an information clerk, who interprets the information request and then collects, processes, and presents the requested data.

In a CBIS, the tasks of the EDP operators and information clerks for activating programs and interpreting and/or post-processing data-system results are typically defined in terms of manual procedures. A CBIS, by definition, contains some number of automated processes, computer programs, which are executed according to the data-system procedures. Note that one program may represent several processes and thus also automate the part of the procedure that controls their execution sequence.

We have already discussed how to model the data component of the data system. We will now present some alternative ways of stating the specifications for the processes and programs. Note that, although we will concentrate on program specification, these specification techniques can also be used to describe manual processes.

Program and process descriptions are required at two stages, first for program design specification and then for documentation of the implemented program. The same presentation techniques can be used for both specification and documentation.

PROGRAM SPECIFICATION

We have already identified the processes of the information system, both those that exist (during system analysis) and those that are needed (during information-system design). The relationships between the processes, in sequence and component parts, have been described in the information graphs (see examples in Figures 5.7, 5.9, and 5.10). A verbal process definition, including an informal statement of the processing algorithm, exists in the process dictionary (Boxes 4.4 and 5.2). And finally, the data requirements for each process have been stated in the data-usage matrix (see example in Figure 8.8). What remains for a complete definition of the processes is a precise statement of:

1. which processes are to be grouped together into programs.
2. the algorithm(s) for each program.
3. the input data required to activate each program.
4. the points in the program where the stored data are used.
5. the output to be generated by each program.

A program can consist of multiple processes. The designer must determine which processes are so related that consolidating them into one program will make processing more efficient. Typically, processes that are closely related in execution sequence can be consolidated. A principal criterion is that a program perform a clearly identifiable function. A program will usually have a relatively simple input, perform a relatively simple set of processes on the input data and possibly stored data, and then produce a well-defined output. A number of programs should be defined for the data processing system.

The program algorithm defines the step-by-step operations the program must execute to perform its function. Programs should be made up of a series of modules, or subprograms, each of which performs some single task. Each module will operate according to its algorithm.

Chapter 7 discussed the design of the system input and output. Generally, getting from a specified input to the required output gives the external boundaries for a program. During program design, it may be necessary to modify the input/output design. However, the designer must take care not to reduce the legibility of either.

Chapters 8 and 9 discussed structures for the stored data. Program design specifies where in the separate programs these data are to be used. Programs for maintaining the data storage structures must also be developed. These programs should be separate from the programs that automate information-system activities.

There are a number of proposed forms for program algorithm specification. These forms can be classified as graphic, tabular, or verbal. Each specification form has problems: graphs tend to have uneven levels of detail; it is difficult to define the data flow in tables; verbal presentations tend to become too verbose, hiding structure. Since no one method has won general support (which might not be desirable), we will briefly present examples of each specification type. Note that there are many specific proposals, particularly for the graphic approach.

Individual organizations generally adopt a standard presentation form for the specification and documentation of their data systems. If the organization has no such standard, the designer is often advised to combine methods or to select a method that will be appropriate for the audience for the specification—for example, graphic presentation for end users, structured English for programmers, or tabular for automated program generators.

Graphic Presentations

Graphic program models are used to show data and program flow and/or program structure. There has been a standard for flowcharting programs since 1963 (ANSI, 1962, 1970). There has also been continual criticism of flowcharting, highlighting what flowcharts cannot easily express (Chapin, 1970). Perhaps the most important criticism is that flowcharting techniques do not force the designer to develop a well-structured design or establish clear program modules. Despite the criticisms, flowcharting, using the ANSI standard or some variant, remains a useful tool for expressing the flow of activities in a program.

Structured programming techniques emphasize top-down program design for specification of the program structure. The emphasis is on describing the processing algorithm as a set of subprocesses that can be implemented separately as program modules. Program flow is the sequence of execution modules, normally controlled by a control module. The structured approach forces the designer to define program modules. Often these can be implemented and tested separately, thus easing system maintenance.

The specification of both program flow and program modules is important for the development of good programs. A pragmatic approach to using graphic program specifications would be to use structured diagrams to identify the program modules, then use flowcharts to document the module algorithm(s).

Flowcharts

The primary objective of a flowchart is to clearly indicate the flow of the program algorithm, giving the order in which operations and program modules are performed and the tests and data included. There are separate flowchart symbols for processing, input/output transfers, decision points, and repetition of operations. Figure 10.1 shows the basic symbols used in an ANSI standard flowchart and gives some of the specialized processing symbols and some of the specialized symbols for data storage and media usage. See (ANSI, 1970) or (Chapin, 1970) for a more detailed presentation.

In general, a flowchart used for program specification should not use the specialized symbols for data storage, as these can be changed when the program is implemented or during program maintenance without changing the processing algorithm(s) specified at design time. A second

Figure 10.1 Flowcharting Symbols

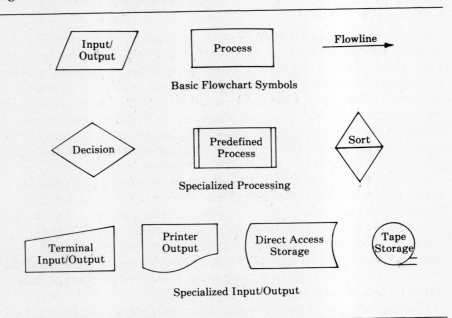

Courtesy ANSI (American National Standards Institute, Inc.), New York.

flowchart, documenting the implemented program, should include these data media symbols.

A good rule for developing a flowchart is to keep the separate pages neat and uncrowded. There should be no more than three columns of symbols, and two is preferable. The flow should be predominantly from top to bottom. Major program modules should be defined in separate charts, referenced from where they are used. Alternative processing should be documented on separate pages, referenced through connector symbols. Short, descriptive names should be used within the symbols. Further explanation should be given in a comments column on the same chart page.

Figure 10.2 illustrates a flowchart that documents an existing program. The chart is constructed to highlight data use. This is a strongly simplified (for reasons of space) example of a program to print the transcript for a given student. The program is named Grade Transcript. Program flow is given in the center column. The data used and the documentation of where these data are stored are given in the left-hand column. The type of data access is given in the comments column on the right.

Note the basic input-process-output (IPO) sequence of the flowchart in Figure 10.2. Using the IPO sequence allows program modules to be identified. Each module has a defined input, does some processing, and produces some output. Complex modules, containing many processes, can be detailed in a separate flowchart and could be implemented independently.

Structured Diagrams

The primary objective of a structured diagram is to illustrate the program structure and to identify relationships between the program modules. A structured diagram is developed in a top-down fashion, starting with the program or process identifier and major control module, then continuing with the major subprograms, their subcomponents, and so on until all system modules are defined.

Structured diagrams use three basic symbols to represent the basic program structures:

1. A sequence of operations
2. A repetition of operations
3. A selection between two (or more) processes

There are several proposed methods of presenting structured diagrams. Figure 10.3 gives the symbols used by M. A. Jackson (Jackson, 1975). In this approach the structured diagram is a hierarchical tree structure of symbols representing sequence, iteration, and task selection.

Figure 10.2 Flowchart Example

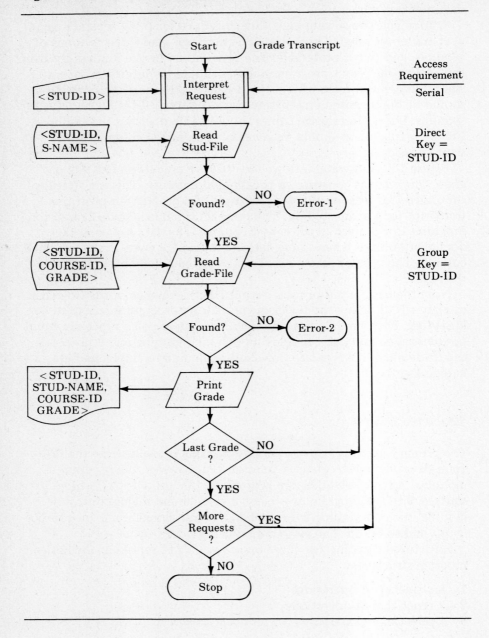

Figure 10.3 Structured-Diagram Symbols

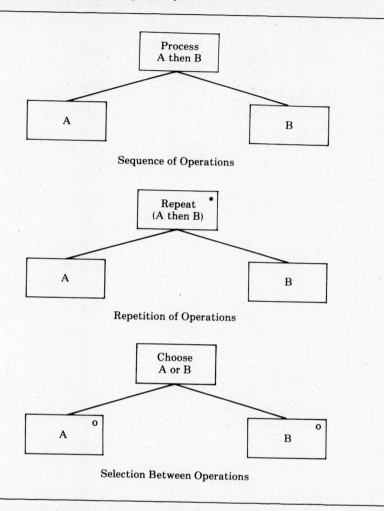

With permission from M. A. Jackson, *Principles of Program Design*, Academic Press, 1975. Copyright Academic Press (London) Ltd.

Each successive level of the diagram represents the subtasks of a higher (parent) level. The diagram is read and the program is to be processed in hierarchic sequence, from top to bottom, left to right. Figure 10.4 shows a structured diagram, using Jackson's symbols, for the same program used in Figure 10.2 (a program to print the transcript for a given student).

Figure 10.4 Structured-Diagram Example

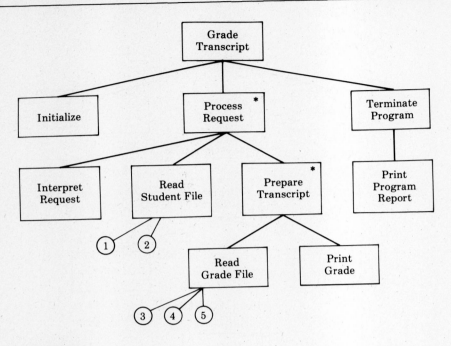

Conditions:
1. Direct access, key = STUD-ID.
2. Error if STUD-RECORD not found, exit.
3. Group access, key = STUD-ID.
4. Error if no grades found, exit.
5. If last grade, prepare for next student.

The form of the structured diagram can be seen in its levels, where level 0 identifies the program, level 1 contains the initiation and termination routines and the major processing initiator, level 2 gives details of level 1, and so on. Special operations or conditions that are relevant to particular tasks are explained through the circled references.

A diagram that uses a hierarchic structure tends to become very wide at the leaf nodes, particularly for medium to large processes (programs). In this situation, it may improve the presentation to use the structured approach to identify program modules, then use a flowchart to present the module algorithm. As a rule of thumb, a structured diagram could be developed for three or four levels of detail, with the explicit aim of identifying the program modules.

Decision Tables

A decision table is a tabular statement of the actions to be taken when given conditions are met. It is a tool specifically for describing decisions of the form "if A, then B," where A may be complex (a-1 *and* a-2 *and* a-3 . . .) and B may involve several tasks.

Decision tables have been used as a program design, implementation, and documentation tool for a long time. In the late 1950s, the first automated decision table processors were developed. These processors accept a decision table as input and produce program code for processing. By 1970, more than 30 different types of processors were in use in many application areas (McDaniel, 1970).

Figure 10.5 gives the basic form for a decision table. Each condition within the program or process that requires action is listed in the upper left quadrant. The decision rules are defined in the upper right quadrant. There must be a rule for each valid combination of conditions. Thus for two conditions there will be four rules, for three conditions, eight rules, and so on. In certain cases, a condition is valid only when some other condition is true; otherwise it is not an applicable condition under the decision rule definition. In this case, a symbol, such as "—," can be recorded in the decision table to indicate that the condition is not applicable. This will reduce the number of rules generated.

All possible actions are listed in the lower left quadrant, ordered in execution sequence. The actions required for each decision rule are indicated in the lower right quadrant by placing an X in the rule column

Figure 10.5 Decision Table Format

Condition Entries	Rules			
	1	2	3	. . .
C-1 C-2 · C-n		Conditions for Each Rule		
Actions				
A-1 A-2 · A-m		Actions for Each Rule		

opposite each selected action entry. Figure 10.6 presents a decision table for the program to print grades for one or more students (see Figures 10.2 and 10.4). The conditions defined for the process are: initialize (start), check for a valid student, process a grade record, and test for more transactions. Rule 1 defines the actions necessary for initialization, rule 2 defines the actions for processing a valid student. Rule 3 defines the actions for processing a grade record for a valid student, and so on. Note that the sequence of actions is serial, from top to bottom of the table; therefore it is necessary to include action 10, defined as "perform action 2."

The action list can be at any level of detail, from process or program names or tasks to program statements. The latter level has been implemented as a program generator.

The use of decision table generators for program development reduces data-system development time and later system maintenance, as changes are easy to make and their impact throughout the decision table can be easily seen. One possible reason that decision tables are not

Figure 10.6 Decision Table Example

Conditions	Rules							
	1	2	3	4	5	6	7	8
Start?	Y	N	N	N	N	N	N	N
Valid Student?	—	Y	Y	Y	—	—	N	N
Grade Record Found?	—	—	Y	N	—	—	—	—
More Transactions?	—	—	—	—	Y	N	Y	N
Actions	1	2	3	4	5	6	7	8
1. Open Files	X							
2. Read Student File	X							
3. Print Student Heading		X						
4. Read Grade File		X						
5. Print Grade Record			X					
6. Read Next Grade Record			X					
7. Print Grade Summary				X				
8. Read Next Transaction				X				
9. Print Error Message							X	X
10. Perform Action 2					X		X	
11. Close Files						X		X

more widely used in program development may be the lack of general information concerning them and/or locally available support systems.

Structured English

Much effort has been directed toward making computers "user friendly," which generally means making the communication languages and program specification tools as comprehensible as possible. English has been used to solve problems for centuries. The main problem with using English (or any other natural language) for program specification is its ambiguities. This is usually not critical when the recipient of the instructions is a human, familiar with the problem area. However, computers are notoriously dumb and require unambiguous statements as processing instructions.

A proposed method of making program specifications comprehensible without using graphs, charts, or tables is to use a highly structured form of English, called *structured English*. Algorithms written in structured English should be comprehensible to any interested person and at the same time specific enough for a programmer to code in some computer programming language.

Structured English program specifications follow the same construction rules as good structured programming and structured diagrams, that is, the program is described as a set of:

1. sequential instructions, using a command form with the verb first:

> ADD 10% to salary.
> PRINT salary.

2. repetition of instructions:

> REPEAT WHILE there are more customers.
> action-1, action-2, . . . action-*n* END.

3. selection of alternatives:

> IF condition
> THEN action-1, action-2, . . . action-*n* END.
> ELSE action-a, action-b, . . . action-*m* END.

Figure 10.7 shows the grade printing program specified in structured English. There are a number of proposed forms of statement structure, differing in the key words to be used and the numbering conventions, if any. A numbering system will help to identify the program modules. It is also good practice, when designing larger programs, to describe the main program structure and specify each module separately.

Figure 10.7 Structured English Example

---

1. INITIATE TRANSCRIPT PRINT PROGRAM.
2. REPEAT WHILE THERE ARE INPUT REQUESTS:
    2.1 READ INPUT REQUEST,
    2.2 READ REQUESTED STUDENT RECORD,
    2.3 IF STUDENT RECORD FOUND
        THEN REPEAT WHILE THERE ARE GRADE RECORDS:
        READ GRADE RECORD,
        PRINT GRADE RECORD,
        SUM GRADES,
        END REPEAT GRADE RECORD COLLECTION.
          WHEN NO MORE GRADES:
        CALCULATE AVERAGE GRADE,
        PRINT GRADE SUMMARY.
        ELSE PRINT "STUDENT RECORD NOT FOUND".
    END STUDENT TRANSCRIPT.
3. CLOSE FILES, PRINT FINAL REPORT.
END PROGRAM.

The use of structured English for program specification is intended to satisfy both the nontechnical user's need to be able to read and understand the program specifications and the programmer's need for detailed, unambiguous specifications. The price of this tool is the verbosity of natural language, and possibly hiding of the program structure.

Comparing Program Specification Tools

Table 10.1 presents a comparison of the tools previously presented. Three major criteria have been considered:

1. Ease of use for the designer
2. Ease of understanding for the user
3. Possibility of automated support

The primary function of program specification tools is as aids in the communication of program specifications and documentation to the user of the program, the implementer, and the system maintenance

Table 10.1 Comparison of Program Specification Tools

Application	Flowchart	Structured Diagram	Decision Table	Structured English
Ease of use:				
Number of symbols	Many	Few	Few	Many
Complexity	High	Low	Low	High
Logic presentation	Poor	Good	Moderate	Good
Program specification	Good	Good	Very good	Good
Ease of interpretation:				
Legibility	Moderate	Good	Moderate	Good
Logic verification	Poor	Good	Very good	Good
User verification	Poor	Good	Good	Moderate
Automated support:				
Machine-readable	Moderate	Moderate	Very good	Good
Machine-editable	Moderate	Moderate	Very good	Good
Alteration	Poor	Good	Very good	Good
Available	Yes	No	Yes	Yes

personnel. A tool must present the program logic clearly, precisely, and legibly.

The system designer may not be able to choose the design tool, as many firms have a standard for all program specification and documentation. Where there is a choice, the specification chosen should take into consideration the users of the specifications. Often it will be advisable to provide more than one presentation form.

PROCESSING MODES

When the application system is defined, all the programs required to support the information-system activities are specified. What remains is a specification of how the system is to operate and the system software required to support this operation. System software includes the operating system, data management system, terminal control systems, and compilers or interpreters used for application program development.

An application system can operate in three modes:

1. As a batch-processing system
2. As an on-line system
3. As a distributed processing system

Not infrequently, different parts of the application system operate in different modes: some routines or programs operate in a batch mode, some as on-line functions, and some as distributed functions.

The system designer must specify the processing modes for the application system and/or its parts. This decision will determine the types of computer hardware and software required to support the system.

For simplicity, we will discuss processing modes in terms of a transaction-processing system. Note, though, that almost any application system can operate in any of the three processing modes. For our discussion we will define a transaction as follows:

Transaction A request for a single information service, such as registration of a sale, delivery of an order, receipt of an order, registration of a (new) customer, modification of data, production of a report, and so on.

Transaction Record The information or data describing a transaction; for example, the transaction record for a sale might include:

⟨customer-name, item-nr, quantity, price⟩

Normally the transaction record will also identify the type of transaction.

When no confusion can arise, transaction records are referred to simply as transactions.

Batch Processing

A batch-processing system is one in which the automated data processing system is activated periodically—each evening, once a week, twice a month, or at some other interval. Between operations, transactions are collected into a batch and then ordered for processing. This batch gives the operation mode its name.

Figure 10.8 presents a typical model of a batch-processing system. Requests for data processing services are collected as system messages. Periodically, these messages are prepared for computer processing, possibly by keypunching input cards or using a data entry medium to transfer the messages. The batch of transaction records is ordered, sorted, in the same sequence as the master file against which it will be processed. For example, if the system is to record student grades in a student file, the transaction records giving the grades to be recorded must be sorted into the same sequence as the student file. The processing system then reads each transaction record and the master file, performs the requested operations, and generates a new master file, the transaction reports, and any file or system reports. The old master file becomes a log of the system status before the batch was processed. This log can be kept for auditing and/or used for backup.

Box 10.1 summarizes the major components of a batch-processing system. Note that the data entry stations are normally at the customer service points. These may be completely manual; for example, a secretary receives a transaction request by telephone or mail. The transaction batch may be collected locally, at the data entry station(s), or centrally within the computer if terminal equipment is used to record the transactions.

The transaction-processing system is commonly an integrated program, with subprograms for the separate transaction processes. The sort and report programs may be integrated with the transaction routines or executed as separate programs.

Batch-processing systems are the oldest processing mode. Their construction, implementation, operation, and maintenance are well known and widely used. With respect to system operation, they are the most secure type of system. Also, batch processing can be implemented on a smaller computer system (see Chapter 11). The relative simplicity of batch-processing systems makes them the least expensive, at least in terms of automated data processing costs.

The major problem with batch-processing systems is that their response time, from initiation of a transaction until its completion, is

Figure 10.8 Batch-Processing System

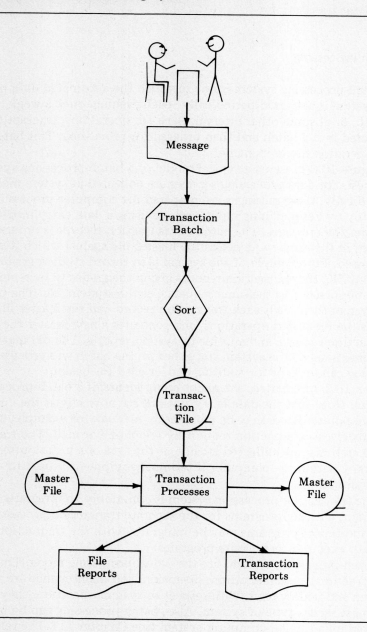

Box 10.1

BATCH-PROCESSING SYSTEM COMPONENTS

1. Data entry stations
   (manual or with automated support, such as terminals)
2. A separate sort process for the transaction file
3. Sequential master files on tape or disk
4. An integrated transaction-processing system
5. Report programs for the master file(s)
6. Regular back-up files as byproducts of processing

---

quite slow (in computer terms). Two bottlenecks can occur, the first at transaction collection and the second at sequential processing.

Despite the slow response time, the low cost of batch processing still makes this a viable option for the system designer. This processing mode is particularly applicable for systems in which response time is not critical, such as any system in which transactions are received through the mail, or in which transactions occur periodically (weekly or monthly reports, for example). Another application area, in which batch processing is often combined with other processing modes, occurs when periodic records of system status are required, such as account auditing, or when high levels of integrity are required.

On-Line Processing

We can define an on-line processing system as one in which the system is continuously available for receipt and processing of transactions. For this system there must be terminals at the transaction generation points to receive processing requests. These terminals are *on-line*, that is, they are connected to the central processing computer through a telephone network, which can be private or public, local and limited to the organization's building or geographically distant. The on-line connection between the users and the transaction-processing system gives this operation mode its name.

Figure 10.9 shows a typical on-line system. Requests for data processing services are received at the many service stations. The operators enter the required transaction records, which are sent over the network to the central processing system. Each transaction is processed upon receipt, and an immediate reply (usually taking between 3 and 10 seconds) is returned to the user, in this case the terminal operator. The

Figure 10.9 On-Line Processing System

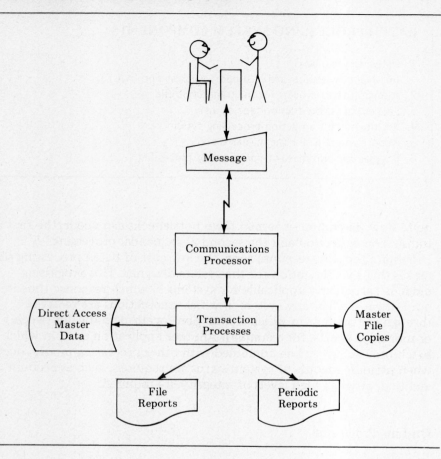

major difference between this system and the batch-processing system illustrated in Figure 10.8 is the immediate transfer of transaction records for processing.

The transaction-processing system commonly consists of individual transaction programs and a control program that activates the required transaction program when an input transaction is received. The transaction programs may be collected in a transaction library, making continuous development of new transactions possible. This feature lies behind the fact that many on-line systems handle a larger number of transaction types than do batch-processing systems.

Since there is no collection of transaction records, there is nothing to sort before processing. Also, the transactions cannot be in any predetermined order, since they are processed as they occur. In this situation, sequential file processing will not provide the required response time, and a direct-access file structure must be used. The control program for the on-line system will normally include a data administration system (file or data base) for storage and retrieval of required data. Traditional batch-processing applications that have been moved on-line will generally use either direct or indexed-sequential files. (See Chapter 9 for file characteristics.) New systems may use a data-base management system if the application system is quite complex.

Transaction replies are sent to the initiating user immediately. File and system reports are run periodically, typically at the close of the business day or at the end of the week. File copies for back-up and auditing must be made by service systems, commonly outside the main on-line system.

Box 10.2 lists the basic components of an on-line system. Note again that the work to be done is the same as for the batch system; the differences lie in the mode of processing, particularly the areas of data entry and file management.

On-line systems have been in use since the late 1960s. These systems work well, normally providing good response times. Response time can be improved by reorganizing and/or restructuring the file system. In large systems, that is, those with many terminals, access conflicts may arise. To solve this problem, the system may allow concurrent processing of transactions. However, if it does, the access control routines must be extended to monitor concurrent update.

When the number of users served by an on-line system becomes large, the total response time tends to degenerate. The system control routines also grow more complex, and adjusting to changing requirements may become difficult. This last problem occurs chiefly because of the difficulties in keeping all routines compatible, particularly with the file system. Users in large systems often feel that the central staff responsible for maintaining the system does not give their jobs satisfactory priority.

Box 10.2

ON-LINE SYSTEM COMPONENTS

1. Automated data entry stations
2. A communications processor with access control
3. Direct-access files
4. A modular transaction-processing system
5. Report programs for the master file(s)
6. Maintenance system for back-up and recovery

Despite the problems, an on-line system is still a good choice for many applications. "Good" applications include those with a well-defined set of 50 to 100 transaction types. These applications should also have a valid on-line response requirement and a relatively diverse system of transaction entry points. An on-line system normally requires a relatively large central computer.

Distributed Processing

A distributed processing system is one in which processing occurs at geographically separate locations. These processing locations are called *nodes* in a network of connected computers. The nodes may be connected directly to one another, or they may be connected through a central computer (or there may be some combination of central and local connections).

Each node in a distributed system is a complete computer with a processing system designed for local processing. In most systems, the node stations can be supported by mini- or microcomputers. A larger central computer may be included in the system to handle overload situations. Data may be stored in a central, common data base or locally at each node. The nodes should have only those data needed for local processing. The transaction programs may be centrally developed and stored, then "down-loaded" to the node stations, or they may be developed locally. Central program development, though slower, will tend to assure processing compatibility. Communication within the network may be handled centrally through the central computer or locally through identical communication programs at each node.

Figure 10.10 illustrates a distributed processing system. Transactions are generated and processed locally at each node. If a nonlocal transaction is required, it can be sent to the node (or the central computer) where the processing routine resides. The output (response) from the transaction will be sent back to the initiating node. If nonlocal data are required, the choices are to (1) send the transaction to the data site for processing, or (2) request that the data be sent to the local (initiating) site for processing.

To the system user, a distributed processing system will seem the same as an on-line system. Response times should be at least as good as in an on-line system. When both the data and the processing program are at the local node, response times should be significantly better. The system user should also notice a marked improvement in adaptation of the processing system to local processing requirements, particularly when processing programs are developed locally. The computer at the local node can be designed for local processing. Either a microcomputer

Figure 10.10 Distributed Processing System

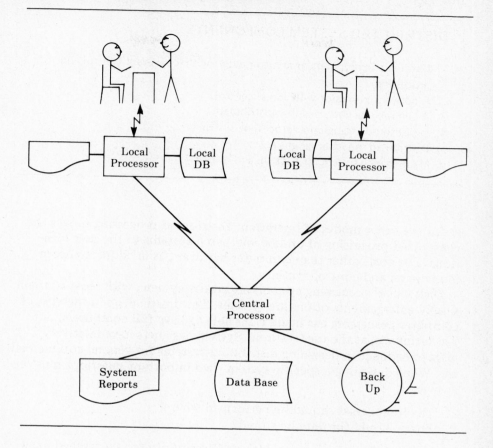

or a minicomputer will usually be sufficient, particularly if a larger central processor is available for larger tasks.

Both the processing-routine library and the data base can be developed and kept centrally, with copies of relevant data and programs sent to the nodes. This will ensure communality throughout the system, and will support the maintenance of data and program integrity. Users at the nodes will often wish to develop their own programs. This should be encouraged so long as programs for general use are developed in accordance with a system standard. Such distributed development should increase the system's adaptability to changing environments. Modifications of the data base should be controlled centrally to ensure that current data values are available at all nodes.

Box 10.3 summarizes the basic components of a distributed system. Note that the work to be done by the information system is the same

Box 10.3

DISTRIBUTED SYSTEM COMPONENTS

1. Local microcomputers or minicomputers with local input control and processing
2. A network processor with access control
3. A central data base, possibly distributed
4. A distributed transaction-processing system
5. Distributed report programs
6. Maintenance system for back-up and recovery

---

as for the other modes of operation. Distributed processing moves the centralized processing of on-line and batch systems to the user locations. The cost, other than computer hardware, is in additional communication and control routines.

Distributed processing systems are relatively new, with most of them simply enlargements of on-line systems. The drastic drop in the cost of computer processors has made it feasible to have full computers, not just terminals, at the user stations. System designers have relatively little experience in designing distributed systems for general commercial use. When designing a specific system, two important questions must be answered:

1. Which processes should be performed where?
2. Where should the data be stored?

Distributed processing provides an opportunity for specialized local processing within a defined larger information system. This should make the system more flexible and provide improved support for the people served by the information system.

Possible good applications include those currently run by on-line systems, and those involving changing and expanding processing requirements. Particularly good applications should be found in distributed organizations with a central administration and locally autonomous divisions.

SUMMARY

We have discussed four techniques commonly used for program specification and documentation: flowcharts, structured diagrams, decision tables, and structured English statements. Flowcharting is very well entrenched and widely used; however, for large systems, this technique tends to produce volumes of charts in which it is difficult to maintain control and consistency. Structured diagrams are strongly preferred, particularly by the academic community, as they clearly show the structure of the system being developed and clearly identify independent modules. We have proposed using a combination of these techniques, first developing a structured diagram for the system, then, where necessary, using flowcharts to specify the details of the modules.

Decision tables are a good tool for identifying the controls and the required actions that follow for complicated systems. An added advantage is that there are systems that can translate a decision table directly into a running program, thus bypassing a time-consuming (and error-introducing) system implementation process.

Structured English is particularly good for documenting an algorithm for the human reader; thus, it is useful for control and communication between the users and the system designer or implementer.

Finally, we have introduced three basic strategies for data-system processing: batch, on-line, and distributed processing. Batch processing is easy, secure, and adequate for periodic processing with relatively long (more than 1 day) response time requirements. On-line processing is necessary for those systems that require an immediate answer. The use of distributed processing is increasing, particularly for systems with relatively disjointed processing requirements.

KEY CONCEPTS

Algorithm	Process
Batch processing	Program
Decision tables	Structured diagrams
Distributed processing	Structured English
Flowcharts	Transaction
On-line processing	Transaction record
Procedure	

DISCUSSION QUESTIONS

1. Define and give an example for each of the key concepts.
2. Discuss the concepts of procedure, process, and program. To what extent do these concepts overlap? Why are these separate concepts necessary?
3. Discuss the differences between application and system programs. Which of these must be specified by the information-system designer? How is the interface with the other system specified?

4. What are the components of a complete process description? Why are there more than one? Who are the readers of these components?
5. What tools are available for program specification? Which is best for the end user? Why? Which is best for the programmer? Why? Which can be most easily automated? Why?
6. Discuss the advantages and disadvantages of each of the processing modes: batch, on-line, and distributed. For what types of systems would each processing mode be best?

PROJECTS

1. Choose a central process in your system and construct a flowchart, structured diagram, decision table, and structured English algorithm for a program to automate this process. Discuss the suitability of each tool for the chosen process.
2. Discuss the advantages and disadvantages of each of the processing modes for your system. Choose a processing mode and defend your choice.

RECOMMENDED READINGS

Chapin, N. "Flowcharting with the ANSI Standard : A Tutorial." *Computing Surveys*, 2 (June 1970).
    Also printed in (Couger & Knapp, 1974). This paper presents the 1970 ANSI flowcharting standard and discusses its acceptance.
Couger, J. D., and R. W. Knapp, eds. *System Analysis Techniques*. New York : John Wiley & Sons, 1974.
    This book contains a number of papers on data-system development techniques proposed and available as of 1974. At that time, system analysis was not commonly separated from system design. Many of the techniques described are principally design and documentation techniques. These approaches are still valid.
Gane, C., and T. Sarson. *Structured Systems Analysis—Tools and Techniques*. Englewood Cliffs, N.J. : Prentice-Hall, 1979.
    Chapter 5 in this book presents a good discussion and comparison of the use of decision tables and structured English for program specification and documentation.
Jackson, M. A. *Principles of Program Design*. New York : Academic Press, 1975.
    This book presents, and illustrates through examples, a graphic approach to structured program design.
Lundeberg, M., G. Goldkuhl, and A. Nilsson. *Information Systems Development—A Systematic Approach*. Englewood Cliffs, N.J. : Prentice-Hall, 1981.
    Chapter 6 in this book gives a detailed illustration of the use of Jackson structured diagrams and their translation to program code.

Martin, J. *Design and Strategy for Distributed Data Processing.* Englewood Cliffs, N.J.: Prentice-Hall, 1981.

In this book, Martin discusses the possibilities and design alternatives that can be developed through distributed processing systems.

McDaniel, H. *Applications of Decision Tables* and *Decision Table Software.* Both by Brandon/Systems Press, Inc., 1970.

These two books include 18 papers and more than 30 processors, respectively, concerned with the use and availability of decision table processors.

PART IV
SYSTEM IMPLEMENTATION

Chapter 11
Computer Support

INTRODUCTION

The data-system design stage is completed when the data and processes required by the application system have been specified. These specifications should be independent of the computer equipment currently available. Computer installations are generally upgraded every fifth year. If the data-system design is computer-independent, it will be robust for the changes in the underlying computer configuration. Ideally, the data-system design should need to be changed only to reflect changes in the external information-system environment.

In practice, many data systems are designed to take advantage of the computer facilities currently available. In the short term, this will tend to

1. reduce system implementation time by reducing the time needed to adjust the data-system design to the available computer facilities.
2. bind the implemented data system to the technical level of the current computer system.

The system implementation stage takes the data-system design and adapts it to and implements it onto a specific computer configuration. Frequently, the organization already has the computer configuration available, either through established contact with a computer service bureau or through the organization's computer service department. If this is the case, the design must be adapted to the available configuration. Occasionally the new application system will require a new computer configuration. In this case, the new configuration must be designed in accordance with the requirements of the new application and of any other applications that will be executed with it.

We will discuss a number of computer facilities that can be used to implement a data-system design. Not all are equally suitable for a given data system. The system designer must choose between advanced techniques, which are likely to require expensive computer components, and less advanced (and costly) techniques, which typically require more processing time.

We define a computer system rather liberally to include both the computer hardware and the system software commonly available from the computer-system vendor. System software includes such systems as the operating system, communications system, data management system(s), compilers, interpreters, and application generators.

COMPUTER-SYSTEM REQUIREMENTS

The data-system design sets minimum computer-system requirements for the processing programs, the processing mode desired, the data to be maintained, and the user interface. The computer system selected should meet at least these minimum requirements. Ideally, the computer system selected should also allow for growth in the scope of the data system.

The processing mode selected will also set minimum computer-system requirements (see Figures 10.8, 10.9, and 10.10). Generally these will include the following:

- For batch-processing systems:
  a. a central CPU
  b. memory for the processing system
  c. serial input and output devices, such as card/printer/tape
  d. serial storage devices, such as tape
- For on-line processing systems:
  a. a central CPU
  b. memory for the active portion of the processing system
  c. terminals for input and output
  d. direct-access storage for the data
- For distributed processing systems:
  a. multiple local CPUs
  b. distributed memory for the local programs
  c. central memory and CPU for the control system
  d. local computers for system-wide communication
  e. local and central direct-access storage

The system software required will depend on the complexity of the hardware system. Batch-processing systems do not need a communication system, and the file I/O routines of their operating system (for serial or sequential file structures) are normally adequate. Distributed processing systems require the most advanced (and complex) communications and data management systems.

The designer must choose a computer system that best meets the real requirements of the organization's data systems. Some trade-offs are given in Table 11.1.

Processing Requirements

The computer-system components necessary to the data system processing programs include the central processing unit(s) (CPU) required to execute the programs, the main memory space required to

Table 11.1 Trade-Offs in Computer-System Configurations

Characteristic	Batch System	Distributed System
Adaptability to changing requirements	Poor	Good
Response time	Long (day)	Short (seconds)
System complexity	Low	High
Cost	Low	High

contain the active programs, the communication network required to reach the end users, and the operating and communications systems.

The system implementor must determine the minimum set of programs required for the resident system, that is, those programs required at any one time. For example, if the system is a transaction-processing system, the minimum resident system would include:

- the communications system
- the input control routines
- the transaction selection routine
- the data management system
- space for the active transaction-processing program

If a number of users are to be served concurrently, enough space must be allowed for the maximum number of concurrent transaction programs and processing control routines. It is also necessary to calculate the amount of memory space needed for the input transaction(s) and the data from secondary storage that the resident system and the active transaction program(s) will use.

The amount of main memory space required for the processing system, then, is found by summing the space required by the control routines, plus one or more transaction-processing programs, plus the data buffers. If more memory space is available, it may be used to maintain more data and/or more processing programs, such as the transaction programs most often used.

Problems arise only when the amount of memory available is less than that required by the resident system. In general, any system can be made into small modules that can overlay one another. This overlay activity takes time and will lengthen processing (and response) time. In a worst-case situation, the overlay activity takes more time than the actual processing. This is called *thrashing* and should be avoided, by increasing the available memory space, whenever possible.

For on-line and distributed processing systems, the processing requirement includes the communication network and the communication control routines. (See pages 264–266, 270.)

Multiple CPUs will be required for back-up in large systems that must be available continuously and for distributed systems. The memory requirement for each CPU must be established; it will depend on the functions to be handled in each.

Data Storage Requirements

The computer-system components required for data storage include the secondary storage units [direct-access storage devices (DASD), or disks, and/or tapes] and the data management system(s). Storage space will be required for:

- the primary data
- any control data that the file and/or the data-base management system need
- the program system
- input logs and back-up copies

Direct-access storage space will be required for the program system and may be required for the active data. Serial storage space will be required for logs and back-up copies. (Note: Input logs and back-up copies of the data are necessary for system maintenance and integrity control. These topics will be discussed further in Chapter 13.)

The number of characters of storage space required for the data is calculated by summing the file space requirements. Each file space requirement can be calculated as:

$$\text{File size} = N \times (\text{record length}) + M \times (\text{record length}) + C$$

where

N = number of records
M = number of new records to be added
C = sum of control data (indexes, pointers)

The number of storage units required will vary depending on their capacity. For example, disk units vary in storage capacity from about 85,000 characters on small floppy diskettes for microcomputers to more than 1,000 million characters on large disk units for mainframe computers. Multiple storage units may also be chosen for efficiency and/or security, in addition to the direct space requirement. The designer is principally concerned with determining the actual amount of data to be stored. Operational efficiency comes later.

User Interface Requirements

The computer-system components required to support the users include the input/output devices—card readers, printers, terminals, and other such devices—and the communications system that serves them.

For batch-processing systems, the computer system only needs to contain at least one card reader and one printer. Other input devices that can be used are tape drives, other data collection units, and terminals.

On-line systems require some number of terminals, usually one for each work station that is to be connected to the computer. If there are many terminals, it may be advantageous to add concentrators to the network. A concentrator collects messages from a relatively small number of terminals and sends the collected messages to the main CPU as a single message. (See Figure 11.4.)

Distributed processing systems will have some number of computers at the user work stations. These computers may serve several users through connected terminals or may be microcomputers serving only one user at a time.

The system designer must consider the type of interface each set of users requires. Some may require the local processing provided by microcomputers with an on-line connection to the main system. Some may be served through screen display terminals, known as CRTs. And some may require a paper terminal medium. Generally some form of local printer will be required to supplement a set of display terminals.

Both on-line and distributed processing systems will need communication-system software. In general, the communication-system software for an on-line system will be less complex than that required for a distributed system.

COMPUTER CONFIGURATIONS

A computer configuration is that set of computer units, or, more correctly, hardware units that function together to provide computing power to an organization or organizational unit. For a good configuration, the design must be based on the processing requirements of the organization's data system(s). There are many possible configurations.

The size of a computer configuration is measured in processing speed, storage capacity for active programs, storage capacity for data, and number of different hardware units. The price of a computer configuration is directly related to its size. The physical space required for different computer configurations ranges from the area of a desk top to a large room or hall.

Table 11.2 Relationships* Among Microcomputers, Minicomputers, and Mainframe Computers

Characteristics	Microcomputer	Minicomputer	Mainframe
Price (minimum)	$1000	$20,000	$1,000,000
Number of users	1–2	10+	100+
Memory capacity	64–512KB	128KB–10MB	1MB+
DASD storage	100KB–50MB	100MB+	1000MB+
Operative staff	0(1)	2+	20+
Physical area	6 ft²	20 ft²	200 ft²
Number of computer units	2–5	5–10	25+

*All numbers are only approximations, giving common (1983) values for characteristic machines of each type. KB equals 1024 bytes; one byte equals 8 bits of information. MB equals 1 million bytes.

Computers come in three different "sizes": mainframes, minicomputers, and microcomputers. The boundaries between these classes of computers, as measured in computing speed and storage capacity, are constantly changing. In particular, speed and capacity in each class are increasing. However, there is an informal relationship between these systems that can be given as:

- A microcomputer is approximately one-tenth the size of a minicomputer.
- A minicomputer is approximately one-tenth the size of a mainframe computer.

Although prices are falling, the same approximate ratio exists between the system types. A similar ratio also holds for the owning organization or organizational unit, measured in number of employees directly engaged in data processing. Table 11.2 gives some of the attributes that characterize microcomputers, minicomputers, and mainframe computers. Note that the numbers are only approximate and subject to development changes. However, the relationships between these classes should remain relatively constant.

Basic Architecture

All computers have the same basic architecture, as given in types of devices or hardware units. A computer will have each of the following:

- central processing unit (CPU)
- memory unit
- input unit
- output unit
- secondary storage unit

Figure 11.1 illustrates the basic architecture. The CPU is the actual processing unit where all operations are executed. It is connected to one or more memory units in which the active programs reside. Instructions are passed from memory to the CPU for execution. Data are also stored in the memory during program execution. The CPU is

Figure 11.1 Basic Computer Architecture

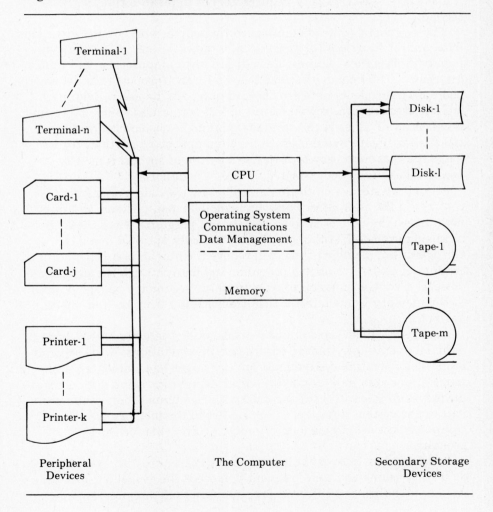

connected to the input/output units and secondary storage units and can send execution commands to activate each. Data are transferred directly from the input/output or secondary storage units to the main memory.

The main memory is reused for each program. Data and programs that are to be reused must be stored on some unit external to the CPU and main memory.

Users communicate with the CPU and main memory through peripheral devices, which include such input/output units as card readers, printers, paper tape readers, card and tape punches, magnetic tape readers and writers, optical readers, and terminals. The primary function of the peripheral units is to transmit data, by character or line (card image), to and from the computer. Their capacity is measured in transmission speed, usually in characters or bytes (8-bit units) per second.

The peripheral units are controlled by people, who enter transactions, data, and/or programs for processing in the computer (CPU and main memory). It is through these devices that the computer has its "human interface." The human interface is given by the format of the messages and data transmitted between the computer and its users. Examples include card formats, screen forms, report forms, and so on. The communication routines in the computer can make the computer quite talkative with a terminal user. Good communication routines try to make the computer easy to use. The measure of success is usually described as the system's degree of "user friendliness."

Secondary storage units are controlled by the data management routines in the computer. These units include disks, drums, and magnetic tapes; they are used to store data and programs when these are not being executed. Although they are actually optional in a basic configuration, including them will relieve the human user of the time-consuming task of reloading programs and data through the peripheral devices. Also, transmission of data from the secondary storage devices to the memory is much faster than transmission from the peripheral devices.

In order to make the computer operational, there must be at least a minimal operating system to coordinate the operations of the separate units. The operating system must include at least a rudimentary communications system to control the peripheral units, and a data management system to control the secondary storage units. These systems are part of the system software, which resides in the memory when the computer is in use. Extra memory must be available for the user programs.

In established EDP environments, the time required to execute the data systems one at a time frequently exceeds the available clock time. A computer with one CPU can process more than one program at a time by utilizing the CPU idle time, which occurs while data are being transported between the memory and the peripheral and secondary storage units. If more than one program is resident in main memory, the CPU can process one while the other(s) wait for data. When the active program requests data, the CPU initiates the I/O request, sets this program on a wait queue, and then is available to process another program. This is called *multiprogramming*.

Time-sharing is a form of multiprogramming. In time-sharing, the concurrent programs are assumed to be from on-line systems, which sets an additional requirement, namely that of maintaining acceptable response times for the users.

Systems used for multiprogramming and time-sharing require more memory to accommodate the multiple programs. The program control routines of the operating system must be expanded to include routines for administering the alternation of CPU processing among the programs and controlling the separation of the active programs.

Figure 11.2 illustrates a multiprogramming configuration. It is typically a larger system than the basic configuration, in terms of number of peripheral and secondary storage units, size of main memory, speed of the CPU, and, implicitly, number of users and their programs.

In large organizations, one CPU may not have enough capacity for all the processing required. Several CPUs may be used in a configuration. The CPUs may be assigned to process separate programs or may be used to process separate sections of the same program. This type of configuration is called a *multiprocessing* system. A multiprocessing system is also a multiprogramming system. Again, the operating system must become more complex to control the assignment of CPUs to programs.

Figure 11.3 illustrates a multiprocessing system. The "extra" CPUs can usually be given special tasks. This figure shows two CPUs used for program execution; one, a "front-end processor," used to control the transport of data to and from the peripheral units; and a fourth, a "data-base machine," controlling the transport of data to and from the secondary storage units.

Both the front-end processor and the data-base machine may be independent computers, with their own memory, peripheral devices, and secondary storage units. Alternatively, they may share secondary storage units with the main computer. The front-end processor and data-base machine are connected to the parent machine by high-speed communication lines for the transport of data. When they are independent computers, major portions of the communications routines and data management routines can be moved to these machines, freeing memory capacity in the central machine.

Figure 11.2   Multiprogramming

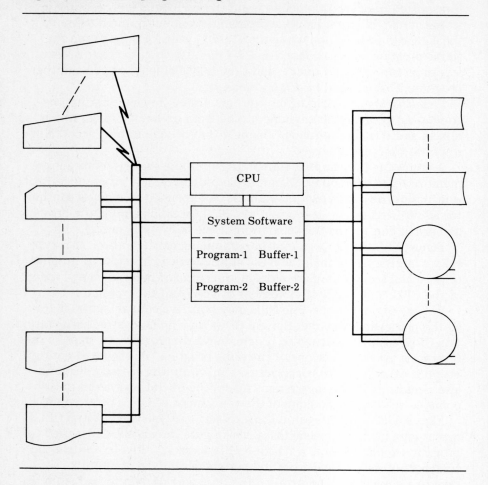

Microcomputers

Microcomputers are the smallest computers. In a business processing situation, a microcomputer typically serves one or two people. In has a simple operating system with minimal communication and data management systems. The system software is commonly burned onto a computer chip, becoming *firmware*. The memory area for the system software is called ROM, for read-only memory; it is generally not available for user programs.

In 1984, microcomputer memory ranges from 64K to 512K bytes

Figure 11.3 Multiprocessing

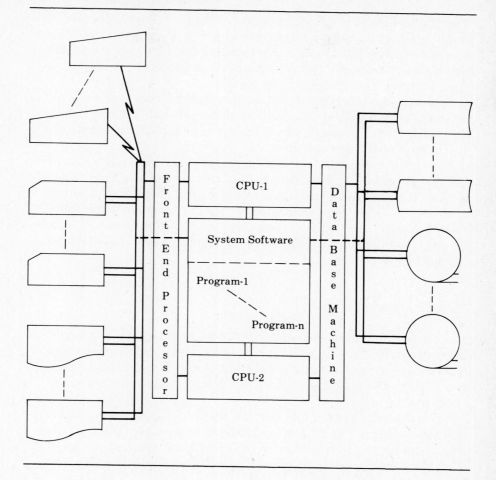

(K equals 1024 bytes). Available peripheral units include the keyboard, CRT screen, printer, and cassette tape. Secondary storage units include cassette tapes, floppy disks, and hard disks. Hard disk storage capacity ranges up to 50 million characters (bytes).

Microcomputers are being sold as independent computers for small businesses (those with fewer than 5 employees). They are also used for word processing stations in automated offices, and as home computers. A microcomputer can function as an independent computer, a terminal in an on-line system, a concentrator, or a node in a distributed processing system.

Minicomputers

The minicomputer is a medium-sized computer. It has moderate CPU speed, memory capacity, and storage capacity. It has a relatively simple operating system with moderately complex communication and data management routines. Minicomputers can be used in both single programming and multiprogramming modes.

A typical configuration would include a card reader, one or two printers, and a few (less than 50) terminals. Secondary storage units include disks and magnetic tapes. Disk storage capacity is normally 100 million characters and up.

Minicomputers are used in medium-sized firms and in divisions of large organizations (ten to one hundred employees) as a main computer facility, for administrative data processing, text processing, scientific data analysis, and engineering applications (for example, computer aided design or CAD). These computers are also used as concentrators for large numbers of terminals and as node computers in distributed processing systems.

Mainframe Computers

Mainframe computers, including the supercomputers, are the largest of the computers. They have the greatest CPU speed, largest memories, highest-capacity storage units, and greatest number of types of peripheral devices. The mainframe computer usually has a multiprocessing configuration.

Typical configurations include card and paper tape readers and punches, printers, optical readers, diskette readers, terminals, and terminal communications with microcomputers and minicomputers. Secondary storage units include magnetic tape stations, disk stations, and drums.

Mainframe computers are used in large organizations, those with from 100 to thousands of employees. The central processor in an on-line or distributed processing system is usually a mainframe. Mainframe computers can be and often are linked together in intercontinental distributed processing networks.

On-Line Systems

An on-line system is one where many terminals are connected to the central processing computer for input/output. Processing is on-line in the sense that the user, at a terminal, has direct contact with the processing program. Typically data and/or transactions are entered and replies and/or reports are received.

The central computer in an on-line configuration is usually a mainframe computer, possibly a multiprocessor, with a large secondary storage capacity. There may be multiple clusters of on-line user sites. This configuration, called a *star network*, is illustrated in Figure 11.4.

Terminals may be either directly connected to the CPU or connected through a multiplexer, concentrator, or local (to the user) computer.

Figure 11.4 On-Line System Configuration

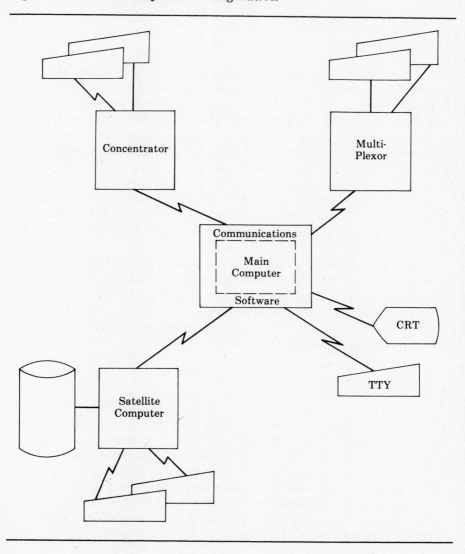

A multiplexer is a hardware device that combines the messages to or from a fixed number of low-speed terminals into a single message that can travel over a higher-speed communication line to the computer. A concentrator is a single-purpose computer that combines low-speed terminal messages onto a higher-speed connecting line and also provides conversion services for "its" terminals. The most flexible connector is the local computer, which can provide some input control services in addition to the communication services. In an on-line system, most processing occurs in the central machine. Applications are typically at the operative level—transaction processing, major data entry, centralized report generation, and so on.

Distributed Systems

Distributed processing systems consist of a number of connected computers. Each computer functions independently in its local environment and can communicate with other computers in the network for transfer of data or programs. The individual computers are configured for the processing requirements of the local environment and have local peripherals and secondary storage units. However, independent computers may share central computer facilities, termed "host computer" facilities, most commonly program libraries and data base(s).

When the independent computers are of different types, a communication network of *node computers* can be used to provide common network translations and communication. Figure 11.5 illustrates such a network configuration.

Node computers are generally of the same type and are dedicated to controlling communications, selecting message routings, and translating messages between the participating machines and the network standard.

In a distributed system, the primary processing requirements are handled by the local machines. Network communications are for nonlocal processing of data or programs.

SYSTEM SOFTWARE

An informal definition of system software is that it is the set of programs needed to manage hardware use, supervise program execution, maintain program libraries and data stores, and translate user data processing requirements into computer-executable instructions. Application programs are those user-defined programs that manipulate data in accordance with information-system requirements. Thus, system software makes the computer available to users, whereas application programs perform user-defined tasks.

Figure 11.5 Distributed System Configuration

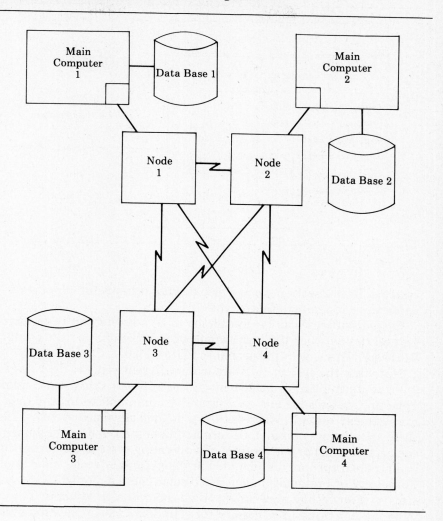

The manufacturers of computer hardware usually provide the system software. These programs can also be obtained from "software houses" that specialize in the development of these programs (usually a specialized subgroup of these programs). They can also be developed within the user organization, although this is generally not feasible because the cost of system software development can seldom be justified.

We have already mentioned several components of system software: operating systems, communication systems, and data management

Figure 11.6 System Software

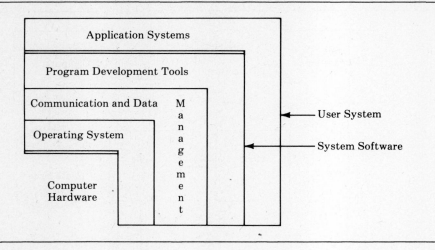

systems. In this section we will also discuss systems for support of
application program development.

System software can be considered to be a layered set of programs
that resides between the user's application programs and the computer
hardware. This view is illustrated in Figure 11.6.

Note that the system software from different vendors does not follow a uniform plan for placement of the different subsystems. Some
operating systems include only primitive communications and data
management systems, whereas others include advanced systems. Also,
there are separate communications and data management systems that
can replace or augment those of the operating system. Sometimes data
management systems are included in the program development tools.
For clarity of presentation, we will discuss these major software systems as though they were independent, coordinated systems. The cu-
mulative functions are necessary for support of the application systems.

Operating Systems

Definitions of an operating system vary; the term may be used to include all system software, or those routines required to monitor hardware use and schedule program execution, or something in between.
For our discussion, we will assume that an operating system includes
programs and/or routines for the following functions:

- Control of input/output (I/O) devices

- Interpretation of user commands
- Selection of user programs
- Supervision of program execution
- Basic read/write functions to secondary storage
- File protection
- Error recovery
- Utility services
- Usage accounting

An operating system has a command language that the user can employ to specify what is to be done. In IBM terminology, the "what is is to be done" description is called a *job*. Using routines for the listed functions, the operating system:

- "reads" a job description, including identification of the user, the desired program, possible secondary storage files, and any input data for the program.
- interprets and checks the job description for valid user, program, and file specifications.
- schedules the program for execution.

During application-program execution, the operating system:

- assigns secondary storage files.
- performs the file I/O as requested by the program, possibly through a data management system.
- allocates main memory space as required.
- routes output.
- maintains usage statistics.

After program execution, the operating system:

- releases the resources allocated to the program.
- records facility usage for subsequent accounting.

The I/O routines of the operating system can work independently of user program execution. Normally, these routines will read and check the job descriptions and set them in a queue to be scheduled and executed.

The operating system has a job scheduler, which is responsible for execution of the programs. It is this routine that can be extended to control multiprogramming and multiprocessing.

Basic file I/O includes file localization, assignment to the user program, allocation of main memory buffers, a serial read/write routine, and a direct-access read/write routine using a user-given relative record number (RRN). To provide file protection, one or more passwords are generally stored with the file description. The user must give a correct password before the file is assigned.

The operating system must also include routines to handle machine errors during execution. The sophistication of these routines ranges from "stop all processing" to an effort to correct the error, check the active programs for damage, recover data, and continue processing.

Communication Systems

The communication system supplements and extends the primitive functions of the I/O routines of the operating system to include interactive communication through terminals between the system and the users. Basic functions include:

- Control of terminal input/output
- Translation of input/output messages
- Routing
- Network protocols
- Network security
- Network statistics

The communication system supports the user at a terminal and provides an interface to the operating system, data management system(s), program development systems, and application systems. The user, at a terminal, may submit a job description for processing that will be handled as described. Depending on the available systems, the user may also:

- Enter data into a file for subsequent processing.
- Enter transactions for immediate processing.
- Query one or more data bases.
- Send messages to other users.
- Use a word processor to develop texts.
- Interact with an interactive compiler to develop a program.

In an on-line system, the communication system handles the transfer of messages between the user and the system and application programs. This includes terminal line control, translation of codes, queuing of concurrent messages, and line error handling.

In a distributed processing system, the communication system must also handle the communication between possibly different types of machines. The network protocols for determining the availability of communication lines, programs, and data are part of the communication system.

Data Management Systems

The data management system handles file and data-base administration for the application systems. There are a variety of data management systems, offering different levels of complexity. Generally, each builds upon the operating system's primitive file I/O routines. A data management system provides at least the following functions:

- File or data-base content definition
- File or data-base structure definition
- Storage space allocation
- Establishment and maintenance
- Data storage and retrieval
- Data integrity and privacy control
- Usage statistics

Given our definition of a file as a collection of records of a single type, a file management system (FMS) is a system that can handle the definition, administration, and I/O facilities for one or more files.

A data-base management system (DBMS) provides all the functions of an FMS along with the definition, establishment, administration, and I/O facilities for inter-record type relationships. A DBMS, as compared with an FMS, assumes that a more complex data collection is used by more, and more varied, users, thus increasing the complexity of the security and integrity routines.

Data definition with an FMS is frequently stated in the application programs. The FMS requires that the record size and the names and lengths of any key fields be known. Defining other data fields is optional with most FMSs.

Data definition with a DBMS requires an external (to the program) definition, using a data definition language (DDL), which is compiled into a *DB schema.* There are a number of data dictionary systems (DDS) that can help the user or system designer to collect data definitions, which can then be compiled for DBMS processing.

Many FMSs and DBMSs can be used both from a program and directly by the user through the communications system. These systems are available from the machine manufacturers (IBM, Sperry UNIVAC, and others), from software houses, and from user organizations. Individual systems vary greatly in facilities offered, operational efficiency, ease of use, vendor support, and degree of portability compared with different hardware and software systems. The application-system designer will have to select an appropriate FMS/DBMS for each application system.

Program Development Systems

Systems to help with the development of programs have existed since the mid-1950s. Although not by any means complete or perfect, they have improved tremendously during these 30 years. Today there is a seemingly endless variety.

The goal of a program development system (PDS) is to translate user data processing requirements into machine-executable code. The PDS should be easy to use and should produce efficient programs. These goals are not directly compatible, and a trade-off between ease of use and machine efficiency is normal. An individual PDS can be classified on a scale ranging from general application generator (easiest to use) to assembly language (most efficient).

We will discuss three types of PDSs: compilers, interpreters, and application generators. These three systems are listed in descending order of programming skill generally needed to use them. Obviously, a programmer could make good use of an application generator. However, the user of an application generator need not have any, or at least only low-level, programming skills.

Compilers

A compiler takes a program, expressed as a number of statements in a programming language, and compiles, or translates, it into machine code for execution. A compiler commonly contains routines for file handling, numeric conversions, arithmetic functions such as SUM, MAX, MIN, AVERAGE, SQUARE-ROOT, and others. These can be added to the user program, relieving the programmer of the need to program these routines repeatedly.

Common compiler languages include COBOL, FORTRAN, PL/1, ALGOL, PASCAL, and ADA. New languages are being developed that have more functions and improved structure and documentation. For a novice, learning a programming language requires 4 to 10 weeks of intensive effort. Becoming an experienced programmer requires several years of practice. However, once a programmer has learned one programming language well, additional languages are far easier to learn; it typically takes a programmer only 2 to 3 weeks to become competent in a new language.

Compilers can produce efficient machine code prior to execution. Many include code optimizing routines and the option of combining assembly routines with the compiled program. Compiled programs should be used for those processes in the data system that are repetitive.

Interpreters

Interpreters also translate programming languages. However, unlike a compiler, an interpreter translates each program statement as it is presented during execution, typically through a terminal. The programmer can develop the program, one line at a time, execute sections of the program, rework these sections, and so on, until the program is complete. This interactive development reduces total development time and makes subsequent modification and extension easier.

There are common interpreters for BASIC, APL, and other languages. Note that there are also compilers for these languages. Learning an interpretive language is usually easier than learning a compiler language. The interpreter commonly includes HELP routines that explain errors, syntax, and so on.

Because the interpreter operates one line at a time, the resulting code will be less efficient than that in a compiled program. The trade-off is between programmer time and machine time. If the program under development is to be used once or infrequently, using an interpreter will facilitate quick completion of the task.

Application Generators

Application generators offer a very high-level problem statement language, which is then translated into machine code or into a programming language for later compilation. The application generator uses a relatively large library of operational routines, each of which has been efficiently coded. The user is not expected to be familiar with a programming language. Commonly, the generator prompts the user for the type of problem specification expected, such as input formats, data names, file access requirements and keys, output formats, processing requirements, and so on.

There are a number of application generators, produced by both machine manufacturers and software houses. The use of an application generator can be learned in a two-day training session. Further skill can be developed over time. Because of the prompting from the system, a user need not use it continually to remain proficient.

Application generators can handle many administrative data processing requirements quite efficiently. Applications that are heavily query bound, that is, those that involve predominantly data retrieval and report generation, are particularly suitable. Complex updating is difficult to specify in a general way, and therefore it is difficult to translate into efficient code.

J. Martin, in his book *Application Development Without Programmers*, describes organizations that have drastically reduced their dependence on COBOL programs (and programmers) by using application generators. This has dramatically improved application-system implementation time, since the users themselves implement the system, rather than waiting for a programming staff to do the implementation in a traditional programming language.

COMPUTER ACQUISITION

Which computer system will be the best choice depends on the organization's total data processing requirements, the required response times for the data systems, and the resources, both financial and personnel, available for data processing. All current systems and those under consideration should be considered when the processing requirements for a new or modified computer installation are determined. Some important considerations include:

1. Data volumes, which will be the basis for calculating the secondary storage capacity necessary, as well as determining the number of input/output units needed to transport data to and from the system.
2. Processing type and volume for each of the separate systems, including the expected work load and whether they are I/O- or compute-bound, to form the basis for determining memory requirements, CPU computational speeds, number of channels for data access, and number of communication lines.
3. Response-time requirements, to determine the extent of on-line system support, the need for distributed processing, and the quantity and location of terminal groups.
4. Organization size, in terms of number of people, geographic distribution, funds available for data processing, to determine the need for and ability to acquire distributed processing capabilities.
5. Processing diversity, to determine whether a centralized computer, with batch or on-line processing, is preferable to a distributed system; high levels of diversity would indicate that local processing in separate, small systems or in a distributed system would be a possibility.
6. Management philosophy may influence the configuration choice; a centralized configuration may be indicated for a strongly centralized organization, whereas a distributed configuration may be more appropriate for a decentralized organization.

Once the processing requirements have been determined and the preferred system configuration established, the system designer may proceed with acquiring the necessary computer-system support. The first decision is where to obtain computer services. There are two main choices: a service bureau or one's own computer system.

Service Bureaus

Data processing service bureaus may offer everything from coding or keypunching of raw data to designing new processing systems, and from providing computer power to execute user-constructed systems to offering packaged processing.

Advantages of using service bureaus include:

- Fixed service costs
- Powerful equipment, normally more so than this system requires
- Back-up
- Standardized processing
- Staff of EDP experts, system analysts, and programmers
- System maintenance

Some disadvantages of using service bureaus include:

- Possibility of higher cost
- External control of data security
- External control of processing priorities
- Remote processing and need for data transmission
- Inflexible systems
- Dependence on the service bureau's continuing existence

Organizations that are new to automated data processing, or those with few systems suitable for automation or with an "extra" system, can be served well by service bureaus. There will be a fixed cost for the processing and contractual agreements concerning delivery of services. The organization need not invest in developing or extending local EDP expertise.

In-House Facilities

Organizations that have many automated data processing systems customarily have an internal computer department that manages the organization's computers, provides system analysis and design for other departments, develops application systems, and provides data processing services.

The advantages of an in-house computer department include:

- Control of data security
- Control of processing priorities

- Sufficient computer hardware, dimensioned for the organization
- Customized design of data systems
- Organizational determination of availability

Some disadvantages include:

- Maintenance of the computer department
- Possibility of high overhead costs
- Maintenance of specialists
- Queues for system implementation

Many organizations that have established automated data processing systems find that having internal control of data processing activities outweighs the costs of maintaining the computer department. These organizations may also make use of external consultants with specialized expertise, possibly from service bureaus, to supplement their computer staff or for internal training courses.

A small organization or one new to automated data processing may choose to acquire its own computer system when local, internal expertise in EDP is needed.

Request for Proposals

Whether an organization is acquiring a computer system or just computer services, three steps should be followed:

1. Request for and receipt of system proposals
2. Evaluation and selection of a system or service
3. Acquisition and test or acceptance of the system

Each of these steps is time-consuming and should be allocated resources proportional to the size of the configuration under consideration.

A request for proposal (RFP) should be sent to more than one vendor or service bureau. The RFP describes the processing requirements and the configuration structure envisioned and invites the recipient to prepare a bid. The RFP may emphasize either the processing requirements or the desired configuration, and thus may influence the form of the incoming bids.

When the RFP specifies the desired configuration, the responding bids will be quite uniform. These bids are relatively easy to evaluate, as each vendor will strive to offer the specified components. The bids will differ in number of units, speed and/or capacity, and price. A major problem may be that the incoming proposals do not reflect new technology or operative methods. Thus, this RFP/bid form will tend to continue the operative practices of the user organization.

When the RFP specifies the desired performance characteristics, the vendor is free to set up a configuration that best meets the performance requirements. The bids may vary considerably, and thus they may be more difficult to evaluate than the configuration bid. However, the organization is more likely to maintain state-of-the-art operations.

Evaluation

In evaluating the bids, each proposal should be analyzed for at least the following criteria:

1. Total system performance, using the stated organization requirements.
2. Component performance.
3. System and component cost.
4. Modularity within the system, that is, how easily individual components can be exchanged and/or upgraded.
5. Compatibility, that is, the problems or possibilities of moving existing systems to the proposed system. An evaluation of the vendor's past development record with compatible systems will help indicate the likelihood that the proposed configuration will be compatible with its predecessors and with its successors.
6. Reliability, the expected percentage of time that the configuration will be available for user processing. A configuration should be reliable enough that the vendor can guarantee up-time of greater than 98 percent. In large systems, reliability is usually provided by duplicating components.
7. Maintainability. All systems fail. The question is how much support the vendor makes available to correct configuration problems, and how quickly the vendor expects to be able to get the system operating. In evaluating this factor, the experience of other users is valuable.
8. Vendor support. In addition to providing maintenance, can or will the vendor support the system by providing new revisions of both hardware and software?

As with previous evaluations, many of these points are difficult to quantify and may be better valued along a scoring scale; for example, 0 to 5 might represent no support to very good support, respectively. (For an additional discussion of evaluation techniques, refer to Chapter 6.)

Note that the evaluation criteria given will be weighted differently in different organizations. For example, an organization with a well-developed systems programming staff should not need the same vendor support as an organization that has concentrated its programming expertise on applications development.

Payment Forms

Most computer configurations can be rented, purchased, or leased. A very general rule of thumb would be:

1. Renting. For new EDP users, the advantage lies in the ability to change and modify the components to tune the configuration to actual processing requirements. Rental vendors also usually offer the greatest support.

   For established EDP users, the tax laws may make renting advantageous, as some countries allow full deduction of rental expenses. The speed with which components may be exchanged as the operating environment changes, may also be an advantage.
2. Leasing involves a longer commitment to the configuration. A more experienced user may retain the tax advantage of monthly payments to an external company, while keeping the flexibility of component replacement, although more slowly than if the system is rented. Leases typically run for 2 to 3 years.
3. Purchasing requires a capital investment and a commitment to retain the configuration for a longer period of time, typically 5 to 8 years. If the processing requirements of the organization are quite stable or the organization is relatively experienced with computer operations, this option provides all the advantages and disadvantages of ownership.

Acceptance Testing

Once the computer is delivered and installed, but before payment begins, the organization should subject the system to an acceptance test. In the case of computer power from a service bureau, the organization should verify that the specified data processing is correct and complete according to the organization's criteria.

Acceptance testing of a computer system usually involves the execution of a test set of jobs, called a *benchmark*, which has certain known characteristics. The results are checked for correctness, processing times, system utilization, and other factors. Once the benchmark runs acceptably, the vendor must provide a demonstration of the up time for the installation. This is often measured over a period of 2 to 4 weeks of normal operation.

Acceptance test procedures and form of payment should be part of the acquisition contract with the vendor.

SUMMARY

We have introduced the broad topic of computer architecture and how one decides which type of computer and what basic system software are necessary for the system being developed. Readers are urged to refer to any of a number of texts on computer architecture for a more thorough presentation of these topics. Our brief discussion is meant to give readers a feel for the possibilities and limitations of various computer architectures so that they can acquire an appropriate computer for the system at hand.

Relatively simple systems for small firms can be developed for microcomputers. These systems will typically have one or two direct users (see Chapter 14). Medium-sized firms and relatively autonomous divisions of larger firms can be served by a minicomputer. Here larger quantities of data and a more varied array of data processing requirements are usually available. Large firms commonly need a central mainframe computer to handle their data processing requirements. These systems will typically have a wide variety of system software available.

Machines of all types may be connected into a distributed network, where a microcomputer can provide local processing for a manager or data analyst, the minicomputer can run department or division reports, and the central mainframe computer can maintain the firm's data base.

During system design, users should take the time to evaluate both the computing requirements for the system being developed and the firm's general data processing requirements.

KEY CONCEPTS

Application generator
Application system
Communication system
Compiler
Computer system
CPU
Data-base management system (DBMS)
Distributed system
File management system (FMS)
Hardware
Input/output (I/O)
Interpreter

Mainframe computer
Memory
Microcomputer
Minicomputer
On-line system
Operating system
Secondary storage
Service bureau
Software
System software
Time-sharing

DISCUSSION QUESTIONS

1. Define and give an example of each of the key concepts. How do these concepts influence the design of automated data processing systems?
2. Construct a model of a minimum system configuration for a batch-processing system, an on-line processing system, *and* a distributed system. Discuss the major differences and the advantages and disadvantages of each.
3. What system software is required for each of the minimal systems modeled in question 2?
4. How are data storage requirements calculated? What hardware requirements do the file structures of Chapter 9 set?
5. Describe a user interface. What characteristics should a good interface have?
6. Describe the similarities between microcomputers, minicomputers, and mainframe computers. How can each of these be used in the minimum configurations modeled in question 2?
7. What processing characteristics determine the choice of a microcomputer, minicomputer, or mainframe computer? What are the chief differences between these computers?
8. What is a node computer? What are its primary functions?
9. What is system software? Why is it necessary? Describe the main functions of operating systems, communication systems, and data management systems.
10. What is an application generator? A compiler? An interpreter? When should an application generator be used?
11. What is the use of service bureaus? To whom?
12. Who needs to own a computer? How should one go about obtaining one?

PROJECTS

1. Design a computer configuration for the student AIS. Prepare an RFP and set up the evaluation criteria.
2. Repeat project 1 using your own system.
3. Evaluate your local microcomputer (or minicomputer or mainframe) market. Prepare an RFP and evaluate costs and components available from at least two vendors.
4. Research your local service bureau market. What services are available? At what costs?

RECOMMENDED READINGS

Martin, J. *Introduction to Teleprocessing*. Englewood Cliffs, N.J.: Prentice-Hall, 1972.

This text presents both the hardware and software components used in on-line and distributed processing systems.

Martin, J. *Design and Strategy for Distributed Data Processing*. Englewood Cliffs, N.J.: Prentice-Hall, 1981.

Martin presents in some detail the environment of distributed processing systems, their components, applications, and design.

Martin, J. *Application Development Without Programmers*. Englewood Cliffs, N.J.: Prentice-Hall, 1982.

Martin reviews the state of the art (1982) in software systems designed to provide support for application development. He identifies seven categories of these systems: simple-query facilities, complex-query facilities, report generators, graphics languages, application generators, very high-level programming languages, and parameterized application packages.

Weldon, J. L. *Data Base Administration*. New York: Plenum Press, 1981.

This book reviews the problems of administering large collections of shared data. DBMSs, data-base administration by a human DBA, the use of data dictionaries, and other such topics are discussed as tools for easing the data administration problem.

Chapter 12

Implementation Planning

INTRODUCTION

At this point in the system life cycle, the existing information system has been analyzed, its weak points have been identified, and an improved alternative has been accepted. A data system to support the new or modified system has been designed, and appropriate computer hardware has been chosen for the system. All that remains is the implementation.

The magnitude of the implementation tasks is directly related to the magnitude of the system changes involved and to the newness of the concepts of the new system. For example, if the new system is a standard data processing application using standard software, implementation could consist of contract negotiations with a service bureau that will do the data processing. The system might also be implemented on the organization's own computer. This could involve purchase of the software, loading of the programs, and training of operators. These procedures will normally take from one day to one week and involve one or two people.

At the other extreme, the system being implemented can be a totally new data processing system running new general data processing applications and using new computer hardware. This type of project can take 3 to 5 years of implementation time and involve hundreds of people and thousands of person-hours.

Obviously, the complexity of the planning and management tasks involved in implementing a system also depend on the magnitude of the project. However, there is a core group of tasks that must be performed in all system implementations, at least to the extent of determining that nothing needs to be done. In this chapter we will discuss these core implementation tasks.

THE IMPLEMENTATION TEAM

The goal of any system implementation is to provide the users of the information and information services with a better information system. The success of the new system will be determined by the users' perception of the degree to which this goal is attained. In order to meet this goal and to maintain realistic expectations of what the system can provide, users must also be represented on the implementation team. User participation is most necessary in project management, program selection and acceptance testing, data collection, and final system acceptance testing.

Again, depending on the size of the project, the implementation team can vary in size from one to several hundred persons. Also, one individual may have more than one role on the team. Typically, the roles the implementation team must cover include:

- A project manager
- Programmers (0 to several hundred)
- Data collectors (0 to 25)
- Hardware technicians and operators (0 to 5)

The project manager is responsible for the system implementation, and also for organizing demonstration and training sessions for those who will be using the system. For a small project, the project manager can be responsible for all the tasks listed. For larger projects, a management structure of several people may be required.

Programmers may be employees of the organization's EDP department, the department that will use the information system, a service bureau, or an independent consultant. When standard software is available, programming may not be needed. If the system is to be implemented by an outside firm, management of programming can be reduced to control of progress, that is, ensuring that the agreed-upon deadlines are met. The number of programmers required is determined by the size of the project and its completion schedule. Increasing the number of programmers will not always result in faster implementation, since the problems of coordination and module testing will become increasingly complicated.

Most administrative systems require the processing of large quantities of data. If these data are not readily available, they must be collected and organized for the new system. Usually only the organization has access to the required data. The organization's data-base administrator (DBA) should be a member of the implementation team. The DBA knows what data are available within the organization and how to incorporate these data into the new system. In the actual loading of the data bases, those persons who will be responsible for data collection once the system is operative should be involved.

If new hardware is required, someone knowledgeable about the computers the organization already has and the organization's plans for computer expansion should be responsible for its acquisition, testing, and operation. This will help avoid acquiring incompatible hardware that can hinder later systems integration. When existing hardware is used, a member of the operating staff should be at least a consulting member of the implementation team to ensure that the resources the new system requires are or will be available.

IMPLEMENTATION MANAGEMENT

Managing the implementation of a system is an exercise in project management. System implementation includes a number of activities that can be performed simultaneously, assuming that personnel are available, and activities that are dependent on the completion of other tasks. It is the project manager's responsibility to identify the tasks required, assign tasks to the available personnel, and organize the tasks so that the project is completed as early as possible.

In the following section we will discuss the core tasks that are part of any system implementation, then discuss some project management tools that can be used to maintain control of task scheduling and follow-up.

Implementation Tasks

There are a number of tasks involved in the implementation of all computer-based systems, regardless of the size of the project. The following seven core tasks must be completed. The time required to complete them will vary, depending on the project, from almost none to several years.

1. Acquisition of computer support
2. Application programming and testing
3. Data-base construction
4. Acceptance testing
5. User training
6. System documentation
7. Conversion to the new system

Acquisition of Computer Support

In Chapter 11 we discussed various facilities that are available to support computer hardware and system software. In the system-design phase, which of these facilities are required to support the current application system was determined. If the organization already has enough computing power to support the new system, this task involves no further activity.

If new (more) computing power and/or facilities are required, the following activities must be initiated:

- Preparation of a request for proposal (RFP)
- Evaluation of received proposals
- Selection and ordering of equipment (hardware and system software)
- Site preparation
- Preparation of test routines
- Installation of equipment (hardware and/or software)
- Acceptance testing

Generally, acquisition of computer support must precede the other implementation tasks; it must at least be initiated before they can be begun in order to provide a test environment for development of the new programs and storage facilities for the new data base.

The time required for this task will depend on the quantity of new equipment needed and the level of computer technology that already exists in the organization. If the new equipment supplements an existing computer system, the acquisition time will depend on the machine vendor's delivery schedule. If a totally new system is required, acquisition time may also include time for RFP evaluation and/or site preparation. For example, site preparation for a microcomputer involves finding desk space, whereas a new mainframe may require a new building.

Normally, once the characteristics of the computer support required have been determined, someone responsible for the organization's computer facilities should be assigned to acquire the needed computer support facilities.

Application Programming and Testing

There are two possibilities for acquiring the application programs required for the system: (1) to use standard application packages, or (2) to develop new programs. The use of standard program packages, when this is possible, can save the organization development and testing time. In many cases standard program packages can be tailored to the particular application by either the software vendor or the organization's own programmers. However, if extensive tailoring is required, this may well take longer than creating new programs. For some applications, standard program packages can be used as the core of the new system, leaving only the special programs to be implemented by the organization.

If the new system is to use a standard program package, two options are open:

1. A service bureau can be contracted with to provide the required data processing services.
2. A standard package can be purchased and run on the organization's own computing facilities.

In either case, the same activities that were involved in acquisition of computer support facilities are involved in procurement of the standard services.

If the new system is to be programmed by the organization, the following activities must be initiated:

- Selection of the programming team
- Development of an implementation schedule for the program modules
- Module programming and testing
- Subsystem testing
- System testing

Programming can be done locally, by the organization's programmers, or by outside consultants or service bureaus who are under contract to the organization. In either case, the project manager should maintain control of the scheduling and follow-up routines and arrange for representatives of the end-user groups to perform module and system testing. Depending on the project size, from one to several hundred programmers may be needed; clearly in the latter case extreme care in subsystem design, programming, and testing will be required.

Programming can be begun as soon as a computer and relevant compiler are available. The computer system need not be the final system, but must be compatible with it. For program or module testing, at least a test data base must be available. If possible, user representatives should be included on the module testing teams.

The time required for programming, with programmers using such traditional programming languages as FORTRAN, COBOL, or PL/1, will vary from one month to several years, depending on the complexity of the system. Progress is being made on the development of application generators (Martin, 1983). These are very high-level problem specification languages that allow the end user to develop application programs directly. When such systems are available, particularly for traditional data processing applications, such as administrative systems or transaction-processing systems, they can drastically reduce program implementation time. However, most systems will also require some programs that will have to be implemented using more traditional programming languages. Module testing will also remain an important task.

Data-Base Construction

In this section, the term *data base* is given its most general meaning, "those data required for the execution of the application system." The decision as to whether or not to use a DBMS to administer the data should have been made during data-system design (see Chapters 8 and 9).

Normally, the new data base will not contain completely new data, but rather data that already exist within the organization, some of which may already be in other automated data bases. Someone in the organization should be responsible for management of the organization's data. This someone, a data-base administrator (DBA), should be responsible for managing the data-base construction activities for the new system.

During system implementation, two data bases need to be constructed:

1. A test data base, which includes all types of data, accurate and erroneous, and which is to be used for testing the program modules as they are completed
2. The real data base, which will receive the organization's data and be maintained through the application system

The activities involved in establishing an application data base include:

- Selection and acquisition of data management software (DMS)
- Adaptation of record and file layouts to the DMS specifications
- Definition of stored data structures
- Collection of data
- Generation of test files/data base
- Generation of operative files/data base
- Specification and generation of data structure maintenance procedures and programs

The data bases can be established at the same time as the programming is done, provided personnel are available. Once forms for data entry and the underlying programs are established, the end users responsible for data entry can begin to develop the data base.

Normally, the data base needed for an application is not new to the organization, but can be transferred from other systems. When this is the case, the time required to establish the data bases will depend on the time required to develop the data transfer program(s). If the data required do not exist within the organization or are not on machine-readable media, data-base construction can be very time-consuming, as the data must be manually collected, coded, entered onto machine-readable media, and edited for errors before they can be used by the automated procedures.

System Acceptance Testing

Once the pieces of the new system—machine, programs, and data base—have been acquired and tested separately, a test of the full system must be performed. The testers should be the end users. The test environment must be as near to the normal operative environment as possible. The implementation team, particularly the programmers and the DBA, must be available to make necessary corrections.

There are two classes of errors that can occur during acceptance testing:

1. Implementation errors, which include program errors, missing program logic for handling erroneous data, errors in file specifications, errors in computer support dimensions, errors in operative procedure specifications, and so on
2. Design errors, based on misunderstanding of the system goals

Care must be taken to ensure that only implementation errors are corrected during the test phase. If design or goal errors are found, the test phase should be halted and a major analysis of the error performed. Many design errors can be corrected and the system test continued. However, correction of goal errors can require such major revisions in the system design that the implementation should be postponed or abandoned. If the current system design is still considered useful, correction of the goal error can be designated as a phase 2 (next phase) system modification.

System testing should proceed for several days or weeks and cover as many conditions, particularly error conditions, as possible. Once the system has passed the test phase, it can be put into operation and replace the current system.

User Training

In this context, training includes presentation of the new system to all those who will be working with it, either directly or indirectly. Actually, "training" began when the various user groups accepted the plans for the new system.

As system implementation progresses, prospective indirect users of the system's information services should be informed of the system's capabilities. This information can be presented in half-day seminars, which should occur shortly before the system is to be accepted.

Users who will be working directly with the system should be represented on the system testing teams. These users must receive training that is intensive enough to enable them to use the system, and they must receive it immediately before the test phase is initiated. This training should involve one day to one week of "hands-on" classes, depending on the variety of interactions to be learned. Users must be given enough time to become familiar with all relevant interactions and feel confident that they can handle any error conditions that may arise.

The general direct user community must receive training in system use before conversion to the new system. Again, the training sessions should give hands-on experience over a time period long enough to enable them to become familiar with the new system's facilities.

System Documentation

Actually the system documentation has been under development throughout the system development process, from the initial goal analysis through system analysis, design, and implementation. The implementation documentation completes the system documentation.
Implementation documentation has three components:

1. Program documentation, including flowcharts, compiler listings, error messages, and procedures
2. Data structures
3. Operative instructions, including user manuals, operator manuals, and program and data-base maintenance procedures

For large systems, it will be advantageous to have someone on the implementation team who is specifically responsible for collection, development, and maintenance of the system documentation. Various components of the documentation can be generated by different individuals, such as system analysts, system designers, programmers, the DBA, trainers, and others. If there is no one person responsible for collecting and coordinating the documentation, the parts can become separated and poorly maintained as the individuals move to other tasks.

Conversion to the New System

Conversion here means the transfer of data processing operations from the old system to the newly approved system. Several strategies for accomplishing this transfer will be discussed in detail later in this chapter.

Conversion is the final task of system implementation; it begins after all other tasks have been completed. The time required to complete conversion depends on the conversion strategy chosen.

Implementation Management Tools

One of the most immediate and hitherto difficult management tasks in system implementation has been completing the implementation on time and within budget. Two major problem areas have been identified:

1. Keeping the developing system acceptable to the users
2. Estimating the programming and testing time requirements

Users generally first get to see the new system in operation during the testing phase. This may be several months (or years) after the design was accepted, and the users' expectations of what the system is to do may have changed. Furthermore, the organizational environment may have changed in ways that require changes in the information system if effective service is to be maintained. The best advice on how to meet and deal with this problem is as follows:

1. Include user representatives on the system analysis, design, and implementation teams in order to maintain, as far as possible, continuous contact with the needs of the users and the organization as they evolve over time. Including users in all phases of the system life cycle will also help to maintain realistic expectations about what facilities are being included in the new system.
2. Allocate time and resources to the initial goal analysis, system analysis, and feasibility studies. Understanding, from the outset, the information problems and the various ways in which these problems can be met ensures an improved and more realistic foundation for the system design.
3. When possible, develop a system prototype to test the system design before full implementation begins. Experience with system prototypes has shown that users discover new information requirements as they become familiar with what an automated system can provide. (Berild et al., 1977).

Estimates of the time required for system implementation are notoriously unreliable, with the worst offender being estimates of the time required to produce correct, operative programs. This problem results from the nature of programming, which many still consider an art rather than a structured, well-understood science. In programming, a person must specify, in great detail, the solution to a problem, identifying all unexpected (error) situations and specifying detailed action to deal with them. This level of detailed specification is not required in our other communications. Tools and techniques for managing the programming task include:

1. Using standard software modules wherever possible, in order to reduce the programming effort by eliminating the reproduction of standard solutions
2. Using high-level languages and/or application generators to develop modules that are prototypes or that are used relatively infrequently
3. Restricting the use of low-level programming languages to modules with critical time requirements

4. Organizing programmer teams who exchange coding and test functions in order to help reduce the time needed to locate logical design and coding errors
5. Requiring structured programming techniques and documentation, in order to maintain control of modules as they develop

Control of the other implementation tasks requires good management. A schedule of the events and tasks that must be performed before the implementation is completed is a necessary project management tool. The project manager must know what tasks are required, the time and effort involved in each task, and the dependency of interrelated tasks.

The implementation schedule must be developed as part of implementation planning, and it must be constantly updated as the implementation progresses. Task execution times are only estimates, and as unforeseen events occur, their impact on the implementation schedule must be determined and corrective measures, such as reallocating resources, taken if the completion date is to be maintained.

Estimating time requirements for human efforts is difficult. One suggestion is to collect several estimates, from programmers or project managers familiar with the type of program to be developed, for each task:

$t(o)$ = an optimistic time estimate, if all goes well

$t(c)$ = a most likely time estimate, assuming normal delays

$t(p)$ = a pessimistic estimate, if everything goes wrong

These estimates can then be combined to form an estimate of the task execution time (TET)—for example, by using the formula

$$\text{TET} = \frac{t(o) + 4t(c) + t(p)}{6}$$

This formula for estimating execution times has been tested and gives quite reliable estimates, especially when the time estimates were provided by individuals who are knowledgeable about the task. In more uncertain situations, a lower weighting of $t(c)$ may be appropriate.

PERT Networks

An implementation schedule can be set up as a PERT (Program Evaluation and Review Technique) network. In this network, each node represents an event and the arcs represent the activities or tasks required to move from one event to the next. Events are considered to be without a time duration and signal a change of state, for example, the completion of one or several activities or the initiation of one or several new activities. Events are used as milestones or control points to check that the project is progressing according to plan.

Each activity or task is characterized by the following parameters:

- TID   the task identification, which is a reference number corresponding to a full description of the task in the implementation documentation
- PE   the preceding event
- SE   the succeeding event
- TET   the estimated task execution time
- D1   the earliest start date for the task
- D2   the latest completion date for the task
- SLT   the slack time available in the schedule:

$$SLT = (D2 - D1) - TET$$

The sequence of project activities can be set up as a PERT network by utilizing the precedent event information. Given a PERT network for the activities, the minimum project completion date can be calculated from the maximum project TET, found by summing the activity TETs along each path to the final event. The critical path (CP) is that sequence of tasks that determines the project completion date, in that a delay in any task on the CP will delay completion of the project. Using the activity TETs and the completion date, the earliest start and latest completion dates for each activity can be calculated.

Figure 12.1 illustrates an event network for the general system implementation tasks. Each event is identified by a reference number and given a name that reflects the completion or start of some activity.

Figure 12.2 shows a PERT network for part of an implementation. Figure 12.2 takes the event network of Figure 12.1 and includes the estimated time for each activity. Each activity (arrow) is characterized by two tuples:

$$\langle TET, D1, D2 \rangle \quad and \quad \langle SLT \rangle$$

Tuple 1, $\langle TET, D1, D2 \rangle$, gives the estimated execution time in weeks. The earliest start and latest completion dates (D1 and D2) are given in week numbers, where $D1 = 1$ indicates the start of week 1 of the project. Correspondingly, $D2 = 1$ indicates the end of week 1. In our example, selection of computer support (activity 1-2), programming of system modules (activity 1-4), and preparation of the test data base (activity 1-3) all begin in week 1 of the project. Their estimated TETs

Figure 12.1 System Implementation Tasks

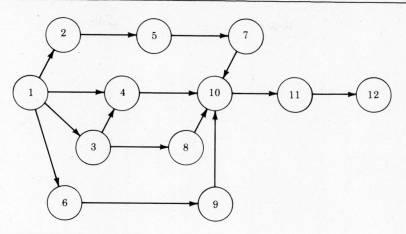

Events:
1 Begin implementation
2 Send order for computer equipment
5 Receive equipment
7 Accept equipment
4 Begin module test (programming completed)
10 Begin system test (all parts completed)
11 Begin system conversion
12 New system in operation
3 DB for test ready
8 Operational DB ready
6 User orientation complete
9 User training complete

are 1, 3, and 2 weeks, respectively. Slack time (SLT) is estimated as 3, 0, and 1 week, respectively. This gives the values for the latest completion date D2 as week 4, 3, and 3, respectively.

The critical path (CP) is along the programming path; this is indicated by the fact that there is no slack time scheduled for these tasks. Project duration, that is, the earliest completion time, can be calculated from the sum of the TETs for the activities along the critical path. In our example, the project is scheduled to take 12 weeks, the sum of activities 1-4, programming; 4-10, program testing; 10-11, system testing; and 11-12, system conversion $(3 + 3 + 2 + 4 = 12)$.

In most system implementations, the CP will follow the programming path. However, if standard software is available, the CP could well follow the data-base construction path.

Once the PERT network has been established, it must be maintained as the implementation progresses. Differences between the estimated

Figure 12.2 System Implementation Schedule—PERT Network

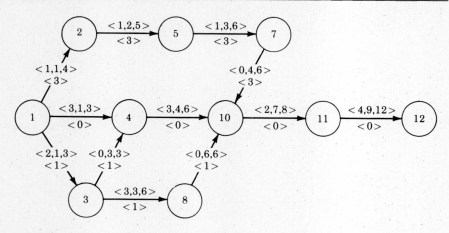

Activities:

1–2	Evaluate and select computer support equipment
2–5	Prepare for delivery of equipment
5–7	Test equipment
7–10	Ready for system test (10–11)
1–4	Program system modules
4–10	Test program modules
10–11	Test system
11–12	System conversion
1–3	Prepare test DB
3–4	Ready for module test (4–10)
3–8	Prepare operational DB
8–10	Ready for system test (10–11)

TET and the actual TET can result in changes in the CP. The project manager must be aware of these changes and determine whether resources should be reallocated to maintain the schedule.

One important advantage of using the PERT technique for implementation scheduling is that there are a number of computer programs that accept a list of the tasks, their preceding event(s), indicating those tasks that must be completed before this task can be begun, and their expected execution times. These programs then construct a PERT network; compute the earliest start, latest completion, and slack times; and indicate the CP through the network.

PERT networks can and should be made at various levels of detail. For example, each node in Figure 12.1 can be represented by its own PERT network.

Gantt Charts

The PERT network is particularly useful for ordering tasks and determining the project completion date. However, it reflects the effort involved in each task only indirectly and gives the parallel tasks implicitly. A more work-specific schedule plan is the Gantt chart.

The Gantt chart is set up with the task list along the left axis and a time axis covering the project duration, usually given in weeks. Each task is represented by a line on the chart, with the starting and completion points of the task marked along the time axis, and work effort, for example, in person-weeks, indicated.

Figure 12.3 illustrates a Gantt chart for a hypothetical implementation. Note that "module programming" is scheduled to begin in week 1 and continue for 3 weeks. The work load is estimated to be 18 person weeks (PW), which translates into a need for 6 programmers. "Machine delivery with site preparation" is scheduled to take 4 weeks but requires only 1 PW effort. This indicates that the person responsible will be free to perform other tasks, either in this implementation or elsewhere. Summing the work loads indicates that during week 1 the implementation team must include at least 2 persons, plus possibly the project manager, whereas during weeks 3 and 4 there must be 17 persons working on the project.

The PERT network and the Gantt chart are complementary tools for implementation management. The PERT network highlights the tasks required, their sequence, and their interdependencies, whereas the Gantt chart highlights the resources required to complete the task and identifies overlapping activities.

SYSTEM CONVERSION

System conversion signals the end of system implementation. It must be planned in such a way that it will disrupt the organization's business activities as little as possible. Ideally, the conversion should be timed well *after* acceptance testing so that the conversion date will not force premature acceptance of the system.

There are four basic strategies for system conversion, illustrated in Figure 12.4:

1. Direct conversion
2. Parallel conversion
3. Modular conversion
4. Phase-in conversion

Direct conversion entails a direct switch from the old system to the new one. This method is most frequently used for major hardware

Figure 12.3　Implementation Schedule—Gantt Chart

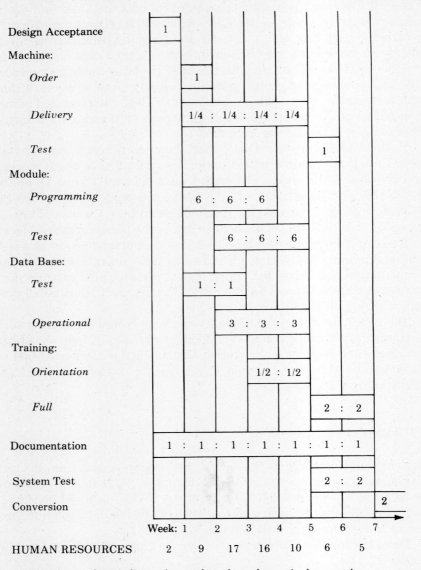

	Week: 1	2	3	4	5	6	7
HUMAN RESOURCES	2	9	17	16	10	6	5

NOTE: The numbers indicate the number of people required per week.

Figure 12.4 Conversion Strategies

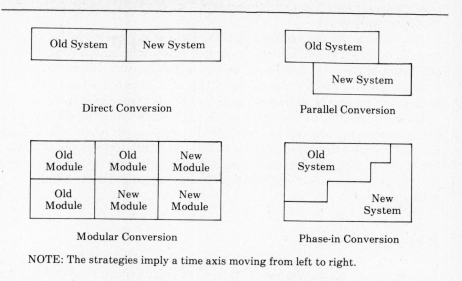

Direct Conversion

Parallel Conversion

Modular Conversion

Phase-in Conversion

NOTE: The strategies imply a time axis moving from left to right.

changes, when the old equipment must be removed before the new equipment and the new systems can be installed. Another situation in which direct conversion is required is when there are no resources for operating two parallel systems. Thirdly, if the system is not critical to the organization, the new system can replace the old and any initial problems can be absorbed without critically affecting other operations. Finally, the new system may be truly new, in which case there is no old system to replace.

Parallel conversion entails maintenance and operation of both the old and the new systems in parallel. This is normally done for critical accounting systems as a final stage of acceptance testing. Parallel conversion can continue over several reporting cycles. Discrepancies between the two systems must be checked and resolved. Unfortunately, some of these apparent errors may actually be errors in the old system that previously had not been located. It is seldom that both systems maintain identical information, and at some point the parallel operation must end.

Modular conversion entails the replacement of program modules with new versions while retaining major portions of the old system. This is most common when facilities are being added to an existing system or when small modifications to existing programs are required. This conversion method is also used when the old system is being translated to another programming environment, or perhaps a data-base environment. It is the "conversion" method used every day during system maintenance.

Phase-in conversion entails replacing the old system with the new one for one user group within the organization at a time. From an organizational point of view, this may be less disruptive than a direct conversion. It also retains some of the advantages of parallel conversion without tying up the extra resources needed for parallel conversion.

Once conversion to the new system has been accomplished, the implementation project can be considered complete. However, the system has just entered the most important and hopefully longest phase of its life cycle. During the system's operative life, it should be reviewed regularly to determine the degree to which the system goals are being achieved.

SUMMARY

The success of system implementation is dependent on the quality of the preceding design specifications and on control of the implementation project. System implementation is normally the most time-consuming of the system development tasks and the one during which there is the highest likelihood of delay. Careful planning and project management are required for the implementation phase.

We have discussed two tools that can be used for planning and managing system implementation: the PERT and Gantt charts. They are complementary in that PERT charts concentrate on the sequencing of events, whereas the Gantt chart highlights the personnel requirements.

KEY CONCEPTS

Acceptance testing
Application generators
Conversion
Critical path (CP)
Direct conversion
Documentation
Gantt chart
Implementation scheduling

Implementation team
Module conversion
Parallel conversion
PERT
Prototype systems
Standard software
System implementation
Training

DISCUSSION QUESTIONS

1. Discuss and give an example of each of the key concepts.
2. What are the tasks involved in system implementation?
3. What skills are required of an implementation team? How many people should be on the team? Where should they come from?
4. Who should be the implementation project manager? Why?
5. Discuss the advantages and disadvantages of using a consultant or a service bureau for system implementation.
6. Discuss the advantages and disadvantages of using application generators for system implementation.
7. Discuss the generation of the data bases. Where do the data come from? Who should collect them and ensure their correctness? What role should the DBA play?
8. What is involved in acceptance testing? Who is responsible? Who are the actors?
9. What is included in system documentation? Who is responsible for it? How can it best be presented and maintained?
10. Discuss the four strategies for system conversion. When should each be used?

PROJECTS

1. Set up PERT and Gantt schedules for the implementation of your system. Discuss the resources required. Where will the people come from?
2. Set up an acceptance test for your system. What major elements are there? How many must meet testing requirements before the system is accepted? Who will be responsible for the acceptance test?
3. Set up a conversion schedule for your system. What strategy is to be used? Why?

RECOMMENDED READINGS

Berild, S., and S. Nachmens. "CS4—A Tool for Database Design by Infological Simulation." *Proc. 3rd Int. Conference Very Large Data Bases*, 1977.
    CS4 is one of a number of systems for developing a prototype system for user testing of a system design. The chief advantage of these systems is that they shorten the time between initial design and availability of an operative, if minimal, system for testing. Development of CS4 has been a major project of the Systems Development Laboratory, SYSLAB, at the University of Stockholm.
Martin, J. *Application Development Without Programmers*. Englewood Cliffs, N.J.: Prentice-Hall, 1982.
    See Chapter 11 readings list for further information.

Szyperski, N., and E. Grochla, eds. *Design and Implementation of Computer-Based Information Systems*. The Netherlands: Sijthoff & Noordhoff, 1979.

This book includes the papers from a symposium on the design and implementation of CBISs. Of particular interest are the papers on implementation planning and implementation research.

Chapter 13
System Maintenance and Growth

INTRODUCTION

An operational computer-based information system (CBIS) requires ongoing maintenance to ensure its continuing performance quality. System maintenance can be defined as follows:

System Maintenance All tasks on existing, operative CBISs that are aimed at keeping the system correct, operating efficiently, and providing the user services desired.

Typical maintenance tasks include:

1. Correction of program errors
2. Conversion of programs to another programming language
3. Adaptation of programs to changes in specifications
4. Correction of data errors
5. Taking periodic copies of data files
6. Reorganization and restructuring of data files
7. Conversion of files to a data base
8. Restoration of the CBIS after a system failure
9. Modification of operative procedures
10. Change in operational mode, for example, from batch to on-line

Computer departments report that 40 to 70 percent of their staff time is absorbed by application-system maintenance. This work load reduces the computer department's ability to participate in the analysis and design of new systems, which in turn leads to dissatisfaction, inside and outside the department, with the department's ability to keep abreast of the organization's changing information-processing service requirements.

Maintenance tasks are frequently viewed negatively as drudgery, correction of errors (which should not have occurred), and tedious copying. Many organizations train their new system programmers by giving them maintenance tasks. This can lead to slower than necessary resolution of problems, and to more errors, because the programmers do not understand the system. The pay, morale, and prestige of maintenance personnel is often low.

Most of the tasks listed are commonly considered to be maintenance tasks. It would help in managing system maintenance and hopefully

improve the perception of the importance and prestige of these tasks if
they were considered as three categories of activities, rather than one.
For example, the maintenance tasks can be seen as falling into the
following categories of activities:

- Error control: prevention, detection, and correction;
    maintenance tasks 1, 4, 5, and 8
- System tuning for operative efficiency;
    maintenance tasks 2, 6, and 9
- System growth: expansion and adaptation;
    maintenance tasks 3, 7, and 10

Error control, as defined here, has two phases. The first is an intensive and relatively short-lived effort to achieve an operative system.
Here task 1, correction of program errors, is the predominant activity.
The second phase continues throughout the life of the system and involves intense activity whenever a data error is discovered or suspected.
The operative actions of the second phase of error control are similar
for all systems and can be considered routine.

System tuning is a positive and potentially exciting activity that involves taking a working system and making it work better—usually
faster. Tuning is required to adapt the operative system to changes in
the activity patterns of the system environment.

System growth is also positive and equivalent in many ways to the
design and implementation of a new system. Growth is a natural adaptation of the system to changing and expanding information service requirements within the user community.

In the following, we will discuss the special tasks pertaining to each
category. We believe that separating maintenance activities in this way
will improve the definition of the maintenance-task time requirements
and will foster a more positive perception of these tasks and their
importance.

ERROR CONTROL

Error control is primarily concerned with the prevention, detection,
and correction of errors. Central tasks of error control include:

- Correction of program errors
- Correction of data errors
- Restoration after system error
- Procedures for back-up copies of the system

Unfortunately, a system is never completely error-free. Errors can
exist in programs along execution paths that are used only in rare
instances, so that these errors were not discovered by the test

procedures. Errors can be introduced when incorrect but possible data values are entered into the system or generated by the system. Errors can also be introduced following computer-system failures or through errors in START/RESTART procedures.

Actually, error control begins with system design, continues through programming and data-base generation, and then becomes a major concern during system test and operation. An important factor in error control is a correct system design with procedures for preventing and correcting errors. Naturally, all programs must operate correctly under clearly stated operative procedures. The inclusion of input screening controls to check that the incoming data are reasonable and, whenever possible, correct is also important.

Once an error occurs, it must be located and corrected, and any erroneous actions the system has taken because of the error must be reversed. Depending on when the error is discovered, system recovery can be very complex.

Program Maintenance

It is generally accepted that programs that have been developed and implemented according to a structured or modular design will be easier to maintain, that is, they will require less maintenance and repair. A CBIS contains a number of subsystems, each of which can contain errors, generate errors, and be used to prevent errors. These subsystems include:

- User interface
- Transaction programs
- Report programs
- Audit routines
- Operating procedures

The User Interface

The user interface allows the user to activate various system facilities. Often the user is presented with a menu of system services, such as data entry forms, transaction types, or report forms, from which to choose an appropriate activity.

The user interface can play a central role in system error control by screening both users (for authority) and data (for validity) as they enter the system. In this error-control capacity, the user interface routines must be supplemented with a register of valid users and the activities they can initiate and a register of valid data value ranges and data formats. The user interface should produce a log, commonly called an *input log*, of the user-generated activities, including:

- Time and location of each user interaction
- Transactions activated
- Data submitted and received

Once established, the user interface should require little maintenance. As the system grows, this subsystem may need to be expanded to offer new services, such as transactions, reports, or analytic routines, to new users over new devices (terminals).

The Transaction Programs

The transaction programs are critical for error control, since it is these programs that actually change the state of the data base from which other programs receive all or part of their data.

Each separate transaction program must be thoroughly tested for correct operation given all possible input data values, correct and incorrect. The structure of the programs must be such that the possibility that an aborted execution will leave erroneous data is minimal. Typically, if multiple data sources are used to calculate output data values, these should be read first, so that the set is controlled for completeness before any changes are made in the data base.

It must be possible to *roll back* a transaction program, that is, return the system to the state it would have had if the program had not been started. This is necessary when the program cannot be completed normally because of erroneous data, or when the system stops the transaction for some reason, such as a conflict between transactions being executed in parallel. See Figure 13.1 and the discussion of data integrity.

It must be possible to *erase* the effects of a transaction when an error is discovered after the transaction has been completed. This can be done through a program that is in effect the negative of the original transaction.

All modifications to existing transaction programs must be carefully tested before they are used in the operative system, to ensure that errors are not introduced.

Transaction-program maintenance is facilitated by keeping an up-to-date version of program documentation that reflects any changes that have been made in the programs. Establishing standards for the programming language used, program form, program comments, and program testing is also helpful.

The Report Programs

From the point of view of preventing system errors, the report genera-tors are relatively safe, since they only take data from the system and present them in a desired way. They do not change system data, and thus their effect on other programs of the CBIS is minimal. Also, new report programs may be added and old ones deleted without affecting the operation of the system.

However, it is generally the report set that defines the system's use-fulness for the users and thus its success. Much (if not most) of the maintenance effort on the report programs is devoted to improving their layout and information content so that they present correct in-formation in as clear a manner as possible.

The Audit Routines

Audit routines are added to an operative system to supply error tests and controls on the processing functions of the system. They test for consistency and correctness of data and for correct functioning of the transaction programs. The audit routines do not themselves alter data values, and thus their effect on the transaction and report programs of the system is minimal.

The Operating Procedures

The sequence in which transactions are executed is usually important in maintaining correct data states. These procedures can be given as manual instructions to the system's users and operators or can be included in the control subsystem. Changes in transaction sequencing or the addi-tion of new transactions may affect the operating procedures.

Data Integrity

Data integrity control includes those activities primarily concerned with maintaining the correctness of the data within the data base (in its most general meaning, "the data required for an application system"). Data integrity is maintained through three activities: keeping logs of correct data-base states and transaction data, monitoring update activity, and restoration when errors are discovered.

Subsystems involved in maintaining data integrity include:

- the user interface, which executes the data input controls and gener-ates input logs

- transaction programs, containing correct data value calculation algorithms
- audit routines, which check the stored data values

Further, the data-base management system (DBMS) should include controls on all data values presented for storage, ensuring that they are within the range and of the type defined as acceptable. Erroneous data must not be accepted, and the transaction generating them should be aborted. This should lead to a rollback of the transaction in order to preserve the previous correct data-base state.

If a transaction has produced an "acceptable" data error, that is, an erroneous data value within the acceptable range, this should be revealed by periodic audit controls. In this case a major corrective action may have to be initiated, depending on the age of the "bad" data and the number of transactions that have used it.

In batch processing or single-user systems, these actions are sufficient. In systems that allow multiple concurrent users (transactions), however, further concurrency control must be taken, usually by the DBMS.

The concurrency problem is illustrated in Figure 13.1a. Here there are two programs, P-1 and P-2, each of which modifies the data values of record A. P-1 and P-2 each read the same values from record A, and both compute new values, with P-1 returning its version of record A before P-2 returns its version. In this sequence, the effects of P-1 have been erased, but no error has been detected by the programs themselves. The error is in the sequencing of the executions of the programs.

Concurrent update situations are controlled by monitoring the data requests of all update programs. When a program, P-2 in the example, requests a record that is already in use, it is put into a wait state until the first program has been completed. One problem with this method is that a *deadlock* situation can arise, as shown in Figure 13.1b. Here P-1 has read record A and P-2 has read record B. P-1 requests record B and is put on a wait queue, waiting for P-2 to finish. So far all is well. Unfortunately, P-2 requests record A and is put on a wait queue, waiting for P-1 to finish. Neither program is in error and neither can continue. The DBMS must detect the deadlock situation and roll back one of the programs, thus allowing the other to finish processing. The rolled-back program is then restarted.

Back-up and Recovery Procedures

Some errors require corrective action that is more comprehensive than simply preventing or rolling back the actions of a single user or transaction. Major errors can occur when there has been a system failure and the exact status of the active transactions is unknown. Or the audit

Figure 13.1 Concurrency Control

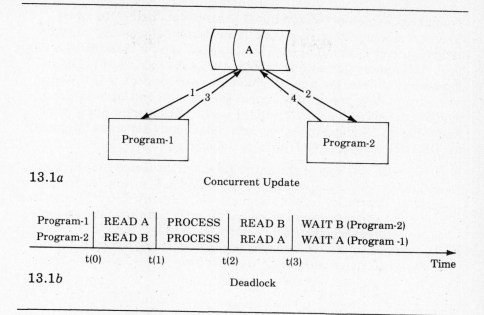

13.1*a*   Concurrent Update

| Program-1 | READ A | PROCESS | READ B | WAIT B (Program-2) |
| Program-2 | READ B | PROCESS | READ A | WAIT A (Program -1) |

| | t(0) | t(1) | t(2) | t(3) | Time |

13.1*b*   Deadlock

routines may uncover erroneous data that are known or suspected to have been used in succeeding transactions. In both these situations the main strategy is to return the data base to some previous correct state, then recreate a current status without the errors.

Back-up and recovery procedures assume that the CBIS can be out of service while the error condition is repaired and the system brought back into operation. Some systems, such as a hospital intensive care system or a spaceship control system, may not tolerate a system failure. For these systems a second (and sometimes third) back-up machine that can work in parallel with the main system must be available. Alternatively, the CBIS can be operated on a fault-tolerant computer system in which the back-up hardware and software is already incorporated.

Occasionally, the computer system sustains such a major failure that the recovery time is measured in days and weeks—for example, in case of fire, explosion, or some other such occurrence. The CBIS can be reactivated on another computer while the original is under repair. To cover such situations, organizations often participate in reciprocal back-up contracts with other compatible organizations.

DB Back-up

To make possible the recreation of a correct data base (DB) when errors are discovered or suspected in the current DB, a copy of some earlier, correct DB must exist. This data-base copy is called the *back-up copy*; it is always assumed to contain a correct version of the DB at some specific time, the time at which the copy was created. It is also necessary to have copies of the input transactions and/or the record modifications that have been applied to the DB since the copy was made. Figure 13.2 illustrates the data collections commonly suggested for DB error recovery. The recovery data include:

1. A full *back-up* copy of the data base taken at regular time intervals, such as the beginning of every day, every week, or some other interval, depending on the volume of data modification. The back-up copy or copies are commonly kept on tape, but they may also be kept on direct-access storage devices (DASDs).
2. An *input log*, initiated immediately after a back-up copy is taken, that logs all transaction input that has been applied to the data base

Figure 13.2 Back-up and Recovery Files

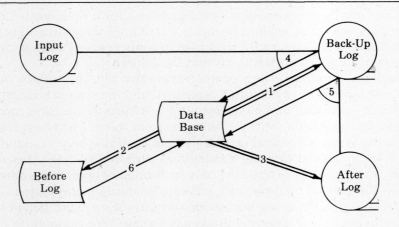

1. Back-Up   Periodic DB copy
2. Before Log   Record copy before change
3. After Log   Record copy after change
4. Long Recovery: Input-log + transaction processing ➔
                      Back-up copy ➔ reconstructed DB
5. Short Recovery: After-log ➔ back-up ➔ reconstructed DB
6. Roll-Back/Restart: Before-log ➔ DB ➔ reconstructed (prior) DB

since the back-up copy was made. There must be an input log for each back-up version.

3. An *after log* (optional), initiated after a back-up copy has been made, containing a copy of all records modified since the last back-up copy was made. Each after-log record contains the date and time of modification and the identification of the transaction that produced the modification.

4. A *before log* (optional), kept from the time the last back-up copy was made, containing a copy of all records prior to their modification. Again, each before-log record is time and date stamped and includes the identification of the transaction that is to make a change.

DB Recovery

Recovery is the process of restoring the data base, and the system, to an earlier correct state as close to the present time as possible. Three basic strategies can be used, indicated in Figure 13.2:

- *Long recovery* uses the back-up data-base copy and reexecutes the transactions recorded on the input log.
- *Short recovery* uses the back-up data-base copy and recreates the data base by rewriting (patching) modified records from the after log.
- *Rollback* uses the current data base and rolls it back by rewriting (patching) records from the before log.

Long recovery is the most time-consuming, since transactions must be reexecuted. This recovery strategy must be used when a program error was the cause of the problem and the erroneous program has been corrected. New transaction programs can affect other programs by producing different data values. In this case, determining the correct system state can be very complex, and must normally be done outside the automated system.

Short recovery (compared with long recovery) can be used when the DB needs only to be recreated and no changes have been made in the transaction programs. This recovery strategy can be used after a computer-system failure. It should proceed up to but not include the transactions that were active when the failure occurred. Normal processing begins with a restart of the last active programs.

Rollback of the data base rolls back the transaction programs that are currently active and any previous transactions that must be erased to return the DB to a correct state. This strategy can be used after a system failure when no major DB damage is suspected. It is the normal strategy for resolving a deadlock.

SYSTEM TUNING

System tuning, in the context of this chapter, includes those activities that change the implementation characteristics of the automated system with the intent of improving system efficiency. System efficiency can be measured in terms of execution speed and capacity requirements. The system users commonly perceive an improvement in system efficiency as an improvement in the system's response time. Response time is the time from the system's receipt of an input transaction or message until the appropriate output has been sent to the user.

Activities that aim at improving system efficiency include:

- Conversion of programs from one language to another to improve the compiled program version
- Recombining the system modules to make the most active modules more readily available
- Reorganizing or restructuring data files to improve data access times
- Conversion of files to a data base to improve data access capabilities
- Change of operational mode to improve total system responsiveness

Not infrequently, an attempt to improve system efficiency leads to an upgrading or replacement of the computer system. This will commonly involve several of these activities.

Program Tuning

Once the programs have been corrected and the system is operational, the programs and their routines can be divided into groups according to their usage characteristics—frequently used routines in one group, seldom used routines in another, and so on. Tuning efforts should be concentrated on the frequently used routines. There are two types of tuning efforts, which may be applied separately or together.

1. Check, correct, and/or modify program flow to minimize the number of statements executed.
2. Reorder the location of program modules to minimize the transport of modules from program libraries to the CPU.
3. Rewrite in a more efficient language to increase the speed of execution.

Programs that execute correctly may still be inefficient. The code should be checked, and modified as required, to ensure that:

- There is a minimal set of branches.
- All constants are assigned outside of loops.
- Unnecessary statements are eliminated.

- Input/output statements are well placed so that the program has work to do while waiting for data transfers.

Many larger CBISs contain a central group of programs that remain resident in the CPU during system execution. Less frequently used programs are kept in program libraries on secondary storage (DASD) and loaded into the CPU when needed. The number of resident programs is commonly limited by the memory space available in the CPU. Therefore which programs to include in the resident set is a design problem. Once the system is operative, program usage statistics may indicate that reordering the resident program set can reduce the amount of library-to-CPU transport and thus improve the system's efficiency.

Once the program flow is deemed efficient, central, highly active routines can be reprogrammed in a more efficient language. For example, routines generated by an application generator could be reprogrammed in COBOL and COBOL programs reprogrammed in assembler.

Program flow control and reprogramming are time-consuming activities that should be reserved for high-usage routines only. A problem that can arise here is that it can be psychologically difficult for the original programmer to do this type of work, since he or she has already produced a good version of the program.

It may be advantageous to have programmers other than those who prepared the original version check for program efficiency. However, care must be taken to ensure that the efficiency of the programs is actually improved and the programs are not just changed. New (that is, different) programmers tend to change programs to align the code with their particular way of programming. This does not necessarily improve the efficiency of the program.

Data Reorganization and Restructuring

Most administrative CBISs are I/O-bound, which means that they spend most of their time waiting for data transfers to and from the secondary storage devices. This is because of the relatively slow speed of the storage devices and the great quantity of data to be processed. Maintaining clean file structures is vital to maintaining the total system's efficiency.

The most common file structures—sequential, indexed sequential, and to some extent direct—are all subject to a reduction in efficiency as new data are added to the overflow areas of the file. Periodically, depending on the rate of new data additions, these files must be reorganized. This is done by making a sequential copy of the file, for example, onto tape, then recreating the original file structure—indexed, sequential, direct, and so on. The file copy can be used as the back-up copy required for recovery.

Occasionally, file usage changes from that anticipated during file design, requiring redesign and conversion to another file structure. This process is called *restructuring*. Common changes can be from sequential or directed to indexed sequential, indexed sequential to linked or inverted, linked to inverted, file system to data base.

File structure maintenance and tuning depend on the information collected from file usage statistics. As illustrated in Figure 13.3, the usage statistics are collected during normal system operation. These statistics are processed periodically to determine whether a file reorganization or restructuring is required. File statistics collected for each file include such data as:

1. Number of records in the file
2. Number of accesses to the file
3. Number of record additions and deletions
4. Average response time for retrieval of one record
5. Average load percent of primary file blocks
6. Number and distribution of overflow records
7. Number of index searches
8. Number of times each field is used as a search argument

Reorganization is indicated when the relative number of overflow records is high (6 to 1 in the list) and the response time has increased (4 in the list). Another indicator for reorganization would be a low load percent for the primary file blocks with a high and/or uneven distribution of overflow records, indicated by items 5 and 6. The activity statistics, items 2 and 3, indicate the frequency with which the quality of the file structure should be checked.

When frequent reorganization cannot maintain acceptable response times, item 4, a restructuring may be required. Restructuring may also be indicated when the number of searches using nonindexed attributes (fields) becomes high (item 8).

Both reorganization and restructuring are time-consuming operations, requiring at least twice the time needed to copy the file. For example, it can take about 40 minutes to copy one whole disk file to a tape file and then recreate a reorganized or restructured file. In addition, a restructuring can affect the way in which application programs access the files, making program changes and/or recompilation necessary.

Normally, these operations are performed when the system is not in use, such as at night or during the weekend. However, there are techniques available that allow reorganization, and restricted restructuring operations, to be performed at the same time as nearly normal system operation (Sockut & Goldberg, 1979). Whether or not concurrent

Figure 13.3 File Maintenance

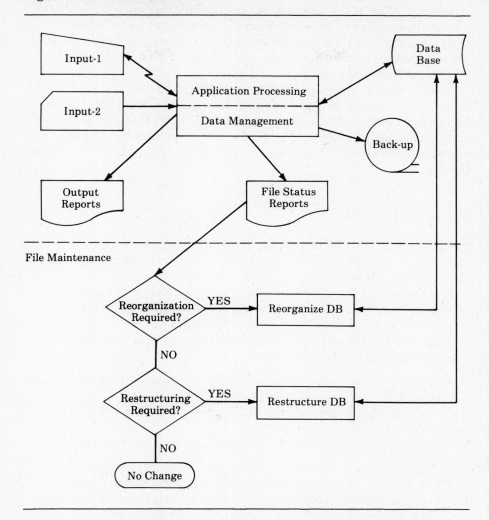

reorganization and/or restructuring are allowed depends on the facilities of the data management system being used. (See Figure 13.3.)

Operational Tuning

System efficiency can be improved by replacing data storage devices with faster units—tape with disk, slow disks with faster ones, disk with drum, and so on. High-usage transaction programs can be made resident in main memory, reducing the time required to fetch the program for processing. More main memory can be allocated to data buffers, reducing the number of transfers from the secondary storage units.

System efficiency can also be improved by restricting particularly time-consuming processing to low-activity times, thus reserving the system for high-usage and short processes.

A more drastic operational strategy would be to convert the system from one processing mode to another, for example, from batch to on-line or from a central processing system to a distributed one. In each case, processing of a user transaction is initiated closer to the user, allowing a perceived improvement in the processing speed and response time.

SYSTEM GROWTH

System growth involves expanding the CBIS to include new processes and/or new data. The boundary between system growth and system maintenance can be indistinct, at least as perceived by the system users. This is because of the degree of change required before the user perceives the modifications as an increase in the facilities of the system rather than an improvement of existing facilities.

Examples of changes that can occur in the gray area between system maintenance and system growth are:

- Changes in tables used for calculations, such as tax tables that change each year
- Changes in algorithms for calculation, such as the algorithm for calculating rebates
- Changes in interpretation of coded data, such as the weighting of scale values

These types of changes are necessary to keep the system current. However, they seldom require either new processes or new data, and thus they will be classified here as system maintenance activities. If we define system maintenance as those activities that aim at keeping the system operative, correct, efficient, current, and within its original scope, then the currency modifications will be the least time-consuming of the system maintenance activities. That is, both error control and tuning, keeping the system operative, correct, and efficient, will normally be more time-consuming than making currency adaptations.

System growth thus encompasses those activities that aim to add new facilities to the system. It is a natural continuation of the maintenance-oriented system modification activities. Typical system growth activities include:

- Modifying programs to new specifications
- Adding new transaction types
- Adding new reports
- Adding new user interface facilities
- Adding new data

Figure 13.4 illustrates two ways in which a CBIS can grow. Quadrant I represents the current system. Changes here can be considered either maintenance or growth, depending on the extent of the modification and the newness of the specifications.

Quadrant II represents new processes, both transactions and reports, that use the existing data. These extensions are common and relatively easy to make, as there will be little, if any, interaction between the new processes and those of the original system.

Quadrant III represents the addition of new data. Normally there will be no activity in this quadrant, since there will be no use for the new data in the existing program set. Occasionally, data can be added to an existing system "for future use," normally as part of the preparation for planned new processes. The main problem with adding new data is extending the administration of the data management system to these data without disturbing the existing processing system's view of the

Figure 13.4 System Growth Model

Programs \ Data	$d(1)\,d(2)\,d(3)\ldots d(n)$	$d(n+1)\,d(n+2)\ldots d(m)$
PROG 1 PROG 2 PROG 3 . . PROG i	I Date-usage matrix	III
PROG $(i+1)$ PROG $(i+2)$. PROG j	II	IV

  I. Current system.
 II. New processes.
III. New data.
IV. New processes with new data.

data-base content. This type of addition is possible with most DBMSs but may require a recompilation of the existing programs.

Quadrant IV represents a real extension of the system, involving new processes that use both existing and new data. Implementing these new processes with the new data requires a preparatory system analysis and design of the type described throughout this book.

System growth should be planned for. The original system design should indicate the areas of growth for the system and can include a preliminary design of the system's phase II (phase III, and so on) extensions. When system growth has been planned for, there is an orderly procedure for implementing phase I (quadrant I), then phase II (quadrant II), and so on.

If system growth has not been planned for during system design, then the new system requirements, as they relate to the existing system, must be analyzed, then a modified system (if applicable) must be designed and implemented. Conceptually, this is the same as a decision to design a new system. Thus, we have completed the system life cycle (Figures 3.1 and 3.3) and are ready to begin again. See Chapter 3.

SUMMARY

The aim of any CBIS system analysis and design project is to develop a system that functions properly and can be used for as long a period of time as possible. Most CBISs are complicated systems with many subsystems. Determining that the total system functions correctly under all circumstances is very time-consuming, if it is possible at all. Furthermore, user information requirements change as the organization adapts to its environment and as the individual users gain experience with the system. As a result, after the system is operational, it needs continuing maintenance.

We have discussed three aspects of system maintenance: error control (maintaining a correct system), system tuning (maintaining an efficient system), and system growth (providing an adaptive system). Each of these aspects requires planning and can be made easier if the original system has a good, modular, well-documented design. Therefore, these topics are important considerations for the designer of a CBIS.

KEY CONCEPTS

Back-up	Integrity
Concurrent update	Log
Deadlock	Operational mode

Recovery
Reorganization
Response time
Restructuring
Rollback

System efficiency
System growth
System maintenance
Tuning

DISCUSSION QUESTIONS

1. Within the framework of system maintenance and growth, define and give examples for each of the key concepts.
2. Discuss and give examples of activities for each of the maintenance tasks given in the introduction to this chapter.
3. Present arguments for and against dividing maintenance activities into the three areas of error control, tuning, and system growth. Discuss the boundaries between these subareas of system maintenance. Are they or can they be clearly defined?
4. Discuss the error control mechanisms that can be included in (a) the user interface, (b) the application programs, (c) the application control system, and (d) the data management system.
5. How can audit routines be used in error control?
6. How can data integrity be maintained?
7. What is a deadlock? How can it be detected and resolved?
8. What back-up and recovery procedures are typically used with CBISs? When are they enacted? By whom?
9. What is system tuning? Who is the benefactor of a tuning effort? How?
10. Discuss the differences between reorganization and restructuring. What criteria are used to initiate these activities?
11. What operational changes can be made to improve system efficiency? When could such a change be considered an example of system growth?
12. Discuss the differences between system maintenance and system growth? Where is the boundary? Give examples.

PROJECTS

1. Set up error control procedures for your system (or for the student AIS discussed in this text).
2. Outline components of phases II and III for your system (or the student AIS).

RECOMMENDED READINGS

Biggs, C. L., E. G. Birks, and W. Atkins. *Managing the Systems Development Process.* Englewood Cliffs, N.J.: Prentice-Hall, 1980.

    This book includes detailed lists of activities for all phases of system development. Sections on system tuning and maintenance are of particular interest for this chapter.

Fernandez, E. B., R. C. Summers, and C. Wood. *Database Security and Integrity.* Reading, Mass.: Addison-Wesley, 1981.

    This book includes chapters on integrity, auditing, and enforcement and their application to distributed data-base systems. Of particular interest here are the concurrent processing algorithms presented.

Sockut, G., and W. Goldberg. "Database Reorganization—Principles and Practice." *ACM Computing Surveys*, 11, No. 4 (1979).

    This paper discusses the reorganization and restructuring problem as it applies to files and data bases, giving procedures for parallel reorganization with normal operation.

Vessoy, I., and R. Weber. "Some Factors Affecting Program Repair Maintenance: An Empirical Study." *CACM*, 26, No. 2 (1983).

    This paper presents a rare empirical study of the effects of time and environment on system maintenance.

Weldon, J. L. *Data Base Administration.* New York: Plenum Press, 1981.

    Part IV of this book discusses the problems of error control and tuning of data-base systems.

PART V

IMPACT OF COMPUTER-BASED INFORMATION SYSTEMS

Chapter 14

Using Computer-Based Information Systems

INTRODUCTION

Computer-based information systems are becoming so numerous and are being used in so many different application areas that everyone is a potential interactor with some CBIS. An individual can, in a short period, interact at different levels with different CBISs. For example, one person can be a:

- recipient of computer-generated output, such as advertisements sent to an address list maintained by a computer or bills generated by a CBIS.
- data supplier, perhaps as a respondent to a national census or owner of credit cards or bank accounts or loans.
- active user of a CBIS, by requesting information from an information service such as The Source, using an automatic bank teller to enter monetary transfers, playing a video game, or learning programming, spelling, math, or history lessons at school.
- designer of a CBIS, perhaps as a participant on a system-design team or by using an automated application descriptor.
- programmer/implementer of a CBIS, by using any programming language, such as BASIC, PASCAL, LOGO, COBOL, or FORTRAN, or an application generator.
- owner of a CBIS, perhaps at home in the kitchen stove, burglar alarm, car, or TV-telephone information services; at play in video games; or at work for data administration and analysis or process control.

In this chapter we will first discuss different classes of CBIS users, paying particular attention to their interest and possible participation in the design of the CBISs they use. Then we will discuss some of the types of application areas where one can expect to find a CBIS. Both discussions are necessarily limited, since the potential CBIS user community includes everyone and the application areas in which CBISs could potentially be used are limited only by our imagination.

USERS

Intuitively, a system user is someone who interacts with a (for our discussion) CBIS. Normally it is assumed that this person has a job-related reason for needing the services of the information system for storing data, retrieving data, processing data, and/or transferring data from one location to another. We have described various categories of such users of administrative information systems in Chapters 2 and 4 (Figures 2.3 and 4.1).

However, there are others who are potentially interested in a CBIS, and whose work or life situation is, or can be, affected by the design or operation of the CBIS. The distinction between the intended users and the other groups interested in a CBIS can be difficult to draw.

In order to design a good CBIS, one that will be perceived as successful, the designer must consider the requirements of all interest groups. Thus, for this discussion, we will define the CBIS user to include all interested groups.

CBIS User Anyone who has some interest in or comes in some contact with a CBIS.

As noted earlier, using this broad definition, everyone is a potential user of some CBIS or set of CBISs. The designer must assume that the potential user community for a particular CBIS is very diverse and that its members will, of necessity, have different degrees of interaction with, and interest in, the system. With such a potentially diverse user community, it is practically impossible to fully satisfy all valid user requirements for information services with one CBIS or even a closely related set of CBISs.

In order to identify types of users and their requirements, it is helpful, and common, to divide the user community into generally separate groups that reflect the period of interest and the type of interaction with or interest in the CBIS. Typical user groups, or interest groups, include:

1. System analysts and designers
2. System implementers, normally programmers
3. System administrators and controllers
4. Direct (or end) users
5. Indirect users
6. Passive users

This book has been primarily directed toward system analysts and designers. We've described a methodology, with related techniques, for the development of CBISs. An underlying assumption of the team approach to system analysis and design is that if users (understood to mean direct users) participate in the analysis and design of a new or modified CBIS, this will ensure higher quality, that is, increased relevance to the application area, and thus the resulting system will be more successful (Ginzberg, 1979).

Most, if not all, of the current concern with user participation in system design has concentrated on the relationship between the system designer and the direct (end) user. In the following discussion, we will take a closer look at these relationships. We will also discuss some of the needs and expectations of the other system users, particularly as these needs are affected by system-design decisions.

System Designers

The system designer is generally thought to be someone other than the direct user for whom the system is to be constructed, usually someone with EDP expertise. It is the designer's responsibility to design a CBIS that fulfills the requirements of the application area *and* is EDP effective, maintainable, operable, and controllable.

It is impossible to design a good, useful (to the application users) CBIS without knowing the usage requirements for the system in detail. This knowledge is part of the direct user's work area, the application area for the CBIS. When the system designer is from outside the application area, he or she must compensate for gaps in knowledge of the application by working closely with the direct users, or at least with user representatives. It is generally assumed that the system designer has the EDP expertise to design an EDP effective, maintainable, and controllable CBIS.

There are a number of models for designer/direct user interaction; the following are examples:

1. The designer works independently, submitting system proposals to users for correction or agreement.
2. The designer and users work on a team in which the designer is dominant because of technical expertise.
3. The designer and users work on a team in which the users are dominant because of application expertise.
4. The user does the design alone using automated design tools.

One CBIS design problem is bringing enough technical expertise and application knowledge to the design project to develop a product that is technically efficient and applicationally complete and usable. What is the "correct" design team will depend on the expertise of the individuals available to participate in the design effort and on the type of CBIS being planned.

Model 1 will be useful when the designer understands the application area well and when the users are not available to participate in the design project. Many software packages are of this type, including such systems as operating systems; data management systems; compilers; application generators; statistical, mathematical, and business analysis systems; all types of games; and many teaching aids. The assumption behind this design model is that the users will be able to adapt their usage requirements to the idiosyncrasies of the implemented system.

Model 2 can be useful when the designer understands the application area well and the users, though available, do not have, and do not need to acquire, EDP expertise. Typical uses of this development strategy would include customizing standard systems for a particular organizational environment, for example, systems for accounting, accounts receivable, or inventory control. The assumption behind this development model is that the designer is competent in the general application area and will be able to adapt the system to a stated set of specific user requirements.

Model 3 will be required when the designer is not sufficiently familiar with the application and when the users have, need, or are interested in acquiring EDP expertise. This design strategy is generally necessary when a new type of system is being designed, when the system is large with respect to the number of functions it supports, when the system will be used for a relatively large part of the users' working day, and/or when the system significantly changes the job definition of its direct users. This model is the one that those interested in participative design advocate most strongly. The assumption behind this design model is that the EDP expertise required is or can be made available within the user community.

Model 4 is appropriate when the user has EDP expertise, at least at the level required by the automated design tools. Current (as of 1983) automated design tools still assume a relatively high level of EDP competence, including at least the workings of computers, the design of files, and the basics of programming. The underlying assumption of this design approach is that it is (or will become) possible to construct automated tools that can translate problem statements describing a system's desired characteristics into a working CBIS. Some predict that in the near future there will be no need for specialized EDP system designers.

System Implementers and Maintainers

Those who are charged with implementing and then maintaining a CBIS will have to live with the system from the time the design is accepted until the system is replaced. They are responsible for implementing the ideas, intentions, and application assumptions that are embedded in the design. They are also responsible for maintaining the CBIS functions and adapting them to ongoing changes in service requirements from the user environment.

To do this job effectively, the implementer/maintainer must understand the application area well, and also understand the ways in which the users want to interact with the system. The implementer/maintainer must also understand the technical requirements and restrictions of the system hardware and software to be used. The system implementer/maintainer is usually not the direct user, but an applications programmer. A good system design must convey the application requirements to the implementation programmer(s).

The way in which a CBIS is implemented will affect the ease with which it can be maintained and adapted to changing requirements. Some writers have strongly suggested that systems developed using a structured or modular design will be easier to maintain (Yourdan, 1975).

Although they are not direct users of the CBIS, application programmers, who are normally responsible for system implementation and maintenance, represent a level of expertise in the design and implementation of automated systems that must be brought to the CBIS design project. It is assumed that the EDP-system designer will have this expertise. If there is no EDP-system designer, then the user/designer must acquire this technical expertise.

System Administrators and Controllers

System administrators live with a CBIS from the time it is implemented and converted until it is replaced. Although they are not normally considered to be direct users of the CBIS functions, they are responsible for sequencing the operative and utility routines of the system, making back-up copies of the data and programs, and initiating recovery procedures should the system fail. In addition, there may be a data administrator who is responsible for enforcing standardization of data terminology and structures, access authority clearance for the users, incorporation of modifications into the operative system, and so on.

The design of the CBIS must include operation and recovery procedures. Again, it is assumed that the EDP designer brings knowledge of these requirements to the design project. The application users must define the security requirements.

The control of a CBIS, the types of data to be included, the allowable processes, and its user community generally lies outside the immediate environment of the operative system. Such control responsibilities lie with the system's owners—the organization's shareholders and board of directors, represented by the organization's management—and must be exercised in accordance with public laws, such as security and privacy laws.

Responsibility for knowing about the external control requirements and enforcing compliance with policy decisions rests with the organization's management. These requirements must be brought to the design project. Typically, neither the EDP designer nor the direct user knows enough about the control requirements. To provide this expertise, management must be involved in the system design decisions.

Direct Users

Direct users are those who, in performing their jobs or satisfying their interests, interact directly with the CBIS to store, retrieve, analyze, modify, and/or transfer data. They are responsible for the quality of the data, and have job-related tasks to perform on the data. A subset of these data-related tasks have been automated into the CBIS.

Indirect users are also active users of the system, but they receive information services through some direct user. Figure 14.1 illustrates the relationship between direct and indirect users. The user groups included are those typically found in business administrative systems (see Figure 2.3). There can, of course, be many other user groups. And there can be other classifications than direct or indirect user.

Figure 14.1 Direct versus Indirect CBIS Users

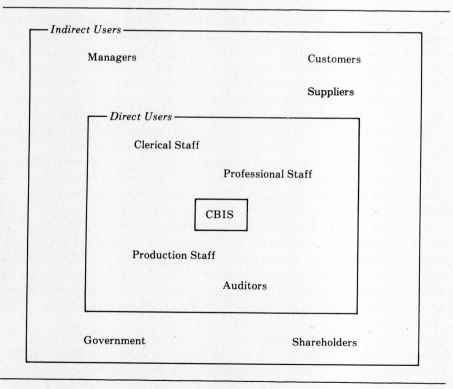

Which user groups will be direct users, with direct interaction with the CBIS, and which will be indirect users, receiving their data processing services through one of the direct users, depends on the design of the particular CBIS. Box 14.1 illustrates one possible distribution of direct and indirect user groups and indicates the types of CBIS service each could have.

One principal difference between direct and indirect users involves the degree to which their job definition is related to the data services the system provides. It is generally assumed that direct users will also be, or become, quite heavily dependent on the CBIS in performing their jobs. This has prompted laws (initially in Scandinavia) requiring direct-user participation in the design of CBISs that will have an effect on their job environment. Concern for workers' job satisfaction also lies behind the efforts to expand user participation in the sociotechnical methods of information-system design.

Direct users, through their job definitions and responsibility areas, define the functions, data, user interfaces, security, and maintenance routines that are to be contained within the CBIS. Their perception of the system's usefulness for performing their jobs is directly related to the system's success, as measured by the degree to which it is actually used (Ginzberg, 1978; Lucas, 1978).

CBISs that are not job-related and cannot have mandatory usage also have direct users. Such systems include library information systems, store directories, airline flight information, general information services

Box 14.1

DIRECT AND INDIRECT CBIS USAGE

User Group	Usage Example
Direct users:	
Clerical staff	Data entry
Professional staff	Data analysis
Production staff	Production control
Auditors	Accounting review
Indirect users:	
Managers	Receipt of reports
Customers	Receipt and payment of bills
Suppliers	Receipt of orders
Government	Receipt of tax statements
Shareholders	Receipt of financial reports

(the SOURCE, CompuServe, and others), home banking systems, home office routines, teaching aids, games, and so on. For these systems, user satisfaction determines the purchase and/or usage rate and thus determines the system's financial success. Perhaps unfortunately for both users and designers, the prospective users of these systems are seldom available to participate in the system design effort.

Indirect Users

Indirect users are users who receive data services from the CBIS through some direct user. An example of an indirect user would be a customer who is offered services or goods through a catalog that is sent using an automated address list. The customer (indirect user) may then send (by mail) an order, receive (by mail) the services or goods and the bill, and make a payment (by mail or in person). A direct user, such as a customer service agent, interacts directly with the CBIS to record the customer's activities. The CBIS maintains the customer account status.

Indirect users receive predefined reports from the system and may or may not take action based on the information in these reports. Generally, their jobs or other activities are not dependent on interaction with the system. The information generated by the CBIS will normally also be available verbally, or in some manually produced form.

Indirect users are seldom consulted during the design of a CBIS. Their needs are assumed to be represented by the direct users. It is unfortunate if the information services the indirect users receive from the direct user or CBIS give them a negative image of the organization and/or its service capability.

Passive Users

A number of CBISs contain data about people and/or organizations that otherwise have no interaction with the system. Common examples of passive participation in a CBIS include national census data, address list membership in third-party companies (companies with which one has not done business), representation in credit reference company files, description as a competitor, representation in a research data base as a result of a previous customer relationship, and so on.

Individuals are normally neither consulted nor informed before they are included in these systems. However, many developed countries have laws that allow individuals to ask an organization whether they are included in a specific CBIS, then monitor the correctness of the data maintained within that system. In some cases, individuals can demand that the data describing them be deleted from the system.

In some countries, particularly in Scandinavia, there are public com-
mittees charged with the task of approving the design of systems that
are to contain personal data. To make their task easier, design guidelines are being developed, and these will give passive users some influence, although quite indirect, on the design of systems in which they
may be included.

APPLICATION AREAS

The use of CBISs has spread from the research applications in technical
and natural sciences, government statistical services, and military systems for which they were initially used in the mid-1950s to virtually all
research areas, government and business administration, health services,
the study and development of dance and music scores, teaching from
pre-school to post-graduate, customer services, home computing, and
other areas. Today it is difficult to find an area which has not been
affected to some degree by automation. And indeed, new application
areas seem limited only by our imagination.

Perhaps not all applications are good in the sense that automation
has improved some facet of the work or leisure activity, or has even
been economically justifiable. However, as the costs of computer power
continue to fall and the available computer power and memory space
continue to increase, the economics of applications will continue to
improve.

In the following discussion, we will list a number of traditional application areas and note a few of the more unusual applications. The idea
is to stimulate the reader's imagination, not to list good application
areas.

Business Applications

The best-established business CBISs are at the operational level of the
organization. These systems capture operating data about products,
customers, suppliers, and employees. They then produce reports such
as inventory status, customer billing, material orders, payrolls, budgets,
and accounts. Traditional CBIS applications are found in:

- production management: production control, engineering support
  (CAD/CAM), project management, inventory management, internal
  accounting.
- marketing: market research, sales support, customer service, supplier
  systems.
- personnel management: payroll, project assignment, personnel development (education, job histories, recruitment).

- planning: decision support systems, operational analysis, project scheduling, forecasting, simulations.
- finance: budget planning, portfolio management, accounts receivable or payable, general ledger.
- office management: word processing for reports and letters, scheduling of meetings, message/memo systems, archives, information retrieval systems.

Within business applications, current CBIS development efforts are directed toward providing office management and office activities with automated tools and toward making the organization's data and data processing facilities more readily available to both tactical- and strategic-level management. Under the name of decision support systems (DSS), management decision aids are being provided for use in forecasting, statistical analysis, econometric analysis, and simulation of decision alternatives.

Improvements in terminal facilities and user interface languages are allowing non-EDP personnel and infrequent users to use DP services. The advent of microcomputers has allowed data processing services to move into the office and into small businesses, such as medical offices, dental offices, or local groceries.

Government and Public Service Applications

Many of the types of CBISs applicable in business administration are also applicable in government administration at all levels, from national to local, and in all sections, including health and social services, communications, justice, military, and others. Examples include personnel administration, finance, customer/client services, and project management.

In addition, specific government and public service operations use a number of CBIS applications. These include:

- law enforcement: criminal and crime registers, court scheduling, law research.
- health services: patient journals, hospital service scheduling, intensive care monitoring, outpatient registers, billing and payment, national health services (Medicare/Medicaid), medical research.
- social services: participant registration (such as Social Security membership), recipient payments, registration of social services and programs, school administration, Social Security administration.
- internal revenue services: personal and business tax management, budgeting.
- statistical services: census, labor statistics, business, export and import.

- military applications: research, space exploration, strategic planning.
- weather forecasting.
- library and information services: recording and making available information about books, articles, and laws; medical information; consumer reports; statistical reports.
- graphic services: constructing maps of states, counties, or cities; presentation of data in graphic form; locating special items, such as fire hydrants, candy shops, or hospitals.

Also, in government and public service areas, as well as in the private sector, organizations are developing CBISs aimed at providing information-processing services to high-level management, office staff, and the general public. Particularly interesting is the development of public information services where "customers," that is, anyone with a terminal, telephone, or TV, will be able to reach a news/information service and receive information covering any of a number of areas, from weather to sports to foreign and local news. Customers will also be able to order anything from airline tickets to food.

Research Applications

Almost all possible areas of research have made or can make use of CBISs. For example:

- Statistical methods are useful for determining relationships between observed phenomena in areas such as weather, stars, public opinions, epidemics, word usage in texts, and many others.
- Computer simulations are useful for analyzing models of functions of people (medicine), animals (biology), organizations and technical systems, and many others.
- Information retrieval techniques are useful for organizing, and selecting individual items from, voluminous quantities of texts, and from reference collections (catalogs) for manuscripts, music scores, descriptions of pictures, museum objects, specialist directories, and so on.
- Graphic techniques can be used for studying almost all physical items from molecules and cells, towns and populations, to the solar system.

The special area of artificial intelligence uses the computer heavily to mimic human behavior in order to better understand how we function, the point being to be able to construct useful robotic helpers. Also, the computer and CBISs are vital to the further development of computers and CBISs.

Educational Applications

There are two important CBIS application areas in the educational sector, one in school administration and the other in support of teaching activities. Both these areas have made use of CBISs and are continuing to expand their use. A primary impetus to the use of automated tools is the advent of microcomputers, providing inexpensive computational power.

School administration, for one school or for a nation's or district's school system, is similar in many ways to business and government administration, including financial and personnel management, student (= customer/client) administration, and course (= product/service) administration. An interesting special application is the problem of scheduling students, teachers, courses, rooms, and time.

Computer-assisted instruction (CAI) programs for drills in spelling and math; simulated experiments in chemistry and physics; language development in English, Spanish, and German; and many other areas are available. CAI programs are also available for a host of teach-yourself courses from programming and typing to history. CAI systems have been developed for the traditional school system, grades 1 through 12, for pre-school learning, for adult education, and for special job training. An example of the last would be the flight simulators used to train pilots.

Home Applications

With the advent of microcomputers, computing has become financially accessible to many homes and families. There are literally thousands of programs available for the microcomputer owner and his or her spouse and children. These include business systems to support home economics, such as check managers, word processors for letter writing, information retrieval systems for recipe collections, address list programs for Christmas card lists, CAI programs for homework and new learning, and, of course, games.

The home market is becoming increasingly interesting to the information-service industry, which is offering home users such services as news and weather reports, stock market services, home banking, mail order services, airline reservations, and access to extensive data bases.

Computers are already used in our cars and stoves. They can also be used to regulate lighting and heating, and as burglar alarms.

SUMMARY

In our industrialized society nearly everyone will come in contact with some CBIS in some capacity. We often hear of user-friendly systems or user-participative design without knowing exactly who these "users" are. In this chapter we have reviewed various categories of CBIS users, from those who design, implement, and maintain a CBIS to those who use its facilities directly, indirectly, or passively. It is important that the system designer have a clear understanding of the people who will come in contact with the system, so that their information requirements can be met.

KEY CONCEPTS

Application area
Direct users
Home computing
Indirect users
Passive users

DISCUSSION QUESTIONS

1. Define and discuss each of the key concepts.
2. Discuss the possibility that system analysts and designers are a disappearing race. For which user groups and system types would this be true? For which user groups or system types will system analysts and designers continue to be needed? Why?
3. How can direct users participate in system design? Why is this desirable?
4. Can indirect users participate in system design? How?
5. Can passive users participate in system design? How?
6. Discuss the pros and cons of business use of CBISs.
7. Discuss the pros and cons of government use of CBISs.
8. Outline how CAI can be used in a pre-school, grade school, high school, university, industrial, or adult education environment.
9. Discuss the pros and cons of home computing.

PROJECTS

1. Using the student administration model, develop a phase 2 plan for extending the system's coverage to at least two neighboring application areas.

2. Set up a level 1 information graph (see Chapter 5) for a CBIS for your local fire department. Develop a goal set for such a system. What would be the machine requirements for your system?

RECOMMENDED READINGS

Brabb, G. *Computers and Information Systems in Business*. 2nd ed. Boston: Houghton Mifflin, 1980.

> Chapters 3, 4, 15, and 16 discuss business applications of CBISs.

Ginzberg, M. J. "Participative System Design." In *Design and Implementation of Computer-Based Information Systems*. Ed. N. Szyperski and E. Grochla. The Netherlands: Sijthoff & Noordhoff, 1979.

> Ginzberg's paper summarizes a conference discussion of three papers on participative system design by Mumford, Clausen, and Podger (also published in the book). Central topics discussed are why and how direct users should and can participate in the design of the CBISs with which they are to interact.

Martin, J. *The Computerized Society*. Englewood Cliffs, N.J.: Prentice-Hall, 1970.

Martin, J. *Telematic Society*. Englewood Cliffs, N.J.: Prentice-Hall, 1981.

> Both of Martin's books discuss application areas for CBISs. Most of the CBIS applications envisioned in the 1970 book are well established today. The 1981 book discusses further CBIS application areas and also takes up topics of current concern involving the impact of CBISs on individuals and society.

Szyperski, N., and E. Grochla, eds. *Design and Implementation of Computer-Based Information Systems*. The Netherlands: Sijthoff & Noordhoff, 1979.

> This book contains papers from an international symposium held in Bonn in 1979. The papers of Ginzberg, Mumford, Clausen, and Podger discuss aspects of direct-user participation in the design of a CBIS.

Chapter 15

Directions in System Analysis and Design

INTRODUCTION

During the past decade an increasing amount of attention has been directed toward the computer-based system analysis and design process. There are a number of reasons for this increasing interest, of which some of the more important are listed here.

- A disturbing number of rather large CBIS projects have failed to live up to expectations in terms of performance and functions.
- A relatively large portion of an EDP center's time (40 to 70 percent) is spent correcting and expanding the functions of operational CBISs.
- There is a growing interest in involving users in the system-design phase in order to ensure that requirements are completely specified.
- There is growing knowledge of the effects users can have on system usage (success) and quality.
- There is a growing awareness of and concern for the negative impacts a CBIS can have on job definitions and work quality.
- There has been general advancement in the understanding of how computer-based systems work and the relationships between design strategies and implementation success.
- An increasing number of automated tools are available to support system analysis, design, and implementation tasks.
- It is generally believed that a good CBIS, one that provides the desired information services at an acceptable cost, is possible only if the design is good.

This increasing attention has led to the development of many system-design methodologies. For example, in 1981 IFIP's (International Federation for Information Processing) working group 8.1 invited researchers and practitioners to prepare papers describing system analysis and design methodologies. Each paper was to include the design of a common system for comparison. There were 76 letters of intent to participate. Assuming that not all groups working to develop analysis and design methodologies were represented, this could mean that nearly 100 methodologies are under development. Obviously, there must be considerable overlap among these methodologies, since the problem is simply to translate a need for information processing into a working system.

Generally, methods for the analysis and design of information systems differ in a number of ways, reflecting an evaluation of the most important tasks that must be included or the underlying theory of the construction of information systems. Important characteristics of design methodologies that distinguish separate approaches and that can characterize schools of system analysis and design include:

1. The definition of the scope of the system analysis and design process—automated program design, data flow design, organizational structure, or some other area
2. The basic approach to system analysis and design—top-down or bottom-up
3. The weight of design attention given to the various system components, such as data, process, process/data flow, user interface, and system input/output
4. The type of information system being designed
5. Who the CBIS users are and how they should or can participate in the design process
6. Who the system designer is
7. The tools available or proposed for use in system analysis, design, and/or implementation

In this chapter we will highlight the general development of system analysis and design methodologies and discuss some alternative approaches. Finally, we will return to the approach presented in this book.

THE DEVELOPMENT OF SYSTEM ANALYSIS AND DESIGN

In the mid-1960s system design was frequently considered an art, dependent on the designer's inherent talent for observation and attention to detail as well as on programming competence. System design was felt to be comparable to literary composition. Nonetheless, tools were developed to assist in system and program design, the most important being program flowcharting (ANSI, 1970), data structuring (Bachman, 1969), matrices for documentation of data use in multiple-program systems, and automatic program generation from decision tables (McDaniel, 1970).

Given these tools and techniques, describing methodologies in which they can be used effectively becomes possible. Underlying the methodologies are theories of systems and system design. As mentioned earlier, the development of methodologies and theories for information-system design has intensified through the 1970s until today we have a multitude of methodologies to choose from, some of which have stood up in practical application.

Techniques for System Analysis and Design

As already mentioned, program flowcharting and data structure diagraming are widely used techniques for designing and documenting programs and files (data bases). The cross-reference matrix documents data use in multiple-program systems.

Other important design techniques include:

- Simulation
- Prototyping
- Decision tables
- Problem statement languages
- Automated program generators
- Data-base systems

Most of these techniques can be used manually, that is, the designer can use paper and pencil to develop the graphs and charts and present the designs for manual control in simulated system environments. However, increasingly, these tools have been automated, making it possible for the designer to control the design of larger systems, have prototype systems available much earlier, simulate an increased number of situations, and automatically generate more of the basic program modules and even the data base.

Methodologies

As indicated in the chapter introduction, there are a number of characteristics that distinguish different system analysis and design methodologies. In the following sections we will discuss them.

Scope

Defining the scope of an information system—just what is to be included in an information system and what functions or data are to be considered outside its concern—has always been difficult. As the information system, meaning the automated parts of the information system, has expanded in scope, so has the analysis and design process.

Initially, system analysis meant the design of programs, usually programs that automated some organizational subfunction, such as payroll processing. Today, the system analysis and design process is commonly thought to extend from the analysis of the problem area requiring the information system to the design of the automated support system for the CBIS. The system analysis and design methodologies have had to expand as the scope of the process has expanded.

Approach

Today, system analysis and design methodologies recognize the need to identify and design system modules. The principal differences among methodologies lie in the manner in which modules are identified. Typically, the methodologies can be said to predominantly take one of two approaches:

- Top-down—define the supersystem, then define successive subsystems until the desired module level is achieved.
- Bottom-up—given a set of low-level functions, group these into basic modules, which can then become components of more complex programs, which can again be combined until the total system is defined.

A number of developers and promoters of system analysis and design methodologies point out that using a pure top-down or bottom-up strategy to design a system is impossible, since the design of a high-level component can be influenced by design decisions required for a lower-level component, and conversely, the design of low-level components requires knowledge of higher-level requirements. As a result, an iterative approach to the design of neighboring component levels is proposed, although an overall top-down or bottom-up strategy is maintained.

There is another dimension to the approach to design that a methodology proposes:

- Design first, then implement.
- Implement a prototype, then fine-tune the design, then refine the prototype, and so on until the system is developed.

The design-first strategy assumes that the major system specifications can be identified during an iterative design phase. The system can then be implemented, with only minor revisions needed to provide for additional requirements.

The implement-first strategy, more accurately termed either *prototyping* or *experimental design*, assumes that it is not possible to capture the major system specifications, because the users will be unable to anticipate CBIS opportunities. The prototype system is an instrument for eliciting user response and determining the system requirements.

Emphasized System Component

Another difference among methodologies lies in the principal concern— identifying the information to be used or identifying the information processes required. Obviously, neither the data nor the programs can exist alone, and therefore a complete design methodology must include techniques for designing both.

Originally, attention was focused on *what* was to be done and *how* to do it, leading to the program orientation for system design. More recently, since the development of data-base management techniques, the emphasis has shifted to identifying the system's total data requirement before designing the programs within the system.

Type of CBIS

Most system analysis and design methodologies assume an administrative CBIS. Recently, these methodologies have been applied to other types of systems, such as official statistical systems (Nordbotten, 1981).

CBIS Users

Most methodologies do not emphasize differentiation among user categories. When users are considered, they are assumed to be direct users.

CBIS Designer

Most methodologies assume that an EDP expert, or group of experts, will design the system.

However, more and more emphasis is being placed on the need for active user participation in the design process, leading to proposals for a system design team. The user groups most commonly included on the design team are the direct users and the system owners, represented by the management of the department responsible for the CBIS that is being developed.

Methodologies whose primary component is an application generator assume that the direct user will be the primary designer. These methodologies give no role to the system owner, the system administrator, or indirect or passive users.

Tools

Most methodologies use graphic models to represent data structures, data flow, and program structure. Tables and matrices are used for documentation of goals and data use.

Simulation and program generators are used extensively in methodologies that emphasize experimental design or prototyping. Data dictionaries, sometimes coupled with automated program generation, can be used for data-base definition.

Most methodologies are based on manual tools and techniques. However, the methodology itself is not generally dependent on the extent to which its tools are automated.

Theory versus Practice

In the previous sections, we identified a number of characteristics of system analysis and design methodologies. Any one methodology is relatively free to combine characteristics, giving a rather large potential variety of methodology types. However, it is common to classify methodologies according to their basic approach. Using this classification, we can claim that a given methodology is basically:

1. top-down, that is, the design is complete before implementation.
2. bottom-up, that is, building blocks are implemented, then used in constructing a larger system.
3. experimental or prototype, that is, an incomplete design is implemented, followed by a revised design, revised implementation, and so on.

Underlying Theories

The underlying theories behind these approaches to system analysis and design can be simply (and incompletely) stated as follows:

- Top-down methodologies assume that a successful system can be constructed only after a detailed analysis of the information-processing requirements has been made. Given a complete set of requirements, a system that is best for the application can be designed and then implemented.
- Bottom-up methodologies emphasize that CBISs have a number of common elements that can be implemented first, then used as needed in particular programs. Programs can then be collected into systems for support of an application.
- Experimental design or prototyping methodologies propose that correct design is a prerequisite to a successful system, but that the initial requirement specifications cannot be complete because users will discover additional requirements as they gain experience with a functioning system. Thus a skeleton or prototype system is quickly constructed so that the users can experiment with it. This is expected to elicit a more complete and accurate statement of system requirements, from which a successful system can be constructed.

Much has been written about the pros and cons of these approaches and about the validity of the underlying assumptions and theories.

Unfortunately, much of the debate is speculative and aimed at supporting the beliefs of the individual writer and promoting the methodology being proposed.

Practice and Experience

A number of specific methodologies have followed each of these approaches. These methodologies have been presented in conferences, books, and courses and on the lecture circuits. The following are some general observations about the current state of the art.

Top-down Methodologies These methodologies have been called *classic* because they follow the system concepts from general systems theory and the belief that systems can be described and analyzed by successive and iterative study of the subsystems that make up a whole system. Current work is based on principles of information systems set up by Langefors (Langefors, 1973).

The development of top-down methodologies has focused on the analysis and design stages of system development, often on basically one aspect of the analysis or design. Currently there are a rather large number of methodologies covering a range of opinions about the scope of system analysis and design. The major criticism of specific methodologies in this group is that they are not complete; no one methodology covers all phases of analysis, design, and implementation to an operative CBIS.

Bottom-up Methodologies These methodologies are a continuation and formalization of system development practice. The generally accepted best advice to new CBIS owners and developers of new types of automated applications is to begin small, with a system that everyone can understand. When this system is running, then add to it, letting the system grow as the users gain experience with it.

This strategy works. The major criticism is that the resulting large system tends to be a patchwork of overlapping programs and redundant data. These systems are difficult to maintain because the effect of modifications on parts that should not be involved is unpredictable. These problems provide the arguments supporting a top-down, complete design approach.

Nonetheless, most application generators build on the observation that there are a number of standard components to CBISs that can be incorporated in new systems.

Experimental Design and Prototyping This approach tries to combine the previous two. Quick (and dirty) systems can be constructed using application generators and common system components. Users can experiment with the prototype system and give modified or more detailed system requirements, which can be used to refine the prototype system. In this way a detailed, total system design can be constructed in parallel with system implementation.

The experimental design approach makes possible the implementation of a useful, if not complete, system earlier than does the classic top-down approach. However, it has some of the same problems as the bottom-up approach in that operative routines need to be constantly modified to reflect changing (more detailed) requirements.

Choosing a System Analysis and Design Methodology   A number of projects have been implemented using each of these design approaches. Unfortunately, there is little literature comparing the resulting systems or their development strategies. One problem in comparing systems and/or their analysis and design strategies is that the systems implemented are quite different and are implemented for different user groups.

Assuming that a choice of system analysis and design methodology is possible, we can offer the following rule of thumb.

- Top-down methodologies are preferable for new types of application for a relatively sophisticated EDP user environment.
- Bottom-up methodologies are preferable for system modifications and expansion. They are also good for a well-known type of application for a sophisticated EDP user environment.
- Experimental design methodologies are preferable for a relatively well-known type of application for an EDP-novice user environment.

As is evident from the approach proposed in this book, this author believes that there is no substitute for a good overall system design in guaranteeing a successful, maintainable CBIS. The design should take into account real application requirements and not be just a documentation of the alternatives chosen for implementation. Although implementation independence in the design phase is thought to be best in a top-down approach, it is feasible to construct such a design using an experimental approach. This will be most difficult in a bottom-up approach.

THIS APPROACH REVISITED

The approach to system analysis and design presented in this book is based on a classic system analysis and design methodology. The classic methodologies are generally attributed to the system analysis work begun by Professor Langefors in the mid 1960s (Langefors, 1973).

Langefors's work has been further developed in the Scandinavian research community and has led to commercial systems, such as ISAC (Lundeberg, 1978, 1979, 1981). Briefly, the classic methodologies propose that a detailed system analysis precede system design. Information systems are considered systems according to general systems theory, and they are analyzed by successive decomposition.

The characteristics of this methodology and the assumptions made are given here in the sequence in which they were listed and discussed earlier in this chapter.

• The scope of the system analysis and design project is seen as covering an information problem analysis, information-system goal development, information-system design, automated data-system design, and implementation and operative-system planning. The organizational structure is assumed to be given and stable from the point of view of the new system.

• The basic approach to system analysis and design is top-down with iterations between development phases. It is assumed that an information system is made up of a set of subsystems, with the goals and objectives of each determined by the supersystem of which the subsystem is a part. Further, it is assumed that the goals, objectives, and requirements for the whole CBIS must be determined before the goals and characteristics for the elementary processing or data modules can be established. It is also assumed that supersystem goals will usually relate to a number of subsystems.

• The dominant system component (the one most important for design purposes) is considered to be the data subsystem. It is assumed that the data collection of an organization is the most stable (in terms of data types, not values) component of a CBIS.

• The target CBIS is assumed to be an administrative system at the operative level of the organization. However, it is believed that this approach is applicable to the design of any CBIS, for example, decision support systems, office automation systems, production control systems, educational systems, and others.

• The CBIS users are assumed to represent all categories (see Chapters 2, 4, and 14): direct, indirect, and passive users, as well as system designers, implementers, and owners/controllers. Each of these user groups must be represented, whenever possible, in the analysis and design project as active members of the design team.

• It is assumed that a system designer who has expertise in the design of CBISs, but who is not a direct user of the CBIS being designed, will coordinate the activities of the design team. It is assumed that the system designer is experienced in CBIS design and project management and that the design team members will provide the application expertise necessary for designing a successful system.

• The tools proposed are manual. They consist of a combination of graphs, tables, and matrices that are used to capture and describe the system components. However, there are many automated tools that could be used within this methodology. A set of automated support tools, specifically tailored for this methodology and implementable on microcomputers, is currently being developed at the Institute for Information Sciences, University of Bergen, Norway.

KEY CONCEPTS

Bottom-up approach
Experimental design
Prototyping
System analysis and design
System analysis and design scope
Top-down approach
Users

DISCUSSION QUESTIONS

1. Why is system analysis and design important? What are the primary reasons for the current interest in this activity? Of these reasons, which are the most important? Why?
2. Why all this interest in system users? How can user concerns affect system analysis and design methodologies?
3. Discuss how graphs, tables, and matrices are used in system analysis and design methodologies. Other tools include simulation, proto- typing, decision tables, problem statement languages, program generators, and data-base systems. How can these be used in sys- tem analysis and design?
4. Of the system analysis and design tools, which can or should be automated?
5. Discuss each of the seven categories of characteristics of system analysis and design methodologies given in this chapter. Which are most important? Why?
6. What are the differences between top-down and bottom-up design? When can each be used to greater advantage than the other? Why?
7. What is experimental design? When and why is it useful? Can it replace traditional top-down design? Why?
8. Discuss the design of systems, data, programs, and user interfaces. Which is most important to system analysis and design? Why?
9. Discuss the theories underlying top-down, bottom-up, and experi- mental design. Is there a best one? If so, which one? Why?

10. Discuss the state of the art in system analysis and design method-
    ologies. Why have none of the approaches been proved best?
11. What type of methodology is presented in this book? Is it a good
    one? Why or why not?

PROJECTS

1. Describe a particular system analysis and design methodology (not
   necessarily the one in this text) in terms of the characteristics
   described in this chapter. Is this a good methodology? Why or why
   not?
2. Locate at least two systems implemented according to the same
   analysis and design methodology. Evaluate these systems. How
   could the analysis and design methodology used be improved to
   give an improved system?

RECOMMENDED READINGS

Olle, T. W., H. G. Sol, and A. A. Verrijn-Stuart, eds. "Information Systems Design
    Methodologies: A Comparative Review." *IFIP WG 8.1 Working Conference
    Proceedings.* Amsterdam: North-Holland, 1982.
        This book presents 25 papers (of 76 announced submissions) describing
    system analysis and design methodologies, each illustrated with a design of an
    information system for an IFIP conference. The papers were chosen to illustrate
    ". . . methodologies which best cover the existing spectrum of methodologies."
    Contrary to the title, there is no real comparison of the methodologies. This has
    been set up as an aim of the next conference.
Schneider, H-J, and A. I. Wasserman, eds. "Automated Tools for Information
    Systems Design." *IFIP WG 8.1 Working Conference Proceedings.* Amsterdam:
    North-Holland, 1982.
        As the title indicates, this book presents papers describing current work on
    developing automated tools for support of system analysis and design method-
    ologies. Most tools are developed within the framework of a specific method-
    ology, but have more general application, with some technical modifications.

APPENDIXES

Bibliography

Alexander, M. J. *Information Systems Analysis.* Chicago: SRA, 1974.

Allen, B. "The Biggest Computer Frauds: Lessons for CPAs." *Journal of Accountancy*, 143, No. 5 (1977).

ANSI, "Standard Flowchart Symbols and Their Use in Information Processing." American National Standards Institute, 1970.

Aschim, F. "IFIP WG 8.1 Case Solved Using SYSDOC and SYSTEMA-TOR." In *Information System Design Methodologies.* Ed. T. W. Olle, et al. Amsterdam: North-Holland, 1982.

Bach, C. G. "Data Privacy—Critical Issues of the 80's." *Telecommunications*, 14, No. 5 (1980), 43–48.

Bachman, C. W. "Data Structure Diagrams." *Data Base*, 1, No. 2 (1969).

Berild, S., and S. Nachmens. "CS4—a Tool for Database Design by In-fological Simulation." *Proceedings of 3rd International Conference for Very Large Data Bases*, 1977.

Bertalanffy, L. von. "The Theory of Open Systems in Physics and Biology." *Science*, 3 (1950), 23–29. Also in *Systems Thinking.* Ed. F. E. Emery. Baltimore: Penguin Books, 1969.

———. "The History and Status of General Systems Theory." In *Systems Analysis Techniques.* Ed. J. P. Couger and R. Knapp. New York: John Wiley & Sons, 1974.

Biggs, C. L., E. G. Birks, and W. Atkins. *Managing the Systems Development Process.* Englewood Cliffs, N.J.: Prentice-Hall, 1980.

Bingham, J. E., and G. W. P. Davies. *A Handbook of Systems Analysis.* 2nd ed. London: The Macmillan Press, Ltd., 1978.

Bleier, R. E. "Treating Hierarchic Data Structures in the SDC Time-Shared Data Management System (TDMS)." *Proc. ACM National Conference*, 1967.

Brabb, G. J. *Computers and Information Systems in Business.* 2nd ed. Boston: Houghton Mifflin, 1980.

Burch, J. G., Jr., F. R. Strater, and G. Grudnitski. *Information Systems: Theory and Practice.* 2nd ed. New York: John Wiley & Sons, 1979.

Chapin, N. "Flowcharting with the ANSI Standard: A Tutorial." *Computing Surveys*, 2 (June 1970).

Childs, D. L. "Feasibility of a Set-Theoretic Data Structure—A General Structure Based on a Reconstructed Definition of Relation." *Proceedings IFIP Congress*, Amsterdam: North-Holland, 1968.

CODASYL. "CODASYL Data Base Task Group Report." *Conference on Data System Languages*, ACM, 1971.

Codd, E. F. "A Relational Model of Data for Large Shared Data Banks." *CACM*, 13 (1970).

Couger, J. P., and R. Knapp, eds. *System Analysis Techniques*. New York: John Wiley & Sons, 1974.

Date, C. J. *An Introduction to Database Systems*. 3rd ed. Reading, Mass.: Addison-Wesley, 1981.

———. *An Introduction to Database Systems, Vol. II*. Reading, Mass.: Addison-Wesley, 1983.

Emery, F. E., ed. *Systems Thinking*. Baltimore: Penguin Books, 1969.

Emery, J. "Cost/Benefit Analysis of Information Systems." In *Systems Analysis Techniques*. Ed. J. P. Couger and R. Knapp. New York: John Wiley & Sons, 1974, pp. 395–425.

Fernandez, E. B., R. C. Summers, and C. Wood. *Database Security and Integrity*. Reading, Mass.: Addison-Wesley, 1981.

Gane, C., and T. Sarson. *Structured Systems Analysis: Tools and Techniques*. Englewood Cliffs, N.J.: Prentice-Hall, 1979.

Ginzberg, M. J. "Finding an Adequate Measure of OR/MS Effectiveness." *Interfaces*, 8, No. 4 (1978), 59–62.

———. "Participative System Design." In *Design and Implementation of Computer-Based Information Systems*. Ed. N. Szyperski and E. Grochla. Alphen aan den Rijn, The Netherlands: Sijthoff & Noordhoff, 1979.

IBM. "Information Management System/Virtual Storage (IMS/VS)" Publications: GH20–1260–3, SH20–9025–2, SH20–9026–2, SH20–9027–2, SH20–9028–1, SH20–9030–2. White Plains, N.Y.: IBM Corp., 1975.

IFIP–ICC. *Vocabulary of Information Processing*. International Federation for Information Processing and International Computation Center, Amsterdam, 1966.

Jackson, M. A. *Principles of Program Design*. London, England: Academic Press, 1975.

Kindred, A. R. *Data Systems and Management*. 2nd ed. Englewood Cliffs, N.J.: Prentice-Hall, 1980.

Kriebel, C. H. "Evaluating the Quality of Information Systems." In *Design and Implementation of Computer-Based Information Systems*. Ed. N. Szyperski and E. Grochla. Alphen aan den Rijn, The Netherlands: Sijthoff & Noordhoff, 1979.

Langefors, B. *Theoretical Analysis of Information Systems*. 4th ed. Lund, Sweden: Studentlitteratur, 1973.

Layard, R., ed. *Cost-Benefit Analysis*. Harmondsworth, Middlesex, England: Penguin Books, 1972.

Lucas, H. C. *Information Systems Concepts for Management*. New York: McGraw-Hill, 1978.

———. "The Use of Interactive Information Storage and Retrieval Systems in Medical Research." *CACM*, 21, No. 3 (1978), 197–205.

———. *The Analysis, Design, and Implementation of Information Systems*. 2nd ed. New York: McGraw-Hill, 1981.

Lucas, H. C., F. F. Land, T. J. Lincoln, and K. Supper, eds. *The Information Systems Environment*. Amsterdam: North-Holland, 1980.

Lundeberg, M. *Systemering—Informasjonsanalyse*. (In Swedish.) Oslo, Norway: Tanum, 1974.

Lundeberg, M., G. Guldkuhl, and A. Nilsson. "A Systematic Approach to Information Systems Development. Part I: Introduction, and Part II: Problem and Data Oriented Systems Work." *Information Systems*, 4, Nos. 1 & 2 (1979).

——. *Information Systems Development—A Systematic Approach*. Englewood Cliffs, N.J.: Prentice-Hall, 1981.

Martin, J. *Introduction to Teleprocessing*. Englewood Cliffs, N.J.: Prentice-Hall, 1972.

——. *Security, Accuracy and Privacy in Computer Systems*. Englewood Cliffs, N.J.: Prentice-Hall, 1973.

——. *Computer Data-Base Organization*. 2nd ed. Englewood Cliffs, N.J.: Prentice-Hall, 1977.

——. *Design and Strategy for Distributed Data Processing*. Englewood Cliffs, N.J.: Prentice-Hall, 1981.

——. *Telematic Society—A Challenge for Tomorrow*. Englewood Cliffs, N.J.: Prentice-Hall, 1981.

——. *Application Development Without Programmers*. Englewood Cliffs, N.J.: Prentice-Hall, 1982.

Martin, J., and A. Norman. *The Computerized Society*. Englewood Cliffs, N.J.: Prentice-Hall, 1970.

McDaniel, H. *Applications of Decision Tables*. Princeton, N.J.: Brandon Systems Press Inc., 1970.

——. *Decision Table Software*. Princeton, N.J.: Brandon Systems Press Inc., 1970.

McLeod, R., Jr. *Management Information Systems*. Chicago: SRA, 1979.

Methlie, L. B. *Information Systems Design*. New York: Columbia University Press, 1978.

Muller-Merbach, H. "The Modeling Process: Steps vs. Components." In *Design and Implementation of Computer-Based Information Systems*. Ed. N. Szyperski and E. Grochla. Alphen aan den Rijn, The Netherlands: Sijthoff & Noordhoff, 1979.

Nordbotten, S. "Introduksjon til Informasjonsvitenskap." (In Norwegian.) Bergen, Norway: Institute for Information and Computer Science, University of Bergen, 1975.

——. "Systems Analysis and Design of Computerized Information Systems." Working paper. New York: United Nations Statistical Office, 1980.

Nordbotten, S., and J. Nordbotten. "Systems Analysis and Design Applied to Statistical Systems." *Proceedings ISI–81*, International Statistical Institute, 1981.

Olle, T. W., H. G. Sol, and A. A. Verrijn-Stuart. "Information Systems Design Methodologies: A Comparative Review." *IFIP WG 8.1 Working Conference Proceedings.* Amsterdam: North-Holland, 1982.

Rockart, J. F. "Chief Executives Define Their Own Data Needs." *Harvard Business Review*, March–April 1979.

Schneider, H. J., and A. I. Wasserman, eds. "Automated Tools for Information Systems Design." *IFIP WG 8.1 Working Conference Proceedings.* Amsterdam: North-Holland, 1982.

Sockut, G., and W. Goldberg. "Database Reorganization—Principles and Practice." *ACM Computing Surveys*, 11, No. 4 (1979).

Solvberg, A. "Analyse av Informasjonssystemer: del I og II." (In Norwegian.) CASCADE, working papers no. 30 & 33. Norway: University of Trondheim, 1977.

———. "A Draft Proposal for Integrating System Specification Models." In *Information Systems Design Methodologies.* Ed. T. W. Olle et al. Amsterdam: North-Holland, 1982.

Sundgren, B. "An Infological Approach to Data Bases." Sweden: National Bureau of Statistics, 1973.

———. "User Controlled Design of Information Systems." Working Paper 77:2. Sweden: National Bureau of Statistics, 1977.

Szyperski, N., and E. Grochla, eds. *Design and Implementation of Computer-Based Information Systems.* Alphen aan den Rijn, The Netherlands: Sijthoff & Noordhoff, 1979.

Teichrow, D. "Automation of System Building." *Datamation*, 17, No. 2 (1974).

———. "Problem Statement Languages in MIS." In *System Analysis Techniques.* Ed. J. P. Couger and R. Knapp. New York: John Wiley & Sons, 1974.

———. "Problem Statement Analysis: Requirements for the Problem Statement Analyzer." In *System Analysis Techniques.* Ed. J. P. Couger and R. Knapp. New York: John Wiley & Sons, 1974.

Tsichritzis, D. C., and F. H. Lochovsky. *Data Base Management Systems.* New York: Academic Press, 1977.

———. *Data Models.* Englewood Cliffs, N.J.: Prentice-Hall, 1982.

Veim, J. C. "DDBS a Dynamic Data Base Systems." *Selected Working Papers.* Bergen, Norway: Institute for Information and Computer Science, University of Bergen, 1979.

———. "An Introduction to Information and File Structuring." Compendium. Bergen, Norway: Institute for Information and Computer Science, University of Bergen, 1980.

Vessoy, I., and R. Weber. "Some Factors Affecting Program Repair Maintenance: An Empirical Study." *CACM*, 26, No. 2 (1983).

Wasserman, A. I. "Information Systems Design Methodology." *Journal of the American Society for Information Science*, January 1980.

Weldon, J. L. *Data Base Administration.* New York: Plenum Press, 1981.

Whiteside, T. *Computer Capers: Tales of Electronic Thievery, Embezzlement, and Fraud.* New York: T. Y. Crowell, 1978.

Wiener, N. *Cybernetics or Control and Communication in the Animal and the Machine.* Cambridge, Mass.: MIT Press, 1948 (2nd ed. 1965).

Yourdan, E. *Techniques for Program Structure and Design.* Englewood Cliffs, N.J.: Prentice-Hall, 1975.

Glossary

This glossary defines the principal terms and concepts as they are used in this text. An effort has been made to use common terminology wherever possible. Term or concept definitions taken from other sources are indicated by the author's name or a reference number in parentheses following the definition or by a footnote. The reference numbers refer to the following sources:

1. Chandor, Anthony, et al. *The Penguin Dictionary of Computers.* 2nd ed. Baltimore: Penguin Books, 1977. Copyright © Anthony Chandor, John Graham, Robin Williamson, 1970, 1977. Reprinted by permission of Penguin Books Ltd.
2. IFIP, *Vocabulary of Information Processing*, 1966.
3. Computer and Business Equipment Manufacturers Association. *American National Dictionary for Information Processing.* X3/TR-1-77, 1977.

Another important source for term and concept definition and discussion is:

Ralston, A., ed. *Encyclopedia of Computer Science.* Van Nostrand Reinhold Co., 1976.

Acceptance Testing The evaluation of an operative CBIS, or any of its parts, to determine that it functions according to specifications. Performed as the next to last task in system implementation, stage V of an ISAD project, before acceptance of the system and payment for it.

Activity Analysis A description and evaluation of those tasks (activities) of an object system that have an effect on the information-system functions. That is, an analysis of the portion of an organization that is to receive an information system. For example, a description and evaluation of the tasks of the personnel department before development of an information system for payroll production.

Activity Graph, A-Graph A graphic model of an object system, in which the nodes represent activities (processes), depicted by dots, and materials and/or information, depicted by rhomboids. Arcs represent the sequence of activities and the flow of materials and/or information. For examples, see Figures 5.3 and 5.5.

Activity Matrix, A-Matrix A matrix in which the vertical axis contains activity identifiers, the central columns contain indicators of information element usage, and the rightmost columns provide usage characteristics. For an example, see Figure 5.4.

Administrative Information System (AIS) An information system, including its information archive and processes, that is to provide information to support management activities in an organization; for example, a system to support personnel administration, accounts receivable and payable, project management, or other such activities.

AIS Acronym for Administrative Information System.

Algorithm "A series of instructions or procedural steps for the solution of a specific problem." (1, p. 30)

Analyst Short form for system analyst. A person or group of persons whose job is to:
1. establish the objectives for an information system.
2. evaluate the performance of the information system.
3. prepare design alternatives for improving the existing system's capabilities.

Analyst Team A group of persons whose collective task is to perform the job of a system analyst. *See* analyst.

Application "The particular kind of problem to which data processing techniques are applied. . . ." (1, p. 35)

Application Area Any area of human endeavor encompassing data processing operations that are adaptable to automation. Examples are personnel administration and production management.

Application Generator A software system capable of creating application programs from problem descriptions given by the user.

Application Program A program designed to perform a user-defined data processing task, such as generating payroll checks.

Application System "A system designed to perform a particular (user defined) task." (1, p. 35) An application system consists of one or more application programs that support or totally provide the data processing for an application area.

Attribute "An inherent characteristic. . . ."* In information systems, a characteristic that describes an object (entity) of interest to the system. For example, name, age, and sex could be attributes of the object type *student.*

    Shared attribute An attribute that describes two or more entities. Such sttributes usually describe the relationship between the "owning" entities. For example, a grade attribute can be a characteristic of both student and course. It actually describes the relationship between student and course; for example, student x received a grade of A in course y.

Auditing "The process of checking source date, processing procedures, and output documents for validity and error control (accuracy)." (Brabb)

*The Merriam-Webster Dictionary. By permission. From the Merriam-Webster Dictionary © 1974 by Merriam-Webster Inc., publisher of the Merriam-Webster® Dictionaries.

Back-up "A facility intended to provide a service in the event of loss of service from some other resource; any resource necessary for effective recovery." (1, p. 44) In this text, back-up is used as both the process and the result of making periodic copies of the data and/or data processes so that in the event of system failure, the data and/or processing system can be reconstructed.

Batch Processing "A method of processing data in which transactions are collected and prepared for input to the computer for processing as a single unit. There may be some delay between the occurrence of original events and the eventual processing of the transactions." (1, p. 47) The generation of periodic reports and data analysis for forecasting are typical batch-processing tasks.

Bottom-up Approach A characteristic of an ISAD methodology that describes the direction of system design as first identifying, describing, and specifying the lowest-level elements of a system, then using these elements in the design and construction of composite elements forming higher-level systems. Systems are constructed in this way from a set of elementary or atomic building blocks.

CBIS Acronym for Computer-Based Information System.

Communication Language In person-machine communications, the set of statements, with syntax, grammar, and interpretation, that is used to relay messages between the human user and the automated parts of the CBIS. The communication language may be restricted to one communication direction, namely, from the user to the CBIS. Communication languages may be classified as the following types: parametric, structured English, natural language, menu.

Communication System
1. That software that directs, receives, and sends messages between the human user and a CBIS.
2. Also, that software and hardware that directs, receives, and sends messages between automated systems.

Compiler A software system that translates programs written in some high-level language, such as FORTRAN, COBOL, PL/1, or BASIC, into machine-executable instructions.

Computer-Based Information System (CBIS) An information system with one or more automated subsystems.

Computer System In this text, the combination of hardware units (the computer) and the system software required to run the hardware, typically including an operating system, one or more compilers, a communication system, and a data management system.

Computer Network A set of computers connected for shared processing and/or interchange of messages.

Concurrent Update More than one process modifying (updating) the same data at the same time. This can occur in multiprocessing and distributed processing systems where more than one user program is active at the same time.

Constraints
1. In system design, limits set by the organization on the resources that can be assigned to the development and operation of a CBIS. These constraints may be economic, legal, social, operative, or technical.
2. In data-base design, the rules that define illegal data values, data-base states, and/or operations.

Conversion   The last stage of system implementation, during which the new or modified system replaces the old system.

Cost/Benefit Analysis   An evaluation of the monetary, operational, technological, social, and legal costs of a system during its life cycle, compared with its monetary, operational, technological, social, and legal benefits. The purpose of a cost/benefit analysis is to clearly state the costs and benefits that can be expected as a result of a given system design. Normally, expected benefits must exceed expected costs before an implementation project should be initiated.

CPU   Acronym for Central Processing Unit, the main component of a computer in which all actual processing occurs.

Critical Path (CP)   In project administration, as illustrated in a PERT diagram, that sequence of events that determines the length of time required to complete the project; if any of the critical path events is delayed, the whole project will be delayed.

DA   Acronym for Data Administrator.

Data   "A representation of facts or ideas in a formalized manner, capable of being communicated or manipulated by some process." (2)

Data Administrator (DA) or *Data-Base Administrator (DBA)*   The person(s) responsible for managing an organization's data resources, including the identification and definition of the data, the establishment of security routines, and the provision for data storage and maintenance in files and/or data bases.

Data Base (DB)
1. In general, the collection of data maintained by a (usually automated) data processing system.
2. Technically, an automated, integrated collection of data representing two or more interrelated entity types.

Data-Base Administrator (DBA)   *See* Data Administrator.

Data-Base Management System (DBMS)   A software system that provides users and/or their application programs with the data administrative services (storage, retrieval, modification, and structure maintenance) necessary for a data base.

Data Definition   The specification of the characteristics of the data elements of a system. The definition should include a data element name, its type, the types of values allowed, length, storage and presentation formats, and security constraints.

Data Dictionary   A collection of the descriptions of data elements and interdata relationships; the set of all data definitions for a system.

Data Dictionary System (DDS)   A software system that stores data descriptions, checks them for consistency, and produces various reports from them. Some DDSs have an interface to a DBMS that allows automated specification of the DBMS schema from the data dictionary data.

Data Element   A single piece of data, such as a name, an address, or a price. Synonym: Data item.

   Data element type   A group of data elements of the same classification; for example, *name-of-employee* would be a data element type that would include the data element *name* from each employee record. Sometimes used as a synonym for attribute.

Data Item   Synonym for Data element.

Data Model   "Defines the rules according to which data are structured." (Tsichritzis, 1982) A data model may be presented as a table or as a graph in which the nodes represent the data elements, attribute or entity types, and the arcs, which may be directed, represent the relationships between the data elements. Common data model types are relational (tabular model), network, and hierarchic (graphic models). See examples in Chapter 8.

Data Processing Characteristics   The data usage requirements defined by the application programs. Processing characteristics include access priority, frequency of use, volume of data, access type, processing type (manual or automated), response time, and type of usage (retrieval, modification).

Data Processing System   Synonym for Data system.

Data System   An information-system subsystem consisting of a data collection and a set of formalized procedures for storing, retrieving, manipulating, transferring, and/or disseminating the data. Synonym: Data processing system.

Data-System Design   Stage 4 in an information-system analysis and design project, during which the preparation of a machine-independent specification for a data system is developed.

Data-Usage Matrix   A matrix that defines the interactions between the data elements and processes of a system. See Chapter 8, Figure 8.8.

DB   Acronym for Data Base.

DBA   Acronym for Data-Base Administrator.

DBMS   Acronym for Data-Base Management System.

Deadlock   A processing situation in which each of two or more programs is waiting for the release of resources held by the other(s). See Chapter 13, Figure 13.1.

Decision Support System (DSS)   A data processing system used to provide data analysis functions to support high-level management decisions.

Decision Table   "A table of all the contingencies to be considered in the description of a problem, along with the actions to be taken for each contingency set." (3)

Development Cycle   The sequence of stages involved in the establishment of an operative information system. The cycle consists of (1) problem analysis, (2) system analysis, (3) information-system design, (4) data-system design, (5) implementation, and (6) operation and tuning. See Chapter 3.

Direct Access   In file processing, the ability to locate a single record within a collection of records (a file) without having to scan the entire collection.

Direct Conversion   In system implementation, the changeover to the new system at some specified point in time, with no processing overlap with the previous system. This is most common when a new machine replaces the old one.

Direct File Structure   A collection of records, or a file, ordered in a way that supports direct access. Normally, a record's location within the file is calculated from the value of its primary key. The key conversion routine may make use of some hashing algorithm.

Direct Users   *See* Users.

Distributed Processing   The ability to execute programs at two or more geographically separate locations, normally connected by a computer network.

Distributed System
1. Two or more computer systems connected through a computer network in such a way that work can be processed at more than one site.
2. An application system that is designed to operate at two or more computer sites, using a computer network.
3. An application system composed of two or more subsystems operating independently at geographically separate sites.

Documentation   The textual and graphic descriptions of a data processing system, consisting of verbal descriptions, flowcharts, cross-reference matrices, program listings, and execution instructions. (Brabb)

Domain   The set of valid values for the data elements of a given attribute, or data element type. For example, the domain for the data element type *salary* might be all two-place decimals between $100.00 and $2000.00.

DSS   Acronym for Decision Support System.

Entity   ". . . Something with separate and real existence."* In information systems, used as a synonym for object, and meaning something of interest to the system. An entity may be tangible, such

---

*The Merriam-Webster Dictionary. By permission. From the Merriam-Webster Dictionary © 1974 by Merriam-Webster Inc., publisher of the Merriam-Webster® Dictionaries.

as a person, motor vehicle, or other object, or intangible, such as a career, contract, or university degree.

Entity class   A group or category of objects (entities) with some common attribute set. For example, a group of persons (entities) may form the entity class *student* through the shared attribute "registered at university *x*." Synonym: Object class.

Entity type   The set of attribute types used to describe the entities of an entity class. For example, the entity-type definition

⟨student–id, name, address⟩

could be used to describe persons of the entity class *student*. Synonym: Object-type.

Error Message   A message generated by a program stating (1) that an error situation has been detected, (2) what that error is, and (3) how the error can be corrected.

Experimental Design   An approach to ISAD in which a simple system is constructed as a demonstration of a possible CBIS. Users are then asked to use the system and comment on it, identifying alterations that would make it more useful to them. A more complex system is then built by modifying the original experimental system. This approach is similar to the prototyping approach, although it involves earlier construction of the system.

Feasibility Analysis   The final task in the problem analysis stage of an ISAD project. The feasibility analysis evaluates the costs and benefits that can be expected as a result of modifying the information-processing system. It is normally assumed that the modification will include automation of some previously manual operations.

Feedback   "The return to the input of a part of the output of a machine, system, or process."* For information systems, it is generally assumed that the system output is processed by some other system before it is returned as feedback to the original system. Feedback can be used to correct or alter system behavior.

Field   In file processing, the storage area for a single data element. A record is made up of some number of fields.

File   A collection of records of a single type. For example, a client file would consist of a set of records, one for each of the organization's clients.

File Management System (FMS)   A software system that provides data administrative services (data storage, retrieval, structure maintenance) for one or more files.

---

*The Merriam-Webster Dictionary. By permission. From the Merriam-Webster Dictionary © 1974 by Merriam-Webster Inc., publisher of the Merriam-Webster® Dictionaries.

File Structure   The order in which records are stored within a file, including possible auxiliary data to facilitate data retrieval, such as indexes and pointers.

Financial Constraint   In system design, the limits on monetary resources that can be used for system development and operation.

Flowchart   "The diagrammatic representation of a sequence of events, usually drawn with conventional symbols representing different types of events and their interconnection." (1) Also called a Flow diagram. Flowcharts are most often used to specify and document programs and fully automated systems.

Formal Information System   An information system whose components are well defined.

Function   ". . . An action contributing to a larger action. . . ."* In the context of an information system, a well-defined activity, process, or task.

Functional Dependency   A relational model concept describing the relationship between two attributes. Formally, "given a relation R, attribute Y of R is functionally dependent on attribute X of R if and only if each X-value in R has associated with it precisely one Y-value in R (at any one time)." (Date) Informally, an attribute is functionally dependent on another if its value is uniquely determined by the value of the second attribute. For example, the value of the attribute *student-name* would be functionally dependent on the value of the attribute *student-id* if for each student id value there is only one possible student name.

Functional Information System   An information system developed and used to support a particular activity (function) within an organization, such as accounting, project management, or forecasting.

Gantt Chart   A graphic presentation of project activities indicating the overlap of activities and the expected amount of effort required, normally given in person/weeks. See Figure 12.3.

Goals   The objectives of a system's activities.

Goal Specification   A task within the problem analysis stage, stage I of an ISAD methodology, during which the user requirements for information services are established.

Goal Statement   The formal specification of a given information system's goals, stating (1) what information the system is to maintain, (2) which processes are to be included, (3) who (which users) has access to the system, and (4) what service levels, for example, response times, the system is to maintain.

---

*The Merriam-Webster Dictionary. By permission. From the Merriam-Webster Dictionary © 1974 by Merriam-Webster Inc., publisher of the Merriam-Webster® Dictionaries.

Graphic Model   In data modeling, a graph in which the nodes represent entity types or record types and the arcs represent the relationships between entity types or record types, respectively. See Chapter 8, Figures 8.1 to 8.4.

Hardware   A generic term for the physical units that make up a computer system.

Hierarchic Data Base   A data-base structure in which records may be linked according to tree, or hierarchic, relationships; a structure in which there is only one access path to any one record.

Hierarchic Model   In data modeling, a graphic model in which the nodes must be related in such a way that there is only one path (sequence of node, arc, node, arc, etc.) *to* any given node. See Chapter 8, Figures 8.3 and 8.4.

Home Computing   The use of a microcomputer or personal computer at home to perform such data processing tasks as diverse as meal meal planning, checkbook balancing, and education, and to gain access to computer networks that provide news, stock-market services, banking, shopping, electronic mail, and so on.

Implementation   Stage 5 of an ISAD project, during which the design for the information system is realized. Implementation includes (1) generation of forms, (2) programming of automated subsystems, (3) program test, (4) establishment of operative procedures, (5) training of users, and (6) conversion to the new system.

Implementation Scheduling   The development of a plan for system implementation.

Implementation Team   Those people involved in system implementation. An implementation team will normally include a system analyst as project manager, one or more programmers, possibly a machine operator or the person responsible for machine operations, and user representatives.

Indexed-Sequential File Structure   A file structure in which the prime data are stored in physical sequence according to some set of data values; this is supplemented by an index, on the sequenced data values, that contains pointers to blocks of prime data. See Chapter 9, Figure 9.6.

Indirect User   *See* User.

Informal Information System   An information system whose components are ill-defined.

Information   "The meaning that a human expresses by or extracts from data by means of the known conventions of the representation used." (2)

Information Archive   A general concept for the total collection of information kept within and maintained by an information system. Commonly used synonym: Data base.

Information Clerk   A person whose job is primarily concerned with processing information and/or data.

Information Dictionary   A collection of descriptions of information elements, entity types and attributes, and information messages, giving names, definitions, components, precedents, and usages.

Information Element   A single piece of information; it may be a message describing several characteristics of an entity, or it may refer to a single attribute.

Information Flow   A description of the movement of information through an information system.

Information Graph (I-Graph)   A graphic model of information relationships. For examples, see Figures 5.7, 5.9, and 5.10.

Information Matrix (I-Matrix)   A matrix cross-referencing information elements and information processes. The I-matrix can also indicate information usage characteristics for the processes, such as frequency of use, volume of information used, response time requirements, and so on. For an example, see Figure 5.8.

Information-Oriented ISAD Methodology   An approach to system analysis and design that emphasizes identification of information and data elements for the total system.

Information Services   Synonym for Information processes.

Information System (IS)
1. A system, including its information archive and processes, that is used to provide information.
2. ". . . Any system, including its processes, that is used to provide information." (Langefors, 1973)
3. ". . . A set of organized procedures which when executed, provide information to support decision making." (Lucas, 1978)
4. ". . . An assemblage or collection of people, machines, ideas and activities that gathers and processes data in a manner that will meet the formalized information requirements of an organization." (Burch et al., 1979)

Information-System Analysis   Stage 2 of an ISAD project, during which the current system is described and evaluated against the goals established for it during problem analysis, ISAD stage 1. System analysis entails (1) a description of the object system, (2) a description of the current information system, and (3) an evaluation of the current system against the goal set.

Information-System Analysis and Design (ISAD)   Those activities that (1) identify the requirements for an information system, (2) evaluate the current information system, and (3) develop specifications for a new or modified information system. There are many ISAD methodologies, varying in the extent to which the ISAD phases are separated. However, an ISAD project must cover at least (1) a requirement study for an information system, (2) an analysis of the current system, (3) specification of a new or modified system, and (4) adaptation of the system specifications to conform with available resources.

Information-System Design Stage 3 of an ISAD project, during which the total information system is specified. Some parts of the data subsystem may possibly be candidates for automation.

Information Value The worth of information to its users. Value can be measured as a function of the level of detail, age, accuracy, and relevance of the information.

Input Signals, resources, directives, information, and/or data put into a system.

Input/Output (I/O) A collective term for the data fed into or received from a data processing system.

Input Supplier A person or group who, by his or her existence or activities, provides information to an information system.

Intangible Costs and Benefits Costs and benefits that are the result of system use, but that have no direct monetary value. For example, public relations can be a cost if the system results in poor relations or a benefit if the system improves relations. However, the monetary value of public relations may be difficult or impossible to establish.

Integrity In data systems, the assurance and maintenance of correct data values within a CBIS.

Interface The contact points and methods for communication between a human user and the automated portions of a CBIS.

Interpreter A software system that translates program statements one at a time as they are received, as opposed to a compiler, which processes the whole set of statements of a program. A common interpreted programming language is BASIC.

Inverted File Structure A file structure in which the prime data are stored as a direct file; it is supplemented by multiple indexes constructed on the data values. See Chapter 9, Figure 9.7.

IS Acronym for Information System.

ISAD Acronym for Information-System Analysis and Design.

ISAD Stages A separation of the activities of an ISAD methodology into groups corresponding to the life cycle of an information system. The stages are:
1. Problem analysis
2. System analysis
3. Information-system design
4. Data-system design
5. System implementation

ISAD Tools Techniques used to support the analysis, design, and/or presentation of information and specifications as they are developed during an ISAD project. Common tools include questionnaires, flowcharts, matrices, dictionaries, data models, scoring models, and texts.

I/O Acronym for Input/Output.

Key   A data element used to locate and/or identify a record occurrence or set of record occurrences.

Primary key   A data element type whose values uniquely identify single record occurrences. For example, Social Security numbers uniquely identify employed persons.

Secondary key   A data element type whose values identify a subset of the records of a record type. For example, *home-city=Bergen* would identify those students living in Bergen.

Sort key   The set of data elements used to sequence a set of records. For example, *student-name* can be used as a sort key to construct an alphabetical list of students.

Legal Constraints   Laws set by society or through contracts with labor unions, limiting the data and processes that may be included in a CBIS.

Life Cycle   The sequence of events during the existence of a system. For information systems, the life cycle consists of conception, goal specification, structure definition, function specification, development, use and adaptation, and replacement (which begins with conception).

Linked File Structure   A file structure in which sequencing and group structures are implemented using pointers from one record to the records related to it. See Chapter 9, Figure 9.7.

Log   In CBIS execution, a copy of all transactions, activities, and/or data modifications processed by the CBIS.

Mainframe Computer   The largest computer, normally including the largest number of peripheral units of the different size groups (microcomputers, minicomputers, and mainframe computers).

Management Information System (MIS)   An information system whose main objective is to provide information services for management.

Material Flow   The movement of materials (products, supplies, and so on) from one task or activity to another within an organization.

Memory   The temporary storage location for active data and programs while they are being processed by the CPU. The amount of memory available in a computer architecture indicates the computer's size. The memory is overlaid for each new program processed.

Menu   A form of user interface (communication language) in which the user, at a CRT screen, selects data processing options from a list presented by the system. For an example, see Figures 7.1 and 7.2.

Microcomputer   A small-sized computer that can be placed on a desk top. In 1983 a typical microcomputer contained 64 to 128K main memory, 2 to 4 floppy disk drives, and a CRT display screen. It is possible to connect, among other peripherals, 1 to 4 hard disk drives and one or more printers. A microcomputer is usually considered a work station for one person.

Minicomputer   A medium-sized computer that can be placed in a normal-sized office. The minicomputer is larger, faster, has more storage capacity, and is more expensive than a microcomputer; it is smaller, slower, has less storage capacity, and is less expensive than a mainframe computer. Minicomputers are considered good tools for small business applications, educational courses, and local stations for large networks.

MIS   Acronym for Management Information System.

Modular Conversion   In system implementation, a method of introducing a new or modified system by replacing separate modules or sets of modules in successive stages.

Module   In programming and system implementation, a small, self-contained subprogram that can be programmed and tested in its own right. An application program, particularly an application system, is (or should be) composed of a set of modules.

Multiprocessing   A computer hardware configuration in which multiple CPUs are connected in such a way that they can share the execution of a single program. Multiprocessing systems aim at increasing machine capacity by allowing more than one CPU to execute parts of a program simultaneously.

Multiprogramming   A computer system with operating-system software that can administer parallel execution of multiple programs. Multiprogramming systems aim at increasing machine capacity by allowing several programs to share main-memory resources. Execution of these programs is alternated so that idle time, for example, while waiting for I/O, in one program can be used by another program.

Network   Generally, a connected set of geographically separate computer systems. The connections may be made over telephone lines or through satellite communications.

Network Data Base   A data-base structure that can support data structured according to the network model, that is, one that allows multiple relationships (links) to and from any record type. Principally, data bases structured according to the CODASYL DBTG proposal. (CODASYL, 1971)

Network Model   In data modeling, a graphic model in which the nodes, representing entity types and/or record types, may be connected by multiple arcs. See Chapter 8, Figures 8.1 and 8.2.

Normalization   In relational data modeling theory, a process described as a set of succeedingly refined normal forms, NF, that aims at simplifying the composition of relations in order to reduce data redundancy and avoid data integrity problems during data updates, insertions, and deletions.

OAS   Acronym for Office Automation System.

Object   Something tangible or intangible of interest. Common synonym: Entity.

   Object class   A group of objects sharing some common attribute set. For example, a group of persons could form the object class *teachers* by having the same value for the attribute "faculty member of university x." Synonym: Entity class.

   Object type   In an information system, the set of attribute types used to describe the individuals of an object class. For example, ⟨student-id, name, address⟩ could be the object type definition for the object class *student*. Synonym: Entity type.

Object System   The system forming the environment for an information system, about which the information system collects and processes information.

Office Automation System (OAS)   A data processing system used to support office activities, particularly manuscript preparation (letters, contracts, reports, and so on), memo (mail) distribution, scheduling, and other such functions.

On-Line Processing   A CBIS processing mode in which the users work at terminals and enter commands and/or transactions for immediate processing by the application system. During on-line processing, the input terminal is "locked" for further input until a result (output) is received. Different users at different locations may have to wait because of overload of the machine resources. Many banking and airline ticketing systems execute as on-line systems. *See also* Real-time processing.

On-Line System

   1. A CBIS that includes a communication interface supporting on-line processing.

   2. A computer system with terminal (CRT) input/output stations.

Operative Constraints   Limits on the design of a CBIS set by the organization, specifying the personnel, space, and supplies available for the development and operation of a CBIS.

Operating System   A software system that administers the execution of programs and the allocation of computer resources, and performs system security activities.

Operational Mode   In reference to CBIS execution, the manner in which an application system is activated: real-time, on-line, or batch processing.

Organization   A group of people cooperating to achieve a mutual goal within a legislative or statutory framework that defines their individual authority and responsibilities.

Output   Materials, responses, data, and/or information generated by a system.

Output Recipient   One for whom system output, reports, answers to queries, graphs, and so on is intended.

Parallel Conversion In system implementation, the method of changing over to a new system in which for a limited period of time the old and new systems are operated concurrently. This method provides a back-up system should the new system not perform to requirements; it also provides an additional test of the correctness of the new system.

Parametric Language A type of communication language through which the user passes commands and data values for processing by the system in the form of a list of data elements in a predetermined sequence. See examples in Chapter 7.

Passive User *See* User.

Password A string of characters, letters and/or numbers used to identify a system user and allow that user access to system facilities.

PERT Network A graph used in project administration to plan the scheduling of activities. Each node event is normally the initiation or completion of the succeeding or preceding activity. Arcs represent activities and the expected duration of the activity. See Chapter 12, Figures 12.1 and 12.2.

Pointer In file processing, a field added to the storage record for prime data that contains an address to another record that is related in some way to the current one. Pointer fields coupled with key fields form the record structure of indexes.

Primary Key *See* Key.

Primary Storage The main memory of a machine, used to store programs and data during execution.

Prime Data Those data that represent the attribute values of the object system. Prime data do not include indexes or pointers included in file structures to facilitate data retrieval.

Privacy The protection of data describing persons or organizations.

Problem Analysis Stage 1 of an ISAD project, during which the environment of a possible information system is studied to determine whether the problems reported are due to errors, delays, or missing information. Problem analysis consists of (1) the definition and analysis of the system goals, (2) development of a goal set for the system, and (3) feasibility analysis of the goal set.

Procedure A specified sequence of processes required to perform some information-system activity. In information systems, the instructions, usually manual, for activating one or more processes.

Process Those operations that are required to perform some unit of work, normally a subtask of an information-system activity. In information systems, an activity that stores, retrieves, manipulates, transfers, or disseminates information or data. (See Figure 1.4.)

Process Dictionary A collection of the definitions of the information and data processes included in an information system. Each process definition should give an identification, the algorithm, the information or data required, and the authorized users. (See Chapter 4.)

Process-Oriented ISAD Methodologies   An approach to the analysis and design of information systems that emphasizes identification of the activities, procedures, and processes of the system.

Program   An automated process or set of processes.

Prototype System   A simple version of a complete CBIS, used as a design test vehicle in the prototype design methodology. A number of successively more complete prototype systems can be generated during the repetitive design and implementation process.

Prototyping, Prototype Design   A system-design technique in which a simple (prototype) system is designed and implemented first, then, after the users gain experience with this system, a more detailed, complete system is designed.

Real-Time Processing   A CBIS processing mode in which execution occurs in actual (real) clock time. The system may be on-line; however, there must not be any delays in execution as a result of overload. Common systems of this type are those used in production monitoring, robotics, medical patient monitoring, and space flight control.

Record   In file processing, a set of fields that contain data describing the attributes of some entity.

   Logical record   The set of fields used by an application program or requested by a human user, not necessarily equivalent to the underlying physical record. The fields of a logical record may be a subset of the fields of the physical record or may span several different physical records.

   Physical record   The set of fields used to store data in files.

Record Structure   The sequence of fields, with data types and lengths, that make up a record.

Record Type   Either fixed or variable, depending on whether the component fields have fixed or varying lengths.

Recovery   In CBIS operation, the process of restoring damaged programs, data values, and/or equipment to a correct and valid state.

Relation   In relational data modeling theory, a set of closely related attribute types that describe an entity type or an interentity relationship. Formally, "given the sets (of data values) $D1, D2, \ldots, Dn$ (not necessarily distinct), R is a relation on these 'n' sets if it is a set of n-tuples each of which has its first element from $D1$, second from $D2$, and so on." (Codd, 1970) See Chapter 8, Figures 8.5 to 8.7.

Relational Data Base   A data base structured in accordance with a relational model of the data. A relational data-base management system will provide operators for manipulating entire relations as well as individual tuples (records).

Relational Model   A tabular data model first proposed by Codd (Codd, 1970). Each entity type being modeled is defined as a relation consisting of a set of attributes. Relations are commonly presented as tables in which the rows illustrate the tuple form expected for the relation. The set of relations describing the set of entity types and their interrelationships constitutes the relational data model.

Relationships Connections between elements of a system. In data modeling, the association between attributes and entity or record types.

  Associative relationships Relationships that define the bindings between entities and entity types.

  Attributive relationships Relationships that define the bindings between attributes and the entity they describe.

  Communicative relationships Relationships that define the information and data paths within the system and between the system and its environment.

  External relationships Relationships that define the structure and interactions between the system and its environment.

  Internal relationships Relationships that define the interactions and structure between the subsystems of a system.

  Structural relationships Relationships that define the organization of the subsystems of a system.

Reorganization In file processing, a process that reorders the physical sequence of the data records, with possible regeneration of indexes, so that the physical sequence more closely matches the logical or usage sequence.

Requirement Matrix A matrix cross-referencing users or processes with the information or data required.

Response Time The time the processing system requires to react to and complete processing of an input message. This time is commonly measured from the moment a user submits a request until the user receives the system output.

Restructuring In file management, the process of changing the file structures so that they better support the observed user requirements. Restructuring may also involve a change in record structure, such as adding a field, deleting a field, changing the sequence of fields, splitting a record into two or more parts, or constructing a record from two or more records.

Rollback In system recovery, a process in which the effects of a program or transaction are erased by returning the data records to the values that existed before the program or transaction was initiated.

Scoring Model A technique for assigning, for subsequent evaluation, quantitative values to qualitative information. For example, "satisfaction with the (current) system" might be a desired evaluation characteristic. The user's opinion is converted to a "score" of, for example, 0 to 5, in which 0 stands for no good and 5 for excellent. See example in Figure 6.8.

Secondary Key *See* Key.

Secondary Storage   Storage units, such as disks, drums, and magnetic tape, that are used for the permanent storage of programs and data.

Security
1. As a general term, all efforts to protect a CBIS, including physical protection, protection against human destruction, and integrity and privacy control.
2. As a specific term, efforts to protect a CBIS against natural disasters, such as fire, flood, or earthquake, and willful destruction, such as bombing or theft of data.

Sequential File Structure   A file structure in which the physical sequence of the records reflects a logical ordering according to the data values of one or more fields. See Chapter 9.

Serial File Structure   A file structure in which the physical sequence of records is not determined by any data value. Common serial files are those in which data records are stored in order of receipt. See Chapter 9.

Service Bureau   A computer firm offering such data processing facilities as system analysis, system design, data-system implementation, execution of specific programs (such as payroll), computer capacity, and others for its customers.

Social Constraints   Limits on the design, development, and operation of a CBIS set by the human environment—workers and their motivation, skills, employment contracts, work definitions, and so on.

Software   A generic term for computer programs, as opposed to hardware. The two major groupings, system software and application software, refer to programs that administer hardware resources and those that perform user data processing, respectively.

Software Package   A standardized program developed to process a certain specific type of task. Examples include payroll production, inventory control, statistical data analysis, report generation, and many others.

Standard Software   A program that complies with accepted standards for programs of its type. Standards exist for file organizations, compilers, telecommunications, and network communications; they can be established for programming style within a given project.

Structure Diagram   A graphic model of a process or program, giving the hierarchic structure of the program modules.

Structured English
1. A communication language that uses a limited set of words and grammar from the English natural language. User queries and instructions are usually presented as single-sentence commands, such as, "List all students of course = system analysis."
2. In process specifications, a method of presenting the algorithm for a process or program that uses English sentences, formed using a restricted grammar, and lists these, using indention to show subprocess activities.

Subsystem   One of several parts of a system.

System

1. "A group of units so combined as to form a whole and to operate in unison. . . ."*

2. A structured, interrelated set of components (subsystems) whose combined goals act to achieve the primary system goals. (Chapter 1)

Closed system   A system with no interaction with its environment.

Open system   A system activated by and responsive to its environment.

System Analysis

1. The study of a system to determine its objectives, components, and structure.

2. Synonym for Information-system analysis.

System Analysis and Design   In this text, information-system analysis and design (ISAD). *See* ISAD.

System Analysis Team   Synonym for Analysis team.

System Analyst   Synonym for analyst.

System Benefits   A benefit is defined as "1. Advantage. 2. A useful aid. . . ."* In the context of a CBIS, a system benefit is an increase in the profitability and/or an improvement in the functioning of an organization, attributable to the existence and/or services of the information system.

Tangible benefits   System benefits to which a monetary value can be assigned; for example, a decrease in the cost of processing a transaction.

Intangible benefits   System benefits to which it is difficult or impossible to assign a monetary value; for example, on-line access to more data than in previous systems.

System Components   The elements of a system, both subsystems and atomic elements. In information systems, the system components are the processing subsystems and the information archive. The processing subsystems consist of the elemental processes for storage, retrieval, manipulation, transfer, and dissemination of information and/or data. The information archive consists of data and/or information describing elemental attributes and entities.

System Costs   Monetary, time, and personnel resources required for the development or operation of an information system.

Tangible costs   Costs that can be given a monetary value; for example, maintenance contracts for computer equipment.

Intangible costs   Costs for which a monetary value is difficult or impossible to calculate; for example, poor employee morale, or the negative impact on customers of a poorly functioning information system.

System Efficiency   A measure of system performance in terms of cost and speed. Low cost and high speed characterize an efficient system.

System Environment   The surroundings with which a system interacts and which determine the purpose and goal set for the system. An information system will contain descriptive information about the environment and process this information and/or data to support activities in the environment.

System Evaluation   In the context of information systems, the comparison of current system facilities or proposed system improvements with system requirements and constraints.

System Growth   Adaptation of system facilities to changing user requirements, usually entailing expansion of data coverage, that is, including more data types and more processing capabilities.

System Implementation   *See* Implementation.

System Interface   The contact points and communication routines between the system and its human users (*see* Interface).

System Maintenance   Those tasks that aim at keeping existing systems correct, efficient, and providing desired user services. Maintenance tasks can be grouped as follows:

Error control   Those tasks concerned with correcting errors in data or programs.

System growth   Those tasks concerned with providing new or extended services and facilities.

System tuning   Those tasks concerned with maintaining or upgrading system efficiency.

System Objects   Things of interest in the context of the system.

System Software   Programs that monitor and allocate computer-system resources, such as the operating system, communication system, data management system, compilers, and so on, as opposed to application software, which actually does data processing for a user application.

System Structure   The organization of subsystems.

Tabular Model   In data modeling, the representation form for the relational model, in which the columns represent the attributes of the relation and the rows represent the tuples or instances of the relation.

Technical Constraints   Limits on the design and operation of a CBIS set by the computer facilities and expertise available.

Terminal   A hardware unit through which a user can activate CBIS processing. Such units normally consist of a keyboard for input and a CRT (cathode-ray tube) for output display. The terminal may also be connected to a printer, or may be a microcomputer or minicomputer.

Time-sharing   A multiprogramming technique in which each active program is assigned a time interval (time slice) for execution, at the end of which the next program is activated for a specific time, then the next, and so on until it is the first program's turn again. As programs are completed, new programs are added to the active set.

Top-down Approach   An approach to ISAD that advocates that systems be perceived as a whole, then decomposed into their component parts. This decomposition continues through successive levels of subsystems until the atomic elements, processes and objects, are identified.

TPS   Acronym for transaction-processing system.

Training   In the context of a system analysis and design project, that activity that teaches the users the capabilities of, and how to operate, the new or modified system.

Transaction Process   A formal process supporting an operational-level activity within an organization.

Transaction-Processing System (TPS)   A set of transaction processes that support a functional area of an organization.

Transaction Record   A set of data elements that constitutes the input to a transaction process.

Transposed File Structure   A file structure in which the data are stored by column rather than by row; that is, each record of the file contains the data values for one attribute type. See Chapter 9.

Tuning   Efforts to improve system efficiency; they may include restructuring files, reprogramming central, often-used program modules, expanding or replacing hardware units, changing the number of concurrent programs, and so on.

User   Of an information system, a person with interest in or need for the processes and/or information or data maintained in an information system. System users can be classified according to the type of contact they have with the system.

   Direct user or *end user*   One who interacts frequently with the system and for whom the system was primarily designed.

   Indirect user   One who interacts with the system through a direct user or another system.

   Passive user   One who has no primary interest in the output of the system, but who is described in some way within the system; for example, a person described in a statistical system as a member of a nation's population.

User Directory   A collection of the descriptions of the authorized users of an information system. The description of each user or user group should include a user identification, the information or data elements available to the user, the information or data processes available to the user, and the general security level for the user.

User Group   In the framework of information systems, a group of persons who share common information or information-processing requirements.

User Satisfaction   In the framework of information systems, the degree to which the users receive the services they expect from the information system.

CBIS Analysis and Design Example: Student Administration

INTRODUCTION

The background example for this text is taken from the administration of a hypothetical university with characteristics similar to those of American and Scandinavian universities. This object system (a university administration) was chosen for a number of reasons:

- It is assumed that readers are familiar with this system.
- The system is representative of the general class of systems for organization administration.

This appendix discusses the hypothetical university administration and its problems to provide a background for the discussion and illustrations provided throughout the text. This appendix does not provide the reports of a completed system analysis and design project. Rather, it gives background information about the object system. The task of designing a CBIS for the university administration is left to the student.

PROBLEM ANALYSIS

The University Environment and Organization

The university, ABC, provides members of the surrounding community with a university-level education in several fields. Graduates of ABC become teachers, businesspeople, and specialists in a number of professions. The student body is growing in size and currently numbers about 7500. Normal study time is 4 to 6 years, depending on the degree sought.

ABC has 1500 faculty members and 500 supporting and administrative staff. The university is organized in a traditional hierarchy, with eight schools or faculties: engineering, social science, liberal arts, math and sciences, business administration, law, medicine, and dentistry. Each school has a number of departments, and each department is responsible for a subject area. Each subject area is presented to students in a sequence of courses. A section of the organization, including the department of information science, which at ABC is placed within the school of social sciences, is illustrated in Figure 1.2.

The central university administration is organizationally placed above the schools. It provides such general services as personnel management, financial administration, faculty/school administration, student administration, and information services, including the library and computer departments. See Figure 2.9.

Faculty administration is responsible for coordinating curriculum development and ensuring that there are enough faculty members to teach the courses in the curriculum. It is this function, curriculum development and execution, which is of special interest for this example.

Information-Processing Problems

The administration of ABC university maintains a number of information systems. Many of them are manual, but some have automated subsystems. The university has hired a team of system analysts to review the university's information-processing requirements and to propose new or modified information systems where necessary. The university has computing facilities and is willing to consider supplementing or upgrading them if necessary.

Since the university's major objective is to provide its students with an education, the university administrators decided to begin with an analysis of the student administrative system. Initially, the system was defined in its broadest sense, and all prospective and possible users were identified. Figure 2.9 illustrates the major user groups interested in the student system. Figure 4.2 illustrates the major users, separating those who provide information to the system from those who require information from the system.

Representatives from each recipient user group were interviewed to determine:

- what information services they needed.
- which information or data elements they needed.
- what problems there were with the current system.

The university administrators gave priority to the direct users of the student system, namely, the faculty, students, and administration members directly involved in recording and processing student academic progress. According to these users, their primary interest and concern centered around class and grade administration. Table 4.1 gives a sample of the problem table derived from the interviews.

The three main problems identified, transcript preparation, grade recording, and generation of timely class rosters, led to concentration on four processes:

1. Registration of students in courses. This registration is the basis for gathering data with which to resolve the identified problems.
2. Grade recording.
3. Transcript generation.
4. Class roster generation.

Each of these processes was analyzed for data requirements, frequency of execution, and priority within the total student administration system. An example of the resulting process/information matrix is given in Figure 4.5.

An entity model was then generated as a tool for describing the entities of interest for the system and the relationships between the information elements. This model, once the users (students, faculty, and student administrators) have agreed to it, provides a basis for structuring the data base for the automated sections of the system. Figure 4.3 illustrates a very much simplified entity model.

Problem

Draw a complete entity model for the four processes listed.

THE EXISTING SYSTEM—A SYSTEM ANALYSIS

ABC has a student administration system that includes, among others, the processes identified during the problem analysis, namely, grade registration, transcript generation, course registration, and class roster generation. A detailed analysis of this system was made to determine where improvements were required to deal with the identified problems.

Documenting the Current System

To begin the analysis, the flow of students and faculty through the university was determined. This flow is simplified and illustrated in Figure 5.3. The major activities and their information requirements were identified and recorded in an activity matrix. Figure 5.4 illustrates this matrix.

Each of the major activities was then analyzed and modeled, giving a set of graphs and matrices. One such detail graph and matrix, that for the class administration system, A–6, are given in Figures 5.5 and 5.6.

An activity analysis includes an analysis of the flow of information, people, and materials (books, money, rooms, etc.) within the object system. This is important, since many problems can be the result of personnel shortages or shortages of resources other than information. Once the source of the problems is clear, those that are based in the information system can be isolated. It is these problems with which the information-system analyst is concerned. Extracting and documenting the information system for ABC's student administration is illustrated in Figures 5.7 through 5.10.

To build and maintain a CBIS, it is necessary to understand the information element and process requirements of the object system. Information element and process dictionaries must be developed; they should be begun (or updated if they were developed during a previous system development project) during problem analysis and activity analysis. Boxes 5.1 and 5.2 illustrate entries in the information and process dictionaries, respectively.

System Evaluation

Once the current information system has been thoroughly understood and documented, it can be reviewed (evaluated) for compliance with the system requirements. This will give a detailed list of problems as a basis for proposals for improvement. Figures 6.3 and 6.5 illustrate a description and evaluation, based on the results of the problem analysis, for the four processes under consideration.

The system analysts presented two alternatives for improving the system.

Alternative 1, S-1   A batch-processing system in which the teachers would compile grades and send them to the administration for recording and processing.

Alternative 2, S-2   An on-line system in which teachers would record grades directly into the system. A query processor would be included to allow various queries to the student system.

These proposals are presented and evaluated in Chapter 6 (Figure 6.8). Given the system service priorities specified in Figure 6.8, the fully automated system is "best" for ABC.

Problems

1. Complete the set of graphs for ABC's student administration system, given the system definition of Figure 5.3.
2. Define the other processes and at least three more information elements, using the layout of Boxes 5.1 and 5.2.

3. Change the priorities assigned to the system characteristics of
    Figure 6.8 so that a semiautomated system would be "best" for
    ABC. Discuss these changes.

INFORMATION-SYSTEM DESIGN

The system analysis and evaluation concluded that no new processes
or information elements were needed. What was required was a system
that would make the existing information available on a more timely
basis. In this situation, the information-system graphs for the new system exist (they were constructed during system analysis). If new processes or new information elements were required, the information
graphs from the system-analysis phase would have to be modified to
include the new processes or information elements.

The Design of the Communication System

For the on-line system, screen forms for data entry and query processing must be designed. Figure 7.1 shows the form for student registration. Figures 7.2 to 7.4 show a sequence of menus for activating various
system processes. The initial menu asks for a function. A reply of 6 will
result in the presentation of the second menu, Figure 7.3. A reply of
633 to the first-level menu (Figure 7.2) will immediately activate the
program for preparation of the grade sheet.

In addition to screen layouts, all report layouts must also be designed.
The system will require layouts for:

- Student transcripts
- Class rosters
- Class evaluations
- Course descriptions

System outputs must be readable and easy to handle. For this system,
the width of all outputs was limited to that of normal typing paper, to
facilitate placement in ring binders.

The Security System

The student administration system is to be a relatively open system.
However, a number of security restrictions are required. These include:

1. Limiting access for grade modification to faculty members, and
    limiting their access to students in classes that they have taught.

2. Limiting student access to grade information to information that concerns themselves.
3. Limiting access to course modification to administration and faculty.
4. Limiting access to faculty information to administration, except that faculty members would have access to information about themselves.

As protection against machine failure, whether from natural or human causes, the system is to be duplicated at another, nearby university. Back-ups of all data will be taken daily during the three weeks following exams and twice a week during course registration.

The acceptance of grades by the individual student is assumed to provide sufficient control of the validity of grades.

Problems

1. Design the report layouts indicated.
2. Evaluate the adequacy of the outlined security system.

DATA-SYSTEM DESIGN

The Data Model

The student administration system will need data describing students, courses, teachers, and faculty. These major entities are related to one another according to the following rules:

- A student will take more than one course.
- A course is taken by more than one student.
- A teacher may teach more than one course.
- A course is taught by only one teacher.
- Each student is a member of only one class.
- A class will have more than one student.
- A class will have only one class advisor.
- A teacher will be an advisor for only one class.

The network data model in Figure 8.1 illustrates these relationships. The relationship between students and courses is a many-to-many ($M:M$) relationship. Such relationships commonly hide an associative entity type, which in our case is the grade entity. Figure 8.2 shows a normalization of the $M:M$ relationship that brings out the associative entity.

Another model, presenting the attributes of importance to the system, can be constructed for this data system. These attributes will be represented by data items in the implemented system. Figures 8.5 through 8.7 illustrate a relational model for our system.

Once the required data items have been identified, their usage characteristics must be determined. Figures 8.8 and 9.2 show versions of the data-usage matrix for the system. A complete matrix would include usage characteristics for all data items by all programs. According to the matrix as it is given, item 1: s–id is the candidate key for student relations and records.

Data Structures

Which data structure to select depends on the data access requirements determined from the process set. In the example, the four processes have the following requirements for access to student data:

Process	Access Requirement
P–1 Student registration	Direct access to one student
P–2 Grade recording	Direct access to one student
P–3 Class roster	Group access to students depending on the courses registered for
P–4 List transcript	Direct access to one student; serial access to grade records for this student

Three of these processes have a direct-access requirement. The fourth, which has a group-access requirement, is executed only once a semester and thus has low priority in determining the data structure. From this very brief analysis, we can conclude that some form of direct-access file structure will best support our processes. The choice will be between direct files and indexed-sequential files.

The data model for our system, illustrated in Figure 8.1, indicates that the data structure is more complex than the four processes that have been illustrated and discussed. Most likely, the full student administration system, supporting queries and processes against teacher, course, and class information in addition to the student data, as well as requiring the information in the relationships indicated in the model, will require a data-base solution, preferably one that supports a network structure. Figure 9.8 illustrates how these data can be structured in a network data base.

Process Design

Figures 10.2, 10.4, 10.6, and 10.7 illustrate four methods of process or program specification: flowchart, structured diagram, decision table, and structured English, respectively. The system designer must select one of these methods, preferably one that both the system user and the implementer/programmer understand. Each process in the system must then be designed and checked for correctness and completeness before programming starts.

Problems

1. Complete the data model for this system.
2. Select data structures for each of the entity sets (student, teacher, course, and class plus any others included in the response to question 1).
3. Specify at least one more process. Better, specify four more processes, using a different documentation method for each.

COMPUTER SUPPORT

The university has a mainframe computer with "dumb" terminals in the administration and throughout the various departments. These are currently used by the administration's accounting department, by faculty members in their research, and by those students taking computer courses.

The existing storage units of the computer have sufficient capacity for a student data base to support the student administration system.

Using the Current Computer System

One alternative is to purchase additional terminals so that all faculty members and students can gain access to the student data base. This may cause some bottlenecks at peak usage times, such as during the period immediately following exams.

An Alternative Implementation

Alternatively, the university could purchase a number of microcomputers that can be connected to the central computer to provide access to the student data base. The data can then be processed locally within the microcomputer.

This decentralized processing is possible and feasible given the security restriction that limits faculty members to modifying student grade data only for their own students. Further security regarding student access could be maintained by placing special access control routines in the microcomputers available to students. However, centralized access control will still be necessary. Why?

Problems

Review the pros and cons of the two proposed implementations.

IMPLEMENTATION PLAN

Implementation Parameters

The university decided on an implementation that used the existing machine and terminal net, with additional terminals purchased as needed.

Further, the university decided to let the EDP department do the implementation, using the DBMS supplied by the computer vendor. In this case, the programs would be implemented in COBOL. A newly graduated computer science major was hired as DBA for the system.

Time estimates for the implementation tasks are as follows:

Task	Time in Person/Weeks
1. Design acceptance	0 (assumed OK)
2. Terminal purchase	1
Terminal delivery	3 weeks
3. Programming	24 PW
4. Program testing	4 PW
5. Data-base generation	8 PW
6. Data-base test	2 PW
7. User training	3 PW
8. Documentation	8 PW
9. System test	3 PW
10. Conversion—direct	1 week

Planned Maintenance

The programs of our system are assumed to be correct at conversion time. However, the system will require a number of maintenance routines. These include:

- Periodic data-base back-up
- Generation of an input log
- Ongoing introduction and training of new users

In addition, we expect the system to grow as new processes are added and as users become accustomed to the facilities provided and discover new uses for the data. We need to allocate one-half of a programmer position for this system growth function. New programs may lead to a need to restructure the data base. This will be a task for the DBA.

Problems

Assume that the implementation team consists of the system analyst, the new DBA, and two programmers.

1. Construct a PERT network graph and a Gantt chart for the implementation project.
2. Debate the pros and cons of direct conversion.
3. What extensions to the system seem most likely?

FOLLOW-UP

The student administration system was designed for use by university administration, faculty members, and current students. These are all direct users of the system. Likely indirect users would include (from Figure 4.2):

- Student organizations
- Alumni organizations
- Parents
- Employers
- Government
- Other universities

For each of these user groups, select at least one process. How will this process affect the design of the student DB?

We've maintained that this administration system is typical of administrative systems in general. Name at least one such system in each of the following application areas:

- Business applications
- Government applications
- Research applications
- Educational applications
- Home applications

Index

Acceptance testing, 278, 287–288
Activity analysis, 101, 102, 104–114
  definition of, 101, 104
  methods for, 104
  objective, 104
  tools for, 101 (*see also* Activity graph;
    Activity matrix)
Activity analysis report, 110–114
  components, 110–111
  example, 111–114
Activity characteristics (AC), 109–110.
    See also Activity matrix
Activity graph (A-GRAPH), 105–108
  definition of, 105
  examples of, 107 (fig.), 112 (fig.)
  notation for, 105–107, 106 (fig.)
Activity matrix (A-MATRIX), 108–110
  components of, 108–110
  definition of, 108
  examples, 109 (fig.), 113 (fig.)
Administrative information system
    (AIS), 22, 29–35
  components of, 32–35, 27 (fig.),
    35 (fig.)
  definition of, 23
  environment of, 29–31, 30 (fig.)
  goals of, 29–32, 32 (table)
  structure of, 29–35
  types of, 35–43
  user requirements, 32 (table)
  users of, 29, 30 (fig.), 45 (fig.)
  see also Computer-based information
    system
Algorithm, 226
Analysis and design, tools, 65–70, 81–
    93, 105–110, 116–120, 137–146,
    177–194, 220–224, 225–238
  automated, 69
  for data modeling, 177–194
  for file design, 220–224
  for the goal statement, 86–93
  for information modeling, 83–85,
    116–120

  manual, 67–68
  in problem analysis, 66 (table), 81–
    82, 84 (fig.), 93 (fig.)
  for program design, 225–238
  in system analysis, 105–110, 116–120
  for system evaluation, 137–146
Analysis team, *see* System analysis team
Analyst, *see* System analyst
Application areas (for CBIS), 22–43,
    329–332
  administrative support, 29–34
  business, 329–330
  decision support, 38–41
  education, 332
  government, 330–331
  home, 332
  office automation, 41–43
  public service, 330–331
  research, 331
  transaction processing, 36–38
Application generator, 69, 273–274,
    286. *See also* Implementation;
    Program specification
Application program, 266
Application system, 285–286
  implementation of, 285–286
Attribute, 10, 83–85, 152–153, 185–
    188
  associative, 10
  attribute value, 83
  definition of, 83, 152
  descriptive, 10
  domain sets for, 85
  model of, 83, 84 (fig.), 185–188,
    185 (fig.)
  shared, 83–85
  see also Entity
Auditing, 170, 305. *See also* Error con-
    trol; Integrity control
Automated data-processing system, *see*
    Computed-based information
    system